European Security Governance and the European Neighbourhood after the Lisbon Treaty

The EU has often been considered to be a weak security actor. However, any assessment of the EU's role in international security is underpinned by a specific understanding of security. This book is based on a broad understanding of security. We consider that security concerns are increasingly triggered by challenges such as terrorism, climate change, mass migration flows, and many other 'non-traditional' security issues. This book tries to capture these aspects of the EU's fast changing security policies following the entry into force of the Lisbon Treaty on 1 December 2009.

There are several common themes stemming from a combined reading of the chapters. Firstly, the EU has sought to simultaneously pursue its security objectives and spread its values, such as democracy, the rule of law, and human rights, by encouraging reforms in its neighbourhood. However, it is increasingly evident that there are tensions and contradictions between these two objectives, which can be illuminated and better understood by considering another strand of literature, with which there has been little engagement in EU studies to date, namely the literature on human security. This book is the first to analyze these hugely topical developments in European security after the Lisbon Treaty.

This book was previously published as a special issue of *Perspectives on European Politics and Society*.

Christian Kaunert is Senior Lecturer in EU Politics and International Relations at the University of Salford, UK and Marie Curie Senior Research Fellow at the European University Institute Florence, Italy.

Sarah Léonard is Lecturer in International Security at the University of Salford, UK and Marie Curie Research Fellow at Sciences Po, Paris, France.

European Security Governance and the European Neighbourhood after the Lisbon Treaty

Edited by
Christian Kaunert and Sarah Léonard

LONDON AND NEW YORK

First published 2013
by Routledge
2 Park Square, Milton Park, Abingdon, Oxon, OX14 4RN

Simultaneously published in the USA and Canada
by Routledge
711 Third Avenue, New York, NY 10017

First issued in paperback 2017

Routledge is an imprint of the Taylor & Francis Group, an informa business

© 2013 Taylor & Francis

This book is a reproduction of *Perspectives on European Politics and Society*, vol. 12, issue 4. The Publisher requests to those authors who may be citing this book to state, also, the bibliographical details of the special issue on which the book was based.

All rights reserved. No part of this book may be reprinted or reproduced or utilised in any form or by any electronic, mechanical, or other means, now known or hereafter invented, including photocopying and recording, or in any information storage or retrieval system, without permission in writing from the publishers.

Trademark notice: Product or corporate names may be trademarks or registered trademarks, and are used only for identification and explanation without intent to infringe.

British Library Cataloguing in Publication Data
A catalogue record for this book is available from the British Library

Typeset in Times New Roman
by Taylor & Francis Books

Publisher's Note
The publisher would like to make readers aware that the chapters in this book may be referred to as articles as they are identical to the articles published in the special issue. The publisher accepts responsibility for any inconsistencies that may have arisen in the course of preparing this volume for print.

ISBN 13: 978-1-138-10921-6 (pbk)
ISBN 13: 978-0-415-62337-7 (hbk)

Contents

Notes on Contributors   vii

1. Introduction: European Security Governance after the Lisbon Treaty: Neighbours and New Actors in a Changing Security Environment
   Christian Kaunert & Sarah Léonard   1

2. The European Commission's Position in the Field of Security and Defence: An Unconventional Actor at a Meeting Point
   Chantal Lavallée   11

3. Is the EP Still a Data Protection Champion? The Case of SWIFT
   Ariadna Ripoll Servent & Alex MacKenzie   30

4. The EU Strategy in Tackling Organized Crime in the Framework of Multilateralism
   Daniela Irrera   47

5. The Transition of Egypt in 2011: A New Springtime for the European Neighbourhood Policy?
   Patricia Bauer   60

6. From 'Villains' to the New Guardians of Security in Europe? Paradigm Shifts in EU Foreign Policy towards Libya and Belarus
   Giselle Bosse   80

7. Reconceptualizing 'Cooperation' in EU-Russia Relations
   Cristian Nitoiu   102

8. Unrecognized and Unwelcome? The Role of the EU in Preventing the Proliferation of CBRN Weapons, Materials and Knowledge
   Kamil Zwolski   117

9. Russia's Energy Leverage over the EU: Myth or Reality?
   Tom Casier   133

Index   149

Notes on Contributors

Patricia Bauer, DAAD-Professor, Faculty of Economics and Political Science, Cairo University, Giza, Egypt.

Giselle Bosse, Assistant Professor, Political Science Department, Maastricht University, Maastricht, The Netherlands.

Tom Casier, Senior Lecturer in International Relations, University of Kent/Brussels, School of International Studies, Belgium.

Daniela Irrera, Assistant Professor of Political Science and IR, University of Catania – Department of Political Studies, Catania, Italy.

Christian Kaunert, Senior Lecturer in EU Politics and International Relations, Centre for European Security, University of Salford, UK, and Marie Curie Senior Research Fellow, Robert Schuman Centre for Advanced Studies, European University Institute, Florence, Italy.

Chantal Lavallée, Visiting Fellow, Robert Schuman Centre For Advanced Studies, European University Institute, Florence, Italy.

Sarah Léonard, Lecturer in International Security, Centre for European Security, University of Salford, UK and Marie Curie Research Fellow, Centre for European Studies, Sciences Po, Paris, France.

Alex MacKenzie, School of Humanities, Languages and Social Sciences, University of Salford, UK.

Cristian Nitoiu, Department of Politics, History and International Relations, Loughborough University, Loughborough, UK.

Ariadna Ripoll Servent, Researcher at the Institute for European Integration Research, Austrian Academy of Sciences (OEAW), Vienna, Austria.

Kamil Zwolski, Lecturer in Politics, Department of Politics and Philosophy, Manchester Metropolitan University, Manchester, UK.

Introduction: European Security Governance after the Lisbon Treaty: Neighbours and New Actors in a Changing Security Environment

CHRISTIAN KAUNERT & SARAH LÉONARD

ABSTRACT *The EU has been making strong inroads into the realm of security over the last few years. This is a remarkable development since security matters used to be the preserve of states. The EU has generally been considered a rather weak security actor. However, it is necessary to remember that any assessment of the EU's role in international security is always underpinned by a specific understanding of security, although this may often be left implicit. This special issue – and, indeed, the European Security and Supranational Governance Conference and the whole EUSIM project – are based on a broad understanding of security. We consider that security concerns are increasingly triggered by challenges such as terrorism, climate change, mass migration flows and many other 'non-traditional' security issues. The articles presented in this special issue all testify to the breadth of the EU security agenda as they all try to capture some aspects of the EU's fast changing security policies following the entry into force of the Lisbon Treaty on 1 December 2009. There are several common themes stemming from a combined reading of the various articles gathered in this special issue. One of the themes that emerges particularly strongly from the various analyses is the existence of a complex relationship between values and security at the heart of several EU policies, particularly in relation to its neighbourhood. As emphasized by the various contributors to this special issue, it appears that the EU has sought to simultaneously pursue its security objectives and spread its values, such as democracy, rule of law and human rights, by encouraging reforms in its neighbourhood. However, it is increasingly evident that there are tensions, and perhaps even contradictions, between these two objectives. We argue in this introduction that it is only one of the challenges faced by the EU that can be illuminated and better understood by considering another strand of literature with which there has been little engagement in EU studies to date – the literature on human security.*

This special issue of *Perspectives on European Politics and Society* derives from an international conference on European Security and Supranational Governance, which was held at the University of Salford, Greater Manchester, on 27–28 January 2011. It was sponsored by the European Commission (EC) and the Manchester Jean Monnet Centre of Excellence (JMCE), which is a partnership between the University of Manchester, Manchester Metropolitan University and the University of Salford. The EC's funding took the form of a grant from the Jean Monnet Programme/Lifelong Learning Programme for the European Union Simulation (EUSIM) Project for 2009–12. Warm thanks are, therefore, due to both the EC and the Manchester JMCE for their generous financial support, without which neither the conference nor this special issue would have seen the light of day. The main aim of the EUSIM Project is to bring the study and research of the EU closer to students of a wide variety of backgrounds. It is often thought that because of the sometimes awkward relationship of Britain with the European Union (EU), students in Britain are not interested in, or might even be hostile to, studying or researching the EU. This project aims to encourage students to increase their critical knowledge of the EU through the application of a problem-based learning (PBL) approach to the 'EU Simulation' Jean Monnet module. The EU Simulation module supports students in becoming independent, enterprising problem-solvers through the examination of real-life EU policy problems. The scenario underpinning the EU Simulation in 2010–11 focused on European security and supranational governance. In addition to more traditional classes that introduced them to policy-making in the EU, students were given a policy scenario and asked to conduct negotiations in weekly sessions akin to Council meetings; these negotiations culminated in a session modelled upon a 'real-life' European Council summit. In addition, all students were given free access to the latest cutting-edge research on the topic by attending the conference and they will gain further insights through the publication of this special issue. Bringing together students, researchers and practitioners representing various institutions, including the EC, and coming from a large number of countries has considerably enhanced the understanding and the enthusiasm of the students, who might not have otherwise become interested in EU matters.

European Security Governance after the Lisbon Treaty

The EU has been making strong inroads into the realm of security over the last few years. This is a remarkable development since security matters used to be the preserve of states. The EU has generally been considered a rather weak security actor. One of the first approaches to the study of the EU's Common Foreign and Security Policy (CFSP) in terms of a 'capability-expectations gap' (Hill, 1993) has had a durable impact on the field, as the EU tends to be more often singled out for its shortcomings than its achievements. However, it is necessary to remember that any assessment of the EU's role in international security is always underpinned by a specific understanding of security, although this may often be left implicit. This is important because those who understand security in military terms are likely to consider the EU a weak security actor; in contrast, those who have a broader understanding of security are likely to see it as an increasingly significant security actor (Zwolski, 2009). This special issue – and, indeed, the European Security and Supranational Governance Conference and the whole EUSIM project – are based on a broad understanding of security. We consider that security concerns are increasingly triggered by challenges such as terrorism, climate change, mass migration flows and many other 'non-traditional' security issues (see notably Sheehan, 2005; Dannreuther, 2007; Dunn Cavelty and Mauer, 2010). To some extent, this is a global trend, but it seems to be particularly relevant to the European context (Cottey, 2007). Indeed, the success of European integration has, amongst other factors, led to a significant decrease in the importance of military threats on the security agenda in the last decades, although they have evidently not disappeared completely (Wæver et al., 1993). Conversely, other 'non-traditional' security threats have received significant attention, notably from the EU (Kaunert, 2007, 2009, 2010a, 2010b, 2010c). In its European Security Strategy (ESS), which was adopted in 2003, the EU identified a wide range of security threats, including disease, poverty, terrorism, global warming, migratory movements and organized crime, alongside more traditional security threats (European Council, 2003). This emphasis on 'non-traditional' security threats was arguably even stronger in the 2008 *Report on the Implementation of the European Security Strategy* (European Council, 2008).

The articles presented in this special issue all testify to the breadth of the EU security agenda, as they all try to capture some aspects of the EU's fast changing security policies following the entry into force of the Lisbon Treaty on 1 December 2009. As will be explained in greater detail later, whilst two of the contributions focus mainly on the changing and growing role of two EU institutions in the EU security architecture – the European Commission and the European Parliament – the others examine how the EU has sought to tackle various security threats in recent years. In that regard, an important characteristic of the EU has been its various attempts at cooperating with third countries, in particular neighbouring countries, to address security threats. Several papers presented in this special issue document the EU's attempts at cooperating with other countries on a bilateral or multilateral basis to tackle security issues as diverse as transnational organized crime, irregular migration flows and energy.

There are several common themes stemming from a combined reading of the various articles gathered in this special issue. One of the themes that emerges particularly strongly from the various analyses is the existence of a complex relationship between values and security at the heart of several EU policies, particularly in relation to its neighbourhood. As emphasized by various contributors to this special issue as well as other scholars (see Dannreuther, 2006; Kahraman, 2005; Bosse, 2007; Joffé, 2008; Balzacq, 2009), it appears that the EU has sought to simultaneously pursue its security objectives *and* spread its values, such as democracy, the rule of law and human rights, by encouraging reforms in its neighbourhood. However, it is increasingly evident that there are tensions and, perhaps, even contradictions between these two objectives. We argue in this introduction that it is only one of the challenges faced by the EU that can be illuminated and better understood by considering another strand of literature with which there has been little engagement in EU studies to date – the literature on human security.

The EU, the Neighbours and Human Security

The various debates on the relationship between values and security in the EU's policies are reminiscent of discussions that have been taking place for years regarding the concept of 'human security'. In our view, drawing upon this literature can shed light in interesting ways on the dilemmas that the EU is facing in its security and neighbourhood policies. This is because, in all but name, these policies are largely underpinned by a 'human security' approach.

The concept of 'human security' is generally associated with the 1994 Human Development Report of the United Nations Development Programme (UNDP). Although this concept actually has historical roots dating back to the pre-modern era (MacFarlane and Khong, 2006), the 1994 Human Development Report gave it a very strong endorsement and considerably raised its profile on the international stage (Tadjbakhsh, 2007, p. 8). In this report, the UNDP argued that human security has two main aspects: 'safety from such chronic threats as hunger, disease and repression' and 'protection from sudden and hurtful disruptions in the patterns of daily life – whether in homes, in jobs or in communities' (UNDP, 1994, p. 23). More precisely, it listed seven components of human security: economic security (e.g. assured basic income), food security (e.g. physical and economic access to food), health security (e.g. safe environment and access to health care), environmental security (e.g. healthy and unpolluted physical environment), personal security (protection from physical violence), community security (protection of traditional identities and cultural and ethnic groups) and political security (protection of civil and political rights). Although some have later criticized this definition of security as being too broad and encompassing 'virtually any kind of unexpected or irregular discomfort' (Paris, 2001, p. 89), the drafters of the 1994 Human Development Report saw the 'all-encompassing' character of this definition of security as a major strength, especially the fact that it recognized the interdependent character of all the components of human security.

Nowadays, this seven-pronged definition remains the starting point for many discussions about human security. However, alternative definitions of human security have also been developed by some governments, such as the Canadian and Japanese governments, as well as academic scholars. This proliferation of definitions of human security has led to a distinction being made between the 'broad school' and the 'narrow school' of human security (see Owen, 2004; Kerr, 2007), which is also referred to as the distinction between the 'freedom from want' and 'freedom from fear' approaches. The broad school advocates an inclusive definition of human security that is at least as broad as the definition advocated by the UNDP. In contrast, for the proponents of the 'narrow school', the concept of human security should only be applied to situations of political violence. According to such a perspective, human security means 'the protection of individuals and communities from war and other forms of violence' (Kerr, 2007, p. 95). In other words, it is concerned only with 'freedom from fear'. This definition is advocated by several scholars, who argue that it is more powerful in terms of both analytical utility and practical impact (Mack, 2004; Krause, 2004; MacFarlane, 2004). Beyond these academic arguments, it is important to note that this narrow conceptualization of human security has also become particularly significant because of its endorsement by the Canadian government, one of the most vocal champions of human security (Canada's Department of Foreign Affairs and International Trade, 2000).

In contrast to the Canadian and Japanese governments, the EU has not, to date, officially adopted 'human security' as a core principle for its activities. This concept is not mentioned in any of the European treaties, despite its mention in the speeches of EU officials (e.g. Ferrero-Waldner, 2006a, 2006b) and the publication of various reports advocating the adoption of a 'human security doctrine for Europe' (Léonard, 2009). However, it can be argued that although the 'human security' label has not been officially adopted by the EU, many EU official documents strongly suggest that the EU's activities are implicitly underpinned by human security ideas. For example, the ESS does not explicitly mention 'human security', but it contains sections that are strongly reminiscent of the 1994 UNDP's Human Development Report and its broad approach to human security, in particular the section on 'global challenges' (European Council, 2003). It notably argues the following:

> Since 1990, almost 4 million people have died in wars, 90% of them civilians. Over 18 million people world-wide have left their homes as a result of conflict. In much of the developing world, poverty and disease cause untold suffering and give rise to pressing security concerns. Almost 3 billion people (...) live on less than 2 Euros a day. 45 million die every year of hunger and malnutrition. (...) New diseases can spread rapidly and become global threats. Sub-Saharan Africa is poorer now than it was 10 years ago. In many cases, economic failure is linked to political problems and violent conflict. Security is a condition of development (European Council, 2003, p. 2).

The same conclusion can be drawn from an analysis of the European Commission's key documents on the European Neighbourhood Policy (ENP), in particular its 2003 and 2004 Communications (European Commission, 2003, 2004). Although they do not explicitly refer to 'human security', 'freedom from want' or 'freedom from fear', the wide-ranging policy agenda that they develop, with its calls for 'actions to tackle the root causes of the political instability, economic vulnerability, institutional deficiencies, conflict and poverty and social exclusion' (European Commission, 2003, p. 6), strongly resembles a 'human security' agenda.

In sum, there has been a growing interest in the concept of 'human security' in the EU, although this label has not been officially adopted as such. Moreover, human security ideas have evidently influenced the development of the EU's security and neighbourhood policies. It appears that the EU is to a large extent seeking to pursue a human security agenda in all but name. One can therefore draw upon the rich literature on human security to highlight a few of the challenges faced by the EU while trying to develop and implement security and neighbourhood policies largely based on human security ideas. First of all, one of the risks inherent to pursuing a human security agenda is that it may not be the most effective in terms of delivering practical results. This is because it encompasses a very large number of policy priorities, which lack a clear hierarchy and would require considerable means to be implemented (Paris, 2001; Delvoie, 2001; Tadjbakhsh, 2007; Huliaras and Tzifakis, 2007). A second challenge associated with the implementation of a human security agenda, which has already been mentioned, is the tensions to which it gives rise between the projection of values and the pursuit of self-interest. In that respect, some have suggested that human security ideas might not amount to much more than rhetoric, as those putting them forward are, in their view, doing so mainly to foster their own interests (Werthes and Bosold, 2006; Khong, 2001). A third problem faced by those seeking to implement human security ideas is the possible passivity or even hostility of the countries that are targeted by the reformist policy agenda that they entail. There are indeed well-known difficulties in trying to promote reforms with governments that view them as threatening to their hold on power (Smith, 2005, p. 765). Thus, the EU faces these considerable challenges when developing its security and neighbourhood policies. These challenges are further explored in relation with specific security threats and particular EU neighbours in the articles that follow this introduction.

Outline of the Articles

This special issue analyses various aspects of European security in the wake of the entry into force of the Lisbon Treaty. It focuses on specific aspects of this fast-changing area, in particular the growing role of two institutions that have traditionally been kept at the margins of the security realm, the European Commission and the European Parliament, and the ways in which the EU has attempted to tackle a wide range of security threats through cooperation with its neighbours or at the multilateral level. The impact of the Lisbon Treaty in these various policy areas is highlighted. The various contributions also identify and analyse the challenges and dilemmas faced by the EU while attempting to address these various security threats.

The first article by **Chantal Lavallée** examines the role of the European Commission in European security governance. This is an under-researched topic, most notably because of the traditionally marginal role of the Commission in the CFSP. In contrast, this article shows the necessity to research the role of the Commission as a security actor because of the growing interdependence of EU external policies, which has increased the interactions between supranational institutions and national governments. Moreover, recent developments in security and defence at the EU level have arguably opened a window of opportunity for several actors, including the European Commission. This article documents and explains the emergence of an increasingly structured European 'field' of security and defence as a result of the interactions amongst a multiplicity of actors. Lavallée's article applies a sociological framework, which enables her to highlight the role of the Commission in relation to that of the other state and non-state actors involved in EU security governance. The article concludes that the Commission has become an important meeting point for actors inside this security 'field' as it plays a coordinating role, which also brings up many challenges.

The second article by **Alexander MacKenzie and Ariadna Ripoll Servent** analyses the role of another EU institution that is becoming increasingly important in European security matters, the European Parliament. The article focuses on the role of the European Parliament as a data protection champion, which has particularly come in the limelight at the time of the recent SWIFT negotiations. MacKenzie and Ripoll Servent suggest that, since the 1970s, the European Parliament has been active in the area of data protection and has tended to favour strong data protection controls within the EU. However, it used to lack strong legislative powers in this policy area. This has changed with the entry into force of the Lisbon Treaty, as the European Parliament has now gained consent over most international agreements.

The case of the EU-US SWIFT Agreement in the field of counter-terrorism has allowed the European Parliament to 'flex its data protection muscles' to some extent for the first time. Nevertheless, those in favour of high data protection standards have been disappointed by the European Parliament's eventual decision to consent to the SWIFT Agreement. MacKenzie and Ripoll Servent explain this evolution by citing the necessity for the European Parliament to appear more responsive than before to the EU member states' security concerns since the entry into force of the Lisbon Treaty.

The third article by **Patricia Bauer** moves our focus to the EU's neighbourhood. It focuses on the ways in which the EU has dealt with the Spring 2011 revolution in Egypt. It locates these recent events in the broader context of the EU-Egypt relations, which have developed in the framework of the ENP in recent years. Bauer argues that the EU's policy towards Egypt has been multilayered, has simultaneously pursued different objectives and has relied on both interest-based and normatively-oriented tools. This ambivalence was particularly visible at the beginning of the Egyptian revolution, when European leaders appeared to be circumspect initially, before eventually supporting the protesters. Thus, this article aptly illustrates the dilemmas faced by the EU in its neighbourhood – and highlighted earlier – as it seeks to simultaneously pursue two goals that may be difficult to reconcile, namely security and democratization. Bauer also draws upon the events in Egypt to reflect upon the democratic power of the EU in its foreign relations and how it may evolve as a result of the 'Arab spring'.

The fourth article by **Giselle Bosse** also focuses on some of the themes raised by the previous article, but investigates them in relation to other EU neighbours, namely Libya and Belarus. Bosse argues that the EU's pursuit of its internal security interests has led it to significantly alter its policies towards the autocratic regimes of these two countries. From a position where they were both ostracized for their repeated violations of human rights, Libya and Belarus have now been identified by the EU as potential partners in tackling some of the EU's security issues, such as 'illegal' immigration, which has given them some leverage over the EU. This could be seen clearly when, in 2011, Colonel Gaddafi threatened European countries with allowing large flows of migrants in reaction to the bombing campaign against Libya. Bosse also uses the findings of her two cases studies to reflect more broadly on the EU's so-called 'normative power' and its future role as a 'successful democratiser'.

The following article by **Cristian Nitoiu** is the first of three in this issue that focus on the relationship of the EU with one of its most important partners, Russia, which has consistently refused to be treated as a mere neighbour in the framework of the ENP. Nitoiu argues that the EU is yet to develop a true common policy towards Russia. In its absence, the bilateral relations between some EU member states and Moscow, which have tended to focus on economic and energy issues, have remained of prominent importance. As a result, the EU has not been able to significantly promote its norms and values in Russia and its Eastern neighbourhood. Nitoiu also emphasizes that the pursuit of enhanced relations with Russia constitutes a *de facto* legitimization of Russia's bid to keep the Eastern neighbourhood in its sphere of influence.

Keeping the focus on Russia, the sixth article by **Kamil Zwolski** examines the role of the EU as an actor in the important case of the non-proliferation of chemical, biological, radiological and nuclear (CBRN) weapons. Russia's extensive CBRN programmes, combined with a bad economic situation, weak non-proliferation standards and a high unemployment rate among CBRN scientists, have been a major source of concern for the international community following the end of the Cold War and in particular after the terrorist attacks of 11 September 2001. Zwolski emphasizes that the EU has been the only non-state actor to get involved in tackling this issue. Drawing upon an original 'actorness' analytical framework, Zwolski examines the past and present role of the EU in combating the proliferation of CBRN weapons in Russia and elaborates upon its future role in the light of the changes introduced by the Lisbon Treaty and the evolving security environment.

The seventh article by **Tom Casier** examines a third element of the EU's relationship with Russia by focusing on the issue of energy. He starts by observing that although the EU is now less dependent on Russian energy today than it was 20 years ago, EU-Russia energy relations are more often understood in terms of power, security and zero-sum geopolitical competition. Drawing upon Keohane and Nye's concepts of interdependence sensitivity and vulnerability, Casier challenges this widespread view by testing the actual degree of EU energy dependence and the extent to which dependence may create Russian leverage. The article shows that the actual EU supply dependence has been overrated and mainly stems from divisions within the EU, while Russia's leverage should not be exaggerated as it is limited by Russia's high dependence on EU energy demand. After examining the prevalence of geopolitical, power-related explanations in the analysis of EU-Russia relations, Casier concludes that, overall, EU-Russia energy relations remain predominantly of an economic and commercial nature.

The final article by **Daniela Irrera** takes us beyond the neighbourhood to consider the EU's interactions with other global actors, such as the US and the UN, when tackling the pressing security issue of transnational organized crime (TOC). Despite the lack of a common definition of TOC and a common strategy to fight it at the global level, the EU has attempted to develop its own advanced strategy against TOC. This article discusses the relationship between TOC and global security in the broader context of multilateralism and analyses the interactions between the EU and the other main players in the global fight against TOC, highlighting the important role of the US. The article demonstrates that even though TOC is still largely perceived as a national law enforcement issue, multilateral cooperation, including at the global level, is required for a coherent and efficient strategy against TOC to be developed. It concludes that the EU has an important role to play in these multilateral efforts, particularly since the entry into force of the Lisbon Treaty.

Thus, the eight articles included in this special issue all document in various ways the EU's significant ambitions as a security actor. However, they also show that there is still a long way to go before these ambitions can be fulfilled, notably because of some persistent internal divisions. In that respect, it will be fascinating to observe the full impact of the Lisbon Treaty and that of the EU institutions that are relative newcomers to the security field, namely the European Commission and the European Parliament, in the years to come. It will be equally interesting to follow political developments as they unfold in the EU's neighbourhood and to see the extent to and the ways in which they may influence EU security policies in the future.

Acknowledgment

This research project was also supported by Marie Curie Intra-European Fellowships within the 7th European Community Framework Programme.

Bibliography

Balzacq, T. (2009) *The external dimension of EU justice and home affairs: Governance, neighbours, security*. Basingstoke, UK: Palgrave Macmillan.

Bosse, G. (2007) Values in the EU's Neighbourhood Policy: Political rhetoric or reflection of a coherent policy? *European political economy review*, 7, pp. 38–62.

Canada's Department of Foreign Affairs and International Trade (2000) *Freedom from fear: Canada's foreign policy for human security*. Ottawa, Canada: Department of Foreign Affairs and International Trade.

Cottey, A. (2007) *Security in the new Europe*. Basingstoke, UK: Palgrave Macmillan.

Dannreuther, R. (2006) Developing the alternative to enlargement: The European Neighbourhood Policy. *European foreign affairs review*, 11 (2), pp. 183–201.

Dannreuther, R. (2007) *International security: The contemporary agenda*. Cambridge, UK: Polity.

Delvoie, L. (2001) Curious ambiguities: Canada's international security policy. *Policy options*. [online], 1, 36–42. Available from: http://www.irpp.org/po/archive/jan01/delvoie.pdf [Accessed 1 April 2011].

Dunn Cavelty, M., and Mauer, V., eds, (2010) *The Routledge handbook of security studies*, Abingdon, UK: Routledge.

European Commission (2003) *Communication from the Commission to the Council and the European Parliament: Wider Europe – Neighbourhood: A new framework for relations with our Eastern and Southern neighbours*, COM (2003) 104 (Brussels, Belgium: European Commission).

European Commission (2004) *Communication from the Commission: European Neighbourhood Policy Strategy Paper*. COM (2004) 373. Brussels, Belgium: European Commission.

European Council (2003) *A secure Europe in a better world: European Security Strategy*. 12 December 2003. Brussels, Belgium: European Council.

European Council (2008) *Report on the implementation of the European Security Strategy: Providing security in a changing world*. 11 December 2008. S407/08. Brussels, Belgium: European Council.

Ferrero-Waldner, B. (2006a) Human security and aid effectiveness: The EU's challenge. Speech given at the Overseas Development Institute – All Party Parliamentary Group on Overseas Development Lunchtime Meeting Series, London, 26 October 2006. Available from: http://www.europa-eu-un.org/articles/en/article_6399_en.htm [Accessed 1 April 2011].

Ferrero-Waldner, B. (2006b) Remarks on democracy promotion. Speech given at the Democracy promotion: The European way' conference organized by the European Parliament's Alliance of Liberals and Democrats for Europe, Brussels, 7 December 2006. Available from: http://www.alde.eu/fileadmin/images/Photo_Library/2006/20061206_Democracy_Promotion/061207_benita_ferrero_speech_on_democracy_promotion.doc.pdf [Accessed 1 April 2011].

Hill, C. (1993) The capability-expectations gap, or conceptualizing Europe's international role. *Journal of common market studies*, 31 (3), pp. 305–328.

Huliaras, A., and Tzifakis, N. (2007) Contextual approaches to human security. *International journal*, 62 (3), pp. 559–575.

Joffé, G. (2008) The European Union, democracy and counter-terrorism in the Maghreb. *Journal of common market studies*, 46 (1), pp. 147–171.

Kahraman, S. (2005) The European Neighbourhood Policy: The European Union's new engagement towards Wider Europe. *Perceptions: Journal of international affairs*, 10, pp. 1–28.

Kaunert, C. (2007) Without the power of purse or sword: The European arrest warrant and the role of the Commission. *Journal of European integration*, 29 (4), pp. 387–404.

Kaunert, C. (2009) Liberty versus security?: EU asylum policy and the European Commission. *Journal of contemporary European research*, 5 (2), pp. 148–70.

Kaunert, C. (2010a) The external dimension of EU counter-terrorism relations: Competences, interests and institutions. *Terrorism and political violence*, 22 (1), pp. 41–61.

Kaunert, C. (2010b) Europol and EU counter-terrorism: International security actorness in the external dimension? *Studies in conflict and terrorism*, 33 (7), pp. 652–671.

Kaunert, C. (2010c) *European internal security: Towards supranational governance in the area of freedom, security and justice*. Manchester University Press.

Kerr, P. (2007) Human security. *In*: A. Collins, ed. *Contemporary security studies*. Oxford University Press, 91–108.

Khong, Y. F. (2001) Human security: A shotgun approach to alleviating human misery? *Global governance*, 7 (2), pp. 231–236.

Krause, K. (2004) The key to a powerful agenda, if properly delimited. *Security dialogue*, 35 (3), pp. 367–368.

Léonard, S. (2009) Values vs security? A human security perspective on the European Neighbourhood Policy. *In*: T. Balzacq, ed. *The external dimension of EU justice and home affairs: Neighbours, governance, security*. Basingstoke, UK: Palgrave Macmillan, 229–247.

MacFarlane, S.N. (2004) A useful concept that risks losing its political salience. *Security dialogue*, 35 (3), pp. 368–369.

MacFarlane, S.N., and Khong, Y.F. (2006) *Human security and the UN: A critical history*. Bloomington, IN: Indiana University Press.

Mack, A. (2004) A signifier of shared values. *Security dialogue*, 35 (3), pp. 366–367.

Owen, T. (2004) Human security – Conflict, critique and consensus: Colloquium remarks and a proposal for a threshold-based definition. *Security dialogue*, 35 (3), pp. 373–387.

Paris, R. (2001) Human security: Paradigm shift or hot air? *International security*, 26 (2), pp. 87–102.

Sheehan, M. (2005) *International security: An analytical framework*. Boulder, CO: Lynne Rienner.

Smith, K.E. (2005) The outsiders: The European Neighbourhood Policy. *International affairs*, 81 (4), pp. 757–773.

Tadjbakhsh, S. (2007) Human security in international organisations: Blessing or scourge? *Human security journal*, 4, pp. 8–15.

United Nations Development Programme (1994) *Human development report*. Oxford University Press.

Wæver, O., et al., (1993) *Identity, migration and the new security agenda in Europe*. London: Pinter.

Werthes, S., and Bosold, D. (2006) Caught between pretension and substantiveness: Ambiguities of human security as a political leitmotif. *In*: T. Debiel and S. Werthes, eds. *Human security on foreign policy agendas: Changes, concepts and cases*. [online]. INEF Report 80/2006. Duisburg, Germany: Institute for Development and Peace at the University of Duisburg-Essen. Available from: http://inef.uni-due.de/page/documents/Report80.pdf [Accessed 1 April 2011].

Zwolski, K. (2009) The European Union as a security actor: Moving beyond the second pillar. *Journal of contemporary European research*, 5 (1), pp. 82–96.

The European Commission's Position in the Field of Security and Defence: An Unconventional Actor at a Meeting Point

CHANTAL LAVALLÉE

ABSTRACT *Due to its indirect role in the Common Foreign and Security Policy (CFSP), the European Commission seems to be a marginal actor in European security governance. As a result, there is little analysis of its role in this field. This approach is somewhat misleading because the EU policy-making process is more complex than it appears. The interdependence between the EU's external policies has increased the interaction between supranational institutions and national governments. Moreover, developments in security and defence at the EU level have opened up a window of opportunity for several actors. This paper will show that the structuring of the European field of security and defence is the result of interaction among various actors. From a sociological standpoint, the paper aims to understand the role of the Commission by shedding light, not only on its position in the field, but also on its relations with the other actors, both state and non-state, involved in EU security governance. Using this relational approach, the paper will argue that the Commission is the meeting point for the actors in the field, playing a coordinating role on the one hand, but facing many challenges on the other.*

Introduction

The European integration process has gradually shaped the European Union (EU) as a polycentric political configuration in which many actors are involved in accordance with different logics of action. As time goes by, the significant fragmentation of policy that has occurred across the EU pillars and institutions is raising a set of challenges for the EU's position in the world. Effectiveness, coherence and the visibility of the EU's role on the international stage, including security and defence, have required ever-closer coordination between the EU member states, institutions, structures and tools, even if they are using different approaches and decision-making procedures. Consequently, this interdependence between EU external policies has increased the interaction between supranational institutions and national governments in this sensitive field where member states remain reluctant to transfer sovereignty to the Union or even to display re-nationalizing tendencies.

Since the European Commission is an unconventional actor in this domain, there is little analysis of the role it plays in security and defence. Moreover, the most visible EU framework of action in this field is an intergovernmental policy, the Common Foreign and Security Policy (CFSP). However, the EU policy-making process in external action is more complex than it appears officially. This paper considers that the structuring of the European field of security and defence is the result of interaction among several actors. From a sociological standpoint, the paper aims to understand the role of the Commission by shedding light, not only on its position inside the EU security governance, but also on its relations with the others actors involved, such as state representatives, European institutions and non-state actors from think-tanks, non-governmental organizations (NGOs), enterprises and lobbies. Using a relational approach, the paper argues that the Commission plays the role of an interface, not only between community and intergovernmental instruments, but also between all the actors in the field. In this respect, the European Commission ensures cohesion across this configuration of relations, due to its innovative approach and instruments.

To understand how the European Commission became part of the EU security governance, this paper will first clarify the emergence of the European field of security and defence. Then, to appreciate in what manner the Commission coordinates, manages and regulates security and defence issues, the paper will analyse three key initiatives: the European Security Research Programme and the Instrument for Stability (both launched in 2007), and the Defence Package adopted by the European Parliament and the Council in 2009. Finally, to evaluate the impact of its involvement in this sensitive domain, the paper will emphasize the practices that structure the field and place the Commission at the pivot of this configuration of relations, a delicate position that throws up a set of challenges.

The European Field of Security and Defence: A Configuration of Relations

The literature about security and defence issues inside the EU focuses mainly on the European Security and Defence Policy (ESDP). Launched in 1999, the ESDP has been constructed step by step with new structures and tools linked with and responsible to the Council. In accordance with the Lisbon Treaty, the ESDP became the Common Security and Defence Policy (CSDP) from 1 December 2009. Although the state representatives agreed to change the word, 'European', to 'Common' (ESDP to CSDP), the Treaty does not create any new responsibilities or transfers of competencies to the EU institutions. The CSDP[1] remains the main component of the Common Foreign and Security Policy (CFSP). According to its decision-making procedure, the CFSP is intergovernmental because decisions are taken by the state representatives in the Council, within the guidelines set up by the European Council.

Nevertheless, academic literature proposes an increasing number of analyses that tend to nuance this strictly intergovernmental approach. Some scholars focus on the transgovernmental process in which diplomats and militaries interact on a regular basis at the EU level (Howorth, 2001; Mérand, 2008; Davis Cross, 2010), underlining the role of several actors in the CFSP/CSDP process. This transgovernmental activity is particularly intense in Brussels. The Council is assisted by the preparation and consultative structures based there: the politico-military organs (the Political and Security Committee (PSC), the Military Committee, Committee for Civilian Aspects of Crisis Management (CIVCOM) and the Military Staff); the Permanent Representatives Committee (COREPER); and working groups. The staffs of the Permanent Representations of the member states can all get in touch with each other and with the EU institutions and politico-military organs easily. In this regard, Howorth (2010, p. 1) has described the CFSP\CSDP as 'supranational inter-governmentalism' because, according to him, 'a supranational culture is emerging from an intergovernmental process'. According to Ojanen (2006, p. 64), the European model of security and defence is supranational due to the socialization between the state actors and the inclusion of the supranational actors in the process. Since the CFSP's inception, the European Commission has been fully associated with its development due to the 'symbiotic relationship between the political initiatives taken by the EU under CFSP/ESDP [CSDP] and the assistance delivered by the Community' (Kirchner and Sperling, 2007, p. 40). The Commission is especially involved in the working group of RELEX counsellors to ensure the coherence of EU external actions (Tonra, 2000; Duke, 2007).

However, the aim of this paper is not to take part in the debate on the intergovernmental or supranational approach concerning the CFSP/CSDP, but to evaluate EU policy-making in security and defence matters as a whole. Firstly, in the last decade, we have seen an ongoing 'brusselisation process' because the formulation and implementation of the CFSP/CSDP increasingly takes place in Brussels by national and European civil servants, even if the competencies continue to be the prerogative of the member states (Müller-Brandeck-Bocquet, 2002). Secondly, the European Council (2003) adopted a European security strategy that made a clear link between internal and external, civil and military security and the need to take advantage of all the EU's tools in order to handle the various threats. Since then, this strategy has become an EU reference document for its action in the world and has confirmed that the fragmentation of policy across pillars, the result of the decision-making procedures, was counterproductive (Biscop, 2008). The effectiveness and coherence of the EU position in the world thus necessitate ever-closer coordination between the EU member states, institutions, structures and tools, even if they were working with different approaches and decision-making procedures (Duke and Ojanen, 2006).

Thirdly, developments in security and defence at the EU level have opened up a window of opportunity for several actors, both state and non-state. In this respect, Howorth (2001, 2003, 2004) has underlined – since the early stages of its formulation – the role of epistemic communities in the CSDP policy-making process at the national and European levels. Besides member state representatives and European institutions, think-tanks, NGOs and consultants, enterprises also go to Brussels to play a role at the European level and to have an impact on politics. They have various reasons for doing so: Some want to act as experts, some as lobbyists and some to interface among these actors, organizing informal meetings, conferences and dinners. There is a socialization process between all the actors concerned with security and defence issues, both formally and informally. They know each other well and, at the end of the day, it is a small world.[2] As a result, Webber *et al.* (2004) describe the EU as a polycentric political configuration in which several public and private actors are regularly in touch at different levels in the governance of European security. Kirchner (2006, 2007) has proposed an application of the EU security governance concept based on the Barcelona Process, TACIS programme, European Neighbourhood Policy (ENP), CSDP and – more generally – on the way in which the EU coordinates, manages and regulates conflict prevention, peace enforcement and peace building.

Based on this rich literature, which opens the discussion on EU policy-making in security and defence, this paper will attempt to understand the role that the Commission plays. I think that this role makes sense only if we can clarify the Commission's relations with the actors involved in security and defence and then identify the new practices that structured this configuration of relations. In this respect, the theoretical concept of 'field' as defined by Pierre Bourdieu is useful. According to Bourdieu (2000), field is a social space, a configuration of relations, of struggles for power and strategies among actors to influence the policy process. As Chouala (2002, p. 522) also argues, the notion of field has the advantage of taking into account the configuration as a whole, it encompasses the plurality and heterogeneity of actors and the links among them. Despite the heuristic value of his approach, Bourdieu did not apply it to international relations (Mérand and Pouliot, 2008) or European integration issues (Kauppi, 2003, pp. 781–782). Nevertheless, the notion has been used to understand the transformation of security at the EU level (Bigo, 2005) and, notably, to comprehend the CSDP policy-making process (Mérand, 2006, 2008). This literature shows the emergence of a transnational or transgovernmental field in which several actors influence, through their interactions, the construction of security policies by their social representations, both organizational and national.

The interdependence between the EU's policies and developments in security and defence at the EU level has opened up a window of opportunity for several actors, both state and non-state. This paper, therefore, considers the European field of security and defence as a whole. The next section emphasizes the contribution of the European Commission in this sensitive field. According to Bourdieu (1989, p. 20), agents' actions depend on their position in the set of connections and on their perception of this. The following section will examine the role of the European Commission through three key initiatives in order to underline its position in the field and the way in which it justifies its contribution to this sensitive matter.

The Multidimensional Role of the European Commission in More Efficient and Coherent EU Action in the World

Since the end of the cold war, the European Commission has been keen to increase its role in external action using community instruments. It has played a central role in the enlargement process and in the cooperation, assistance and development programmes, et cetera (Cameron and Spence, 2004, pp. 122–124). Following this, from the mid-1990s on, the Commission began to link development and security clearly. The Directorate General (DG) of Development first played a role in conflict prevention; this was downsized by the creation of the Europe Aid Cooperation Office and, then, with the progress of the CFSP/CSDP, the DG of External Relations became increasingly active (Stewart, 2008). However, it was really the European security strategy adopted in 2003 that gave a sound basis to the involvement of the Commission in this sensitive field. Since then, the Commission has underlined the added value of its multidimensional role, using various community instruments to support the comprehensive approach of security advocated by the strategy. The following section emphasizes the three new interconnected initiatives set up by the Commission: the European Security Research Programme, the Instrument for Stability, and the Defence Package.

Security Research

Progress in security and defence at the EU level as a result of the CFSP/CSDP and the adoption of the European security strategy have been seen by the Commission as an opportunity to enlarge its competencies in this sensitive domain. The Commission wants to profit from the community instruments in order to support the CFSP/CSDP. In particular, the Commission showed its interest in security research to increase the synergies between defence, security and civil research to take advantage of the duality of technologies, supporting the EU comprehensive approach. According to the Commission (2004b, p. 4), '[H]umanitarian actions and interventions on behalf of the European Union, depends both now and in the future on the availability of leading-edge technologies to maximise the efficiency of the actions undertaken.' To achieve this, the European Commission created the European Security Research Programme (ESRP).

The ESRP was initially based on the recommendations of a report by the 'Group of Personalities in the field of security research', including state and non-state actors with technical expertise in this sector. The primary mission of this group was to propose principles and priorities for this innovative research programme 'in line with the EU's foreign, security and defence policy objectives and its ambition to construct an area of freedom, security and justice' (European Commission, 2004a, p. 4). In this respect, the terrorist attacks in Madrid and the EU enlargement in 2004 strengthened the Commission's conviction of the need to enhance internal security by funding research (Commission, 2004b, p. 3). From then on, the Commission was convinced that the ESRP would fund research activities both for the EU missions outside the Union as well as for the protection of EU territory that was connected.

> In Europe, there has been for long a strong separation between research for civil purposes and that for defence objectives. Today, many technologies are 'dual-use': civil developments adding to defence capabilities, developments originally made for defence purposes leading to major innovations and benefits in the day to day life of the citizen. [...] A coherent security research programme at the level of the European Union can add significant value to the optimal use of a highly competent industry (European Commission, 2004b, p. 4).

To identify security research and technology needs, the European Security Research Advisory Board (ESRAB) acted as a consultative organ between 2005 and 2007, including public and private actors in the field that represented demand and supply. The ESRP was launched in 2007 inside the Seventh Framework Programme for Research with a budget of 1,400 million euro (Europa, 2010). It covered:

> Four security mission areas in which there is a European added value (protection against terrorism and crime, security of infrastructures and utilities, border security, and restoring security in a crisis) and three cross-cutting areas (security systems integration and interoperability, security and society, and security research coordination and structuring) (Europa, 2010).

The scope of this programme was then civil, but the EU comprehensive approach towards security raised a set of challenges, notably about the duality of technologies, civil and military. This twofold use of technology obliged the Commission and the European Defence Agency (EDA) to coordinate closely within the European Framework Cooperation for Security and Defence Research. Once the ESRP was launched, the debate on defence research began. 'In 2010, half way through FP7, it is not so much a question of whether a defence research chapter should be included in the next Framework Programme for 2014–2020, but rather on what terms' (Assembly of Western European Union, 2010, p.17). Due to the civil and defence applications of technologies funded by the research programme, interactions took place on a daily basis among the actors involved in EU security governance. Exchanges between the DGs of the Commission were aimed at clarifying the work of everyone and their needs, while an advisory board committee and other experts from the Commission evaluated the research proposals and projects that were submitted to the sector programme committee of the member states.[3]

Moreover, due to the great complexity of security research, the Commission (2009, p. 2) has since the beginning considered that 'it was indispensable to bring together representatives from industry, public and private end-users, research establishments and universities, as well as non-governmental organisations and EU bodies'. Thus, the European Security Research and Innovation Forum (ESRIF) was set up with the mission to work on a Joint Security Research and Innovation Agenda for the next 15 years. This 'strategic roadmap [...] aimed at bringing greater coherence and efficiency to this area encompassing the EU, national and regional levels' (Commission, 2009, p. 2). Based on this report, the European Commission (2009) presented its own document, *A European security research and innovation agenda – Commission's initial position on ESRIF's key findings and recommendations*, about the strategic orientation of the ESRP for the following years. The Commission encouraged, among other things, the member states to pursue their cooperation towards a European security market in order to become more competitive as well as efficient. Furthermore, to increase cohesion with two other key community instruments in this field, the Commission (2009) proposed an assurance that the Defence Package would be properly applied in security domains and complement the operational funding of the Instrument for Stability by offering research funding to support its activities in crisis response and conflict prevention.

Crisis Response and Conflict Prevention

In its communication on conflict prevention in 2001, the Commission defined conflict prevention using a holistic approach for the first time and identified the long- and short-term EU instruments that would deal with this issue (Stewart, 2008, p. 233). One of these was the Rapid Reaction Mechanism (RRM) launched in 2001. 'The special appeal of the RRM as a funding instrument was that it could use fast-track procedures during critical phases of crisis situations and deliver rapidly' (Ricci, 2008, p. 9). However, the effectiveness of the RRM was limited because it supported projects for up to six months with a budget of 30 million euro per year, thus lending for too small a duration and budget to establish links between short-term crisis response and long-term development assistance (Ricci, 2008, p. 9). In the financial perspective for 2007–13, the European Commission (2004d) submitted a communication to reorganize the assistance and cooperation programmes. It proposed, among other things, to create the Instrument for Stability (IfS) in order to be able to intervene more effectively in crisis situations, together with the other community instruments and the CFSP measures. The Commission took advantage of the adoption in 2003 of the European security strategy, which supported the use of all EU tools against threats linked closely to security development, and it presented conflict prevention as a central theme.

The IfS entered into force in 2007, replacing the RRM, with the agreement of the European Parliament and the Council. The IfS has a large budget of two billion euro for 2007–13 (European Community, 2006, Article 24). It constitutes a short-term component, crisis response with 'assistance in response to situations of crisis or emerging crisis', and a long-term component, with 'assistance in the context of stable conditions for cooperation' (European Community, 2006, Articles 3 and 4). In this regard, this new instrument established tangible links between short-term crisis response and long-term development assistance in order to ensure the coherence of EU external action.

The first component, managed by the DG for External Relations,[4] represents the bulk of the IfS, with a budget of 1.4 billion euro (72 per cent of the budget) for the period, 2007–13 (European Commission, 2010, p. 2). With this component, 'the IfS marks clear progress compared to the RRM in that it is endowed with much larger funds, it can support "exceptional assistance measures" lasting up to 18 months, and it is deployed in close consultation with the Council bodies' (Grevi and Keohane, 2009, p. 97). The scope of the IfS in the crisis response dimension remains civil. The Commission continues to closely link security and development with the aim of complementing CSDP missions (European Commission, 2010, pp. 6–7). While the IfS is a flexible instrument, it can be used only when other EU instruments or policies cannot respond within the timeframe required and when no military action is necessary, in accordance with the subsidiarity principle. It 'can be used in all areas of intervention that come under Community competences, with the exception of humanitarian assistance. This means that it can finance anything that can be financed from one of the geographic or horizontal financing instruments without geographical restriction' (Ricci, 2008, p. 11).

The second and long-term component represents 480 million euro (23 per cent of the budget). The three main priorities identified by the Commission (2007a, pp. 3–4) are: '1) to support international efforts to address the proliferation of weapons of mass destruction [...] 2) to support global and trans-regional efforts to address the threats posed by trafficking, terrorism and organised crime; and 3) to build capacity within the EU and the international community for effective crisis response'. Priorities 1 and 2 are managed by EuropeAid, while priority 3 is overseen by the DG for External Relations (Commission/EuropeAid Cooperation and Development, 2010).

On the whole, the IfS can provide assistance for a broad spectrum of activities:

o *Assessment of Possible Community Responses to a Crisis*. The IfS will deploy technical assessment missions in a range of areas in order to inform the Commission's policy making and planning during a crisis;
o *Preventive Action during Emerging Crises*. The IfS can finance short-term actions as part of a wider package of Community and EU measures to address the immediate and root causes of an emerging crisis;
o *Acute Crisis Management*. The IfS can be deployed during a conflict or in response to a sudden-onset emergency to implement measures to restore stability;
o *Post-Conflict Reconciliation*. The IfS can be used to provide confidence-building measures in support of an emerging or established peace process; and
o *Post-Crisis Reconstruction*. The IfS can be used to spearhead long-term Community cooperation programmes in the immediate aftermath of a war or sudden-onset natural or man-made emergency, and to ensure a smooth transition between humanitarian relief operations, the re-establishment of civil administration and the rule of law, and subsequent rehabilitation and development programmes (Ricci, 2008, p. 11).

The high political impact of this instrument and the interdependence that it creates between all the EU external policies explain the relative autonomy of the Commission in its management. The elaboration of IfS programmes needs to take place in close collaboration with a series of actors. First, and in contrast to the RRM, it requires consultation with the member states, given that the Commission is obliged to respect the committee procedure, in which the EU member state representatives can exert control. The Commission cooperates closely with the Council and EU structures, notably the PSC and CIVCOM. CIVCOM has been specially 'created in order to improve relations between the military and the civilian components, including instruments from the first pillar' (Kirchner and Sperling, 2007, p. 69). In the crisis response, the Commission works closely with its delegations in third countries, which 'often provide project proposals to the Commission in Brussels and are directly responsible for the management of adopted exceptional assistance measures' (Commission, 2010, p. 6).

Besides closer consultation with actors inside the EU, the Commission is in touch with appropriate authorities in third countries, the international community and civil society. This consultation 'is an important part of the decision-making process' (Commission, 2010, p. 3). The European Commission works principally with the United Nations, its key partner in conflict prevention, and nearly 50 per cent of 'IfS funds are implemented through UN agencies, which in many cases have existing field structures able to deliver first responses in crisis and conflict affected countries'

(European Commission, 2010, p. 4). To be more effective, the Commission also works with NGOs and 'almost a quarter of all Instrument for Stability (IfS) funds, some 60 million euro, is implemented by NGOs worldwide, in more than 80 actions' (Ricci, 2010, p. 41). For the crisis-preparedness component, the Commission cooperates with NGOs based on the Peacebuilding Partnership, consisting of 'a broad-based network of specialised European NGOs with expertise in early warning, conflict prevention, peacebuilding and post-conflict and post-disaster recovery' (European Commission, 2007a: 18). For many years, the European Commission (2001a, p. 28) has claimed that NGOs are the 'key actors in long-term conflict prevention' because they are on the ground with wide knowledge of local issues and contact networks. Since the Commission has increased its contribution to conflict prevention with a clear need of external expertise, we have seen a growing interest on the part of NGOs, think-tanks and the academic world to provide information and analyses in this field (Stewart, 2008, p. 235). In conflict prevention, crisis management and peace building matters, for example, the European Commission financed the Conflict Prevention Partnership (CPP) for one year from September 2005; the CPP was composed of the International Crisis Group, the International Alert, the European Policy Centre and the European Peacebuilding Liaison Office.

Funded by the EU, the CPP was a cooperative effort, drawing on the specific expertise of each participating organization. It provided EU and national policy-makers with timely and focused information and analysis and practical policy recommendations through the publication and presentation of a series of studies on conflict-related issues. The CPP covered a diverse range of themes from supporting the reintegration of ex-combatants in post-conflict settings to the EU's peace building efforts in Darfur, the Democratic Republic of Congo (DRC) and the Southern Caucasus. (European Peacebuilding Liaison Office, 2010)

The measures and missions adopted under the IfS since 2007 have confirmed the EU's holistic approach towards conflict prevention and peace building, covering a broad range of issues concerning emerging conflict and post-conflict situations:

- Short-term advice to develop and kick-start post-conflict security sector reform (CAR, DRC, Guinea-Bissau, Lebanon, occupied Palestinian territory, Pakistan, Timor-Leste);
- Enabling or supporting measures in areas where CSDP missions are deployed (Afghanistan, Chad, DRC, Georgia, Horn of Africa/piracy, Kosovo, occupied Palestinian territory);
- Support to the UN and/or regional organizations-led peace keeping missions and peace building activities (MINURCAT in Chad, AU-UN Mediation in Darfur, AU in Somalia);
- Rule of law and transitional justice (Afghanistan, Colombia, Kyrgyzstan, Lebanon, Sierra Leone, Solomon Islands, Timor-Leste, Western Balkans);
- Support to interim administrations and special tribunals (ICO Kosovo, Lebanon Tribunal, Sierra Leone SC, ODIHR /ICTY programme in the Balkans);
- Support to conflict resolution and reconciliation (Colombia, Georgia, Republic of Moldova, Myanmar/Burma, Nepal, occupied Palestinian territory, Peru, Sri Lanka, Southern Thailand, Uganda, Zimbabwe);

- Support to fragile electoral processes (Africa-wide, Bolivia, Comoros, Haiti, Republic of Moldova, Pakistan);
- Post-conflict and post-disaster recovery programmes (Bangladesh, Cuba, Eastern DRC, Gaza Strip, Haiti, Lebanon, Myanmar/Burma, Nicaragua, Peru) and funding of joint United Nations (UN)/World Bank/EU needs assessments (eight joint post-crisis needs assessments undertaken); and
- Support to displaced populations (Georgia, Lebanon, Syria) (European Commission, 2010, p. 4).

From the RRM to the IfS, the Commission has justified its role in supporting the progress of the CFSP/CSDP and in increasing the efficiency and visibility of the EU on the international stage. During the same period, the European Commission has argued that the EU has also needed a competitive defence industrial base to increase the CSDP's capacities. It was for this reason that the Commission proposed the Defence Package to the European Parliament and the Council.

Defence Procurement

For many decades, the European Commission has published many studies on the relevance of including defence procurement in the community domain, invoking the subsidiarity principle. In the last few years, the Commission has worked more concretely to establish a European Defence Equipment policy in order for the CSDP to be more efficient and effective in its actions. The Commission has referred to its exclusive competency in the internal market and taken advantage of the European security strategy and – most of all – of the large cuts in national defence budgets. Its aim is to introduce concurrence into the defence equipment market and limit any appeals to the former Article 296 of the Treaty of European Community (TEC), which became Article 346 of the Treaty on the Functioning of the European Union (TFEU). This Article authorizes derogation from internal market rules for member states in particular circumstances, invoking their essential security interests (Irondelle, 2005, pp. 52–53).

In 2003, the European Commission submitted a communication *European defence industrial and market issues: Towards an EU defence equipment policy*. According to the Commission (2003, p. 19), '[T]his Communication is intended as a further contribution to greater efficiency in the defence equipment industry, which is both an objective in itself and an important challenge if the Union is to develop a successful ESDP [CSDP].' Moreover, the Commission wants to end the fragmentation of markets and industries at the national level in order to ensure a European defence market that is more competitive in the world, notably with respect to the American defence market. In 2004, it presented the *Green Paper on defence procurement. Green Paper* launched a public consultation and invited experts from EU member states, institutions and agencies and also think-tanks and industrial and professional organizations to submit their proposals on 'the establishment of an appropriate regulatory framework for the procurement of defence equipment' (Commission, 2004c, p. 3). Then, based on the findings of the public consultation, the Commission proposed two initiatives. First, in 2006, it proposed the *Interpretative communication on the application of Article 296 of the Treaty in the field of defence procurement* in order to limit the use of this derogation to exceptional cases. The Commission allowed the member states to evaluate if their essential security interests were compromised case by case. However, the Commission (2006b, pp. 8–9), as guardian of the Treaty, could investigate and 'bring the matter directly before the Court if it considers that a Member State is making improper use of the powers provided for in Article 296 TEC [later Article 346 of the TFEU]'. Then, in 2007, the Commission presented the Defence Package to the European Parliament and the Council.

> With a view to facilitat[ing] the development of a European defence equipment market: Directive 2009/43/EC on intra-EU transfers of Defence products simplifying terms and conditions of transfers of defence-related products within the Community and the Defence and Security Procurement Directive on the coordination of procedures for the award of certain works contracts, supply contracts and service contracts awarded by contracting authorities or entities in the fields of defence and security. The package also consists of the Communication "Strategy for a Stronger and More Competitive European defence Industry". (European Commission/Enterprise and Industry, 2011)

In this strategy, the Commission (2007b, p. 3) 'recognises the special character of the industry and its unique relationship with governments but argues that much can be done to unleash its full potential to ensure that it provides value for money to Member States and delivers the capabilities needed in an efficient and effective manner for the ESDP [CSDP]'. After some negotiation and amendments, the Defence Package was finally adopted in 2009 by the European Parliament and the Council in accordance with the co-decision process. The Defence Package was adopted in the context of the international economic and financial crisis, which placed public funding under huge pressure. The member states have had until the end of June 2011 to transpose these directives into their national legislation. They will start to apply them from 30 June 2012 (European Commission/Enterprise and Industry, 2011).

In sum, the Commission proposes, coordinates, manages and even regulates programmes and instruments concerning security and defence issues. It argues for the added value of its multidimensional role to increase the efficiency of the CFSP/CSDP and the EU as a whole on the international stage. To achieve this, it proposed these three complementary community instruments through an innovative approach to improve the competitiveness of the European security and defence industry, as well as the capacity of the EU to respond to crises and prevent conflict. The next section will analyse how the Commission plays the role of an interface between the actors, ensuring cohesion across this configuration of relations and structuring the European field of security and defence.

An Unconventional Actor at a Meeting Point

The previous section showed the role of the European Commission by shedding light on its position through its relations with the others actors involved in EU security governance. From this relational approach analysis, it would appear that the Commission forms a crossroads between the interactions of actors inside the field as well as a bridge between the internal and external security dimensions, ensuring the coherence of the field, but also facing various challenges. In this section, I will clarify the practices that structure the European field of security and defence.

Structuring through the Networking of Actors

First, it should be pointed out that the European Commission is not a homogeneous actor: It is divided into several Directorates General (DGs). Each DG has different needs, priorities and visions, according to its function. Thus, the efficiency of the external actions of the Commission as a whole depends on its capacity to coordinate the activities, needs and resources among, at least, the DGs for Trade, Humanitarian Aid, Development, Enlargement, External Relations and its delegations around the world. For example, the success of the IfS programme and the coordination between short- and long-term components begin with close cooperation and exchange of information between the DGs for External Relations and EuropeAid and the delegations in the third countries.

Besides its own organization, in order to be efficient, the Commission needs to coordinate ever more closely between the European and national levels. A study of the security research, crisis response/conflict prevention and defence procurement initiatives confirms the close cooperation that takes place between the Commission and the state representatives through formal and informal committee procedures. As Christiansen (1997, pp. 84–85) argued, there is a 'phenomenon of quasi-intergovernmentalism' inside the European Commission, with the control and the influence of state representatives inside the supranational system and in the whole of European policy-making. While the European Commission is playing a growing role in the field of security, its autonomy remains relative. According to the Commission (2008, pp. 4–5), the Instrument for Stability

> while remaining a first-pillar instrument decided upon by the Commission, the practice of close political co-ordination with EU Member States (notably in the Political and Security Committee, but also in the geographic working groups) has made it a politically responsive EC instrument.

The member states continue to be reluctant to give wide room for manoeuvre to the Commission and fear any possible interference between community instruments and the CFSP/CSDP, notably on the civil security dimension. They are, therefore, present from the initial stage of elaboration to the implementation of the three key initiatives, notably through the Council.

Regarding its relations with the Council, closer coordination, and even shared policy-making, 'requires sufficient dialogue, coordination of policy and shared objectives' (Stewart, 2008, p. 230). The Commission also works closely with the preparation and consultative structures of the Council, such as the PSC, to assure complementarity with the CSDP missions and CIVCOM to avoid interference between the civil missions of the CSDP and the IfS activities, for example.

Although this level of interdependence justifies the need for a high level of coordination, inter-institutional tensions are sometime inevitable, particularly when the sharing out of competencies is unclear or when the time arrives to choose among the EU tools for external relations (Dijkstra, 2009, p. 442). Thus, if cooperation exists due to the added value of the role of the Commission and its budget, conflicts can appear between the Commission and the Council. Within each institution, there are different visions and understandings of the notion of security, different backgrounds and cultures. These differences influence the priorities and strategies of each institution when the time arrives to choose among the EU's instruments of intervention. The European Commission, which traditionally plays a role in development, attaches more importance to the link between short- and long-term action to prevent crises, insists on the collaboration of all the actors involved in EU security governance, and wants to use the IfS.[5] Through the CFSP\CSDP, the Council often reacts on a case by case basis in a national approach. Crisis management by means of the CSDP depends on agreement among member states to intervene in a short-term perspective. This kind of decision implies the deployment of civilian staff or military from member states and the tendency is often to choose military intervention.

Moreover, the Commission cooperates closely with the other European institutions and agencies. In the three initiatives studied in this paper, the Commission needs to keep the European Parliament and the Council informed from the elaboration stage to the implementation stage of the programmes, in accordance with the community method. In addition, the three case studies represent three areas in which the European Commission and the EDA are closely in touch. Regarding the IfS, the Commission keeps the EDA informed about its needs to respond to crises. Regarding security research, the Commission and the EDA collaborate within the European Framework Cooperation for Security and Defence Research to coordinate their research programmes. The EDA is an intergovernmental agency and is perceived by the European Commission as a tool for the member states to use, even if for many member states, the EDA is simply another European agency.[6] However, the balance of power is not so clear between the Commission and the EDA. According to the Assembly of the Western European Union (2010), the Commission has an annual budget of €200 million for security research, while the EDA's annual budget for research on defence stands at €eight million: There is thus a ratio of 25:1. With the possible inclusion of defence in the ESRP after 2013, the Commission (Commission/Enterprise and Industry, 2010) justifies its role in research and defence as follows:

> to develop an innovative and competitive European Defence Technological and Industrial Base (EDTIB). Such an EDTIB is an important prerequisite for an effective European Security and Defence Policy (ESDP) [CSDP] which is designed to provide the EU with the capacity for autonomous action in order to respond to international crises, without prejudice to actions by NATO.

Furthermore, in order to contribute to their effective cooperation and to ensure their complementarity, a representative of the Commission sits alongside the HR and defence ministers of member states (except Denmark) on the EDA's Steering Board, the agency's decision-making body. While the Commission is a non-voting member, it is fully associated with the work of the Agency.

Beyond the debate on intergovernmental and supranational approaches, at the end of the day, 'the EU contains elements of both – it always has and it always will. [...] [It is a] complex system of "multi-level-governance" where powers are shared amid institutions and across different levels' (Šefčovič, 2010). In this respect, in its emphasis on practices, this paper shows that due to the Commission's approach and instruments, it plays a crucial role in the interface between the community and the intergovernmental methods used within the European field of security and defence.

Outside the EU member states and institutions, the efficiency of the work of the Commission depends on close coordination with the other actors on the international stage, such as third countries and international and regional organizations. For example, in the framework of the IfS, the Commission works closely with the UN and the third countries concerned. Israel has been closely involved in security research since the beginning of the European research programme.[7] Moreover, since the adoption of the White Paper on European governance, in 2001, the Commission has attempted to open up policy-making to civil society in order to create more transparency, leading to greater democracy, legitimacy and efficiency in EU action.

In all community policies, the Commission bases its approach with all the actors involved in EU governance on a culture of consultation, dialogue and collaboration. We have seen through the case studies that this is also true of security and defence even though this is a traditionally sensitive field. Since it plays a role in its activities and wants to be recognized as a legitimate actor in it, the Commission needs the technical, practical and theoretical know-how that is generated through these. Therefore, as we have seen, the Commission is particularly careful to stay in touch with public and private actors specializing in security research, crisis response/conflict prevention and defence procurement from the elaboration to the implementation stages of its projects. In addition, the Commission encourages actors from civil society to work closely together and to stimulate debate.

While we can see that the Commission's priority is to gain legitimacy and the recognition to play a role in security and defence through its collaboration with expertise holders, the central issue for some of these actors is to share a privileged relationship with it. There can, therefore, be a real battle of ideas and interests between the various actors relating to this new and competitive market of expertise on the international and European levels. In order to avoid conflict of interest, the Commission is careful about the kind of contact that it maintains with the EU civil society. To this end, in the context of the European Transparency Initiative, the Commission launched a voluntary Register of Interest Representatives and a code of conduct in 2008. This Register includes different kinds of actors, including those involved in security and defence, as, for example, enterprises such as Thales and European Aeronautic Defence and Space (EADS), NGOs such as the European Peacebuilding Liaison Office, professional organizations such as the AeroSpace and Defence Industries Association of Europe and think-tanks such as the Open Society Institute of Brussels (European Commission/Register of Interest Representatives, 2011).

As we have seen, the European Commission does not act directly on the ground, but needs partners within the European field of security and defence and beyond at all stages of its programmes. There are relations of interdependency due to the resources of each actor in the field. The cooperation between state representatives, European institutions and civil society is about sharing expertise and ensuring coherence, efficiency and cost reduction, among other things. It would be pointless to deny that this field is also one of competition between the different positions, visions and perceptions about the goals, priorities and strategies of all the actors. At the same time, the Commission is in a delicate situation – one of dependence. On the one hand, its activities depend on the support of the member states, which, through the European Council, determine its competences, and again, through the Council, renew, with the European Parliament, its programmes and budgets. On the other hand, the legitimacy of the Commission depends on its capacity to base its work on appropriate expertise, which generally comes from experts in civil society. Despite everything, the coordination, consultation and cooperation with all the actors in a formal and informal context place the Commission in the middle of their activity, allowing it to stimulate the interactions in the field.

Structuring through Connections between Internal and External Security

The three case studies show that the European Commission structures the field of security and defence not only by stimulating the interactions among actors in the field, but also by providing a concrete and tangible link between internal and external security issues as well as between the community instruments associated with them. To justify its role in these sensitive matters, the Commission has taken advantage of the European security strategy, which argues the need for a comprehensive approach to security and the use of all EU instruments when facing threats. In general, the Commission (2003, p. 8) argues that the 'failure to enhance the contribution of Community policies, especially on trade, development, internal market, research, and competition policy, will result in sub-optimal solutions in terms of the effectiveness of the ESDP [CSDP]'.

Besides the CFSP/CSDP, the Commission (2006a, p. 7) aims at 'improv[ing] the internal coherence and effectiveness of its input to EU external policy across the full range of its responsibilities. Action to improve strategic planning and priority setting will be pursued in order to ensure the right policy mix on external issues, whether geographical or thematic.' Thus, the Commission emphasizes the link between short- and long-term actions, clearly confirmed with the IfS, but generally in its activity as a whole. Above all, the multidimensional role of the Commission allows it to ensure the connection between internal and external security. In this respect, the Commission generally refers to an integrated approach for security in order to include both dimensions of security in its activities. For example, concerning security research, the Commission (2009, p. 3) refers to the 'societal dimension of security', and for crisis response, the Commission (2003, p. 7) insists on the link between development and security. Moreover, some community instruments, such as the IfS, as we have seen, and security research, are used for both internal and external security. In this respect, the European Commission argues for the added value of its role, which contributes to the coordination of all the actors as well as activities within the European field of security and defence.

Conclusion

An analysis that emphasizes the European Commission's position runs the risk of overestimating its role and its impact on the field of European security and defence. However, this paper considers that the structuring of the field is the result of interaction among several actors, both state and non-state. In this respect, we have seen how the interdependence between EU external policies, confirmed in the European security strategy, has increased the interaction between supranational institutions and national governments in a field where member states are historically reluctant to transfer sovereignty to the Union. I have shown how the implementation of the CFSP and the CSDP offers a window of opportunity for several actors, the EU institutions and also non-state actors, from civil society. Thus, the European Commission has strengthened its role and it has become a player in EU security governance. However, in order to gain the legitimacy to act in this sensitive field, the Commission needs appropriate expertise, and to be efficient, it must work with credible partners. As a result, it has developed relations with relevant actors from member states, EU bodies and civil society.

This paper has skimmed over the European Security Research Programme, the Instrument for Stability and the Defence Package, showing how the Commission coordinates, manages and regulates security and defence issues. The paper has analysed not only the Commission's position in the field and its perception of this, but its relations with the other actors involved in EU security governance. It has emphasized the practices used to evaluate the impact of the Commission's approach and the application of its instruments. At the end of the day, the European Commission plays a crucial role as an interface between various kinds of actors within the field, placing it in the middle of these interactions in order to ensure the coherence of the European field of security and defence.

The next steps will be to evaluate the impact of the Lisbon Treaty on the position of the European Commission in the field of security and defence. The Treaty made major institutional reforms in order to simplify the EU framework. While it officially abolished the pillar system, it did not completely abandon the logical basis on which it was founded. This institutional simplification brings together all the tools that the EU uses for its international role. Nevertheless, the European Commission is facing a huge challenge with the implementation of the new provisions of the Treaty. Its implementation of it will tell us if the role of the European Commission will be limited or reinforced by the new institutional reforms and structures, notably by the European External Action Service and the new hybrid position of the High Representation/Vice-President of the Commission. At the same time, the main ambition of the Lisbon Treaty is to improve and facilitate coordination between member states and EU bodies, as well as among EU external action policies and instruments. According to the Treaty, this role of coordination comes under the responsibility of the High Representative and the Council; we will see how the application of the Treaty will transform the position of the Commission at a meeting point of interactions and its room for manoeuvre within the European field of security and defence.

Notes

[1] To avoid any confusion, this paper will only refer to the CSDP even if some allusions concern this policy before the entry into force of the Lisbon Treaty in December 2009.
[2] Interviews conducted with actors from think-tanks, NGOs, enterprises and lobbies in Brussels in 2007 and 2010.
[3] Interviews conducted at the European Commission in October 2010.
[4] Since the coming into force of the Lisbon Treaty on 1 December 2009, the DG for External Relations moved to the European External Action Service (EEAS). The EEAS was launched officially on 1 December 2010. However, this paper will refer to the DG for External Relations to simplify the analysis.
[5] Interviews conducted at the European Commission in October 2010.
[6] Interviews conducted at the EDA and the European Commission in 2007 and 2010.
[7] Interviews conducted at the European Commission in October 2010.

References

Assembly of Western European Union, (2010) Security research in the European Union: Evaluation of the Seventh Framework Programme – Reply to the annual report of the Council. *Document A/2094*, 1 December.
Bigo. D., (2005) La mondialisation de l'(in) sécurité? Réflexion sur le champ des professionnels de la gestion des inquiétudes et analytique de la transnationalisation des processus d'(in) sécurisation. *Cultures et conflits*, 58, pp. 53–101.
Biscop, S. (2008) La Stratégie Européenne de Sécurité: Mettre en œuvre l'approche holistique. In: C. Lavallée, ed. *L'Europe de la défense: Acteurs, enjeux et processus*. Paris, France: La Documentation Française, pp. 25–38.
Bourdieu, P., (1989) Sociological space and symbolic power. *Sociology theory*, 7 (1), pp. 14–25.
Bourdieu, P., (2000) D.G. Dimitrakopoulos, ed. *Propos sur le champ politique*. Lyon, France: Presses Universitaires de Lyon.
Cameron, F., and Spence, D., (2004) The Commission-Council tandem in the foreign policy area. In: D.G. Dimitrakopoulos, ed. *The changing European Commission*. UK: Manchester University Press, pp. 121–137.
Chouala, Y.A., (2002) Le paradigme du champ à l'épreuve de l'analyse internationaliste. *International review of sociology*, 12 (3), pp. 521–544.
Christiansen, T., (1997) Tensions of European governance: Politicized bureaucracy and multiple accountability in the European Commission. *Journal of European public policy*, 4 (1), pp. 73–90.
Davis Cross, M.K., (2010) Cooperation by committee: The EU Military Committee and the Committee for Civilian Crisis Management. *Occasional Paper 82*. Paris, France: EUISS.
Dijkstra, H., (2009) Commission versus Council Secretariat: An analysis of bureaucratic rivalry in European foreign policy. *European foreign affairs review*, 14, pp. 431–450.
Duke, S., (2007) The role of committees and working groups in the CFSP area. In: T. Christiansen and T. Larsson, eds. *The role of committees in the policy-process of the European Union*. Cheltenham, UK: Edward Elgar, pp. 120–151.
Duke, S. and Ojanen, H., (2006) Bridging internal and external security: Lessons from the European Security and Defence Policy. *European integration*, 28 (5), pp. 477–494.
Europa, (2010) Specific program cooperation [online]. Available from: http://europa.eu/legislation_-summaries/research_innovation/general_framework/i23026_en.htm (accessed 11 April 2011).
European Commission, (2001a) Communication from the Commission on conflict prevention, COM (01)211, final.
European Commission, (2001b) European governance: A White Paper, COM (01)428, final.
European Commission, (2003) European defence industrial and market issues – Towards an EU defence equipment policy, COM (03)113, final.
European Commission, (2004a) Research for a secure Europe – Report of the Group of Personalities in the Field of Security. Brussels, EUR2110, March.
European Commission, (2004b) Communication from the Commission to the Council, the European Parliament, the European and Social Committee and the Committee of the Regions Security Research: The next steps. COM (04)590, final.

European Commission, (2004c) Green Paper on defence procurement, COM (04)608, final.
European Commission, (2004d) Communication from the Commission to the Council and the European Parliament on the instruments for external assistance under the Future Financial Perspective 2007–2013, COM (04)626, final.
European Commission, (2006a) Communication from the Commission to the European Council of June 2006: Europe in the world – Some practical proposals for greater coherence, effectiveness and visibility, COM (06)278, final.
European Commission, (2006b) Interpretative communication on the application of Article 296 of the Treaty in the field of defence procurement, COM (06)779, final.
European Commission, (2007a) The instrument for stability strategy paper 2007–2011 [online].Available from: http://ec.europa.eu/europeaid/where/worldwide/stability-instrument/documents/ifs_strategy_ 2007-2011_en.pdf [Accessed 13 April 2011]
European Commission, (2007b) A strategy for a stronger and more competitive European defence industry, COM (07)764, final.
European Commission, (2008) Report from the Commission to the Council and the European Parliament: Annual report from the European Commission on the Instrument for Stability in 2007 – Executive Summary, COM (08)181, final.
European Commission, (2009) Communication from the Commission: A European security research and innovation agenda – Commission's initial position on ESRIF's key findings and recommendations, COM (09)691, final.
European Commission, (2010) Report from the Commission to the European Parliament, the Council, the European Economic and Social Committee and the Committee of the Regions: 2009 Annual Report from the European Commission on the Instrument for Stability, COM (10)512, final.
European Commission/Enterprise and Industry, (2010) Defence industries working together to support Europe's defence [online]. Available from: http://ec.europa.eu/enterprise/sectors/defence/index_en.htm (Accessed 11 April 2011).
European Commission/Enterprise and Industry, (2011) Defence industries: Reference documents [online]. Available from: http://ec.europa.eu/enterprise/sectors/defence/documents/index_en.htm (Accessed 22 March 2011).
European Commission/EuropeAid Cooperation and Development, (2010) Instrument for Stability [online]. Available from: http://ec.europa.eu/enterprise/sectors/defence/documents/index_en.htm (Accessed 13 April 2011).
European Commission/Register of Interest Representatives, (2011) Register of Interest Representatives [online]. Available from: https://webgate.ec.europa.eu/transparency/regrin/welcome.do?locale=en (Accessed 30 March 2011).
European Community, (2006) European Parliament and Council Regulation (EC) No. 1717/2006 of 15 November 2006 on establishing an instrument for stability. *Official journal of the European Union*, L327/ 1-L327/11.
European Council, (2003) *A secure Europe in a better world – European Security Strategy*. Brussels, 12 December.
European Defence Agency, (2009) EDA and Commission to work closely together on research [online]. Available from: http://www.eda.europa.eu/newsitem.aspx?id=471 (Accessed 11 April 2011).
European Peacebuilding Liaison Office, (2010) Conflict prevention partnership [online]. Available from: http://www.eplo.org/conflict-prevention-partnership (Accessed 18 April 2011).
Grevi, G., and Keohane, D., (2009) ESDP resources. *In*: G. Grevi, D. Helly and D. Keohane, eds. *European security and defence policy: The first 10 years (1999–2009)*. Paris, France: EUISS, pp. 69–114.
Howorth, J., (2001) European defence and changing politics of the European Union: Hanging together or hanging separately? *Journal of common market Studies*, 39 (4), pp. 765–789.
Howorth, J., (2003) Ideas and discourse in the construction of a European security and defense policy for the twenty-first century. *In*: A. Moens, L.J. Cohen and A.G. Sens, eds. *NATO and European security: Alliance politics from the end of the Cold War to the Age of Terrorism*. Westport, USA: Praeger, pp. 37–54.
Howorth, J., (2004) Discourse, ideas and epistemic communities in European security and defence policy. *West European politics*, 27 (2), pp. 211–234.
Howorth, J., (2010) The Political and Security Committee: A case study in supranational inter-governmentalism. *In*: *Les Cahiers Européens de Sciences Po*, 1, pp. 1–23. Paris: Centre d'Etudes Européennes.

Irondelle, B., (2005) L'Europe de la défense à la croisée des chemins? *Critique internationale*, 26, pp. 45–55.

Kauppi, N., (2003) Bourdieu's political sociology and the politics of European integration. *Theory and society*, 32, pp. 775–789.

Kirchner, E. J., (2006) The challenge of European Union security governance. *Journal of common market studies*, 44 (5), pp. 947–968.

Kirchner, E.J., (2007) EU security governance in a wider Europe. *In*: P. Foradori. et al., eds. *Managing a multilevel foreign policy: The EU in international affairs*. Lanham, UK: Lexington Books, pp. 23–41.

Kirchner, E.J., and Sperling, J., (2007) *EU security governance*. UK: Manchester University Press.

Mérand, F., (2006) Social representations in the European security and defence policy. *Cooperation and conflict*, 41 (2), pp. 131–152.

Mérand, F., (2008) *European defence policy: Beyond the nation state*. UK: Oxford University Press.

Mérand, F., and Pouliot, V., (2008) Le monde de Pierre Bourdieu: Éléments pour une théorie sociale des relationsi nternationales. *Revue Canadienne de science politique*, 41 (3), pp. 603–625.

Müller-Brandeck-Bocquet, G., (2002) The new CFSP and ESDP decision-making system of the European Union. *European foreign affairs review*, 7 (3), pp. 257–282.

Ojanen, H., (2006) The EU and NATO: Two competing models for a common defence policy. *Journal of common market studies*, 44 (1), pp. 57–76.

Ricci, Andrea, ed., (2008) *From warning to action: Reportage on the EU's Instrument for Stability*. Brussels, Belgium: Publications of European Communities.

Ricci, Andrea, ed., (2010) *Making the difference? What works in responses to crises and security threats – The debate continues*. Brussels, Belgium: Publications European Communities.

Šefčovič, M., (2010) The Treaty of Lisbon – One year on cooperation in a mature institutional framework [online]. Speech at the European University Institute. Available from: http://www.europa-eu-un.org/articles/en/article_10361_en.htm (Accessed 16 December 2010).

Stewart, E. J., (2008) Capabilities and coherence? The evolution of European Union conflict prevention. *European foreign affairs review*, 13, pp. 229–253.

Tonra, B., (2000) Committees in common: Committee governance and CFSP. *In*: T. Christiansen and E. Kirchner, eds. *Committee governance in the European Union*. UK: Manchester University Press, pp. 145–160.

Webber, M., et al., (2004) The governance of European security. *Review of international studies*, 30 (1), pp. 3–26.

Is the EP Still a Data Protection Champion? The Case of SWIFT

ARIADNA RIPOLL SERVENT & ALEX MACKENZIE

ABSTRACT *Since the 1970s, the European Parliament (EP) has been active in the area of data protection, even though it lacked the legislative power to have significant impact. The EP favoured strong data protection controls within the EU and it demonstrated this in the case of the EU-US Passenger Name Record (PNR) Agreement, for example. With the introduction of the Treaty of Lisbon in 2009, the EP gained, among other things, consent over most international agreements. Whereas the EP was relatively powerless in previous international agreements concerned with data protection, the EU-US SWIFT Agreement allowed the EP, for the first time, to flex its muscles. Even so, the EP appears to have disappointed the proponents of data protection by consenting to the second (permanent) SWIFT Agreement. In this article, we demonstrate that although the EP's previous stance was one of advocacy of strong data protection controls, it could afford to prioritize this without a concern for how such preferences would affect the EU member states. However, now that the EP has the burden of legal powers granted to it by the Treaty of Lisbon, it must be responsible to the member states' security concerns. SWIFT highlights that the EP maintained higher standards of data protection than the Council, but these data protection controls did not deal with major issues such as the transfer of 'bulk data' to the US.*

Introduction

Historically, the European Parliament (EP) has been a strong proponent of human rights and data protection within Europe. This stance has often brought it into conflict with both domestic and external actors, particularly the Council and the US. For instance, the EP condemned the EU-US Passenger Name Record (PNR) Agreements in 2004, 2006 and 2007 because of data protection concerns.[1] However, this opposition was expressed before the EP had any responsibility in legislating or ratifying agreements on internal security matters. With third states. In response to gaining power and influence, it appears that the EP has in fact moderated its stance in later times. In the Society for Worldwide Interbank Financial Telecommunications (SWIFT) case, the EP raised fundamental objections to the US's use of European bank data through its Terrorist Financing and Tracking Programme (TFTP) by passing resolutions that set out recommendations for an EU-US agreement.[2] Once more, this was before the EP had gained consent over international agreements, which it received from 1 December 2009 in the Treaty of Lisbon (Art. 218 TFEU). As it turned out, there were two EU-US SWIFT Agreements in 2010. The EP rejected the first (interim) Agreement in February 2010 due to what it felt were insufficient data protection safeguards. However, it then accepted a re-negotiated second (permanent) Agreement in July 2010.

In past scenarios, the EP had led opposition to unpopular agreements that infringed upon civil liberties and human rights. However, once granted an increased role and enhanced legal powers, the EP has often adopted a more consensual position towards the Council. The purpose of this article is to ascertain whether in the SWIFT case, the EP followed the same pattern as it had in earlier data protection cases. On the one hand, the EP accepted a permanent SWIFT Agreement that, in our opinion, was not considerably different from the first interim Agreement. In this way, the EP did behave consensually towards the Council and the US. On the other hand, the EP, for the first time, pushed the US to make concessions and forced its way into playing a more important role in the procedure of EU-US agreements.

We demonstrate this argument by looking back at EU counter-terrorism policies and the EP's historical role in data protection. Secondly, we give a brief history of the SWIFT Agreement. Thirdly, we examine the EP's 17 September 2009 resolution on SWIFT and extract the key points of the EP's data protection concerns. Fourth, we compare the main demands of the EP with the reality of the second Agreement, looking at the concessions granted by the US. Fifth, we look at other reasons why the EP accepted SWIFT, including issues of responsibility, inter-institutional affairs and the EP's nascent relationship with the US.

1. The Role of the EP in Counter-Terrorism: A Rising Data Protection Champion

The battle around SWIFT is not a new incident in EU debates. The Agreement exemplifies the tensions of a growing policy area: EU counter-terrorism. Therefore, it is important to anchor the events of SWIFT in the wider development of this EU policy area and to understand the role of the EU institutions – and more specifically of the EP – in it.

The EU's Role in Counter-Terrorism

Currently, EU counter-terrorism literature consists of two strands: The first, demonstrated by Bures (2006), suggests that the EU's counter-terrorism policies amount to a 'paper tiger', while the second strand recognises that the EU at least has the potential to play a more significant counter-terrorism role, as shown by Zimmermann (2006). Although we take the latter view, there are significant restrictions on the competences and range of activities that the EU can fulfil. For instance, several scholars have observed that although the EU can do much in counter-terrorism and its involvement has increased rapidly since 2001, it is not a national government and does not have many of the powers associated with one, including the power to arrest suspected terrorists (Edwards and Meyer, 2008; Keohane, 2005; Zimmermann, 2006). Furthermore, while it has been argued that the EU is not a significant actor in external counter-terrorism cooperation (Keohane, 2008), there is a growing body of literature that suggests that the EU is in fact becoming more active, especially in co-operation with the US (Argomaniz, 2009; Kaunert, 2010b; Kaunert and Leonard, 2011; MacKenzie, 2010; Occhipinti, 2010; Rees, 2006, 2008). Whereas the EU's place in counter-terrorism has seen significant scholarship, the respective roles played by the EU institutions in counter-terrorism – and security, more generally – have been overlooked, as Kaunert (2007, 2010a) demonstrated in the case of the European Commission with the European Arrest Warrant (EAW) and the Area of Freedom, Security and Justice (AFSJ). We shall, instead, focus specifically upon the European Parliament (EP), which has been neglected in EU counter-terrorism literature.

There is, however, an emerging literature on the role of the EP in counter-terrorism agreements with third states, especially on the Passenger Name Record (PNR) saga and the SWIFT Agreement (Argomaniz, 2009; Brouwer, 2009; Guild and Brouwer, 2006; Hailbronner et al., 2008; Koesters et al., 2010; Monar, 2010). In the past, the EP had no role in such agreements, since it could only give its opinion. The Treaty of Lisbon empowered the EP by giving it the right to ratify international agreements relevant to and motivated by counter-terrorism. Therefore, whereas with PNR, the EP was legally impotent with no formal powers to affect the Agreement, SWIFT saw the EP gain an essential veto power, giving it the right to say 'yes' or 'no' to the final text. Because these enhanced powers are recent additions to the EP's arsenal, it is perhaps unsurprising that the EP has gone unnoticed in the EU counter-terrorism literature.

The new power of consent over international agreements opens new opportunities for the EP in this policy area. However, given that the EP has its own set of interests, which have often been at odds with those of the Council (especially in data protection), the EP it has the potential not just to be an important institution in counter-terrorism cooperation with the US, but to redefine relations completely.

Data Protection as an Institutional Battlefield

Indeed, data protection has been a long-term concern for the EP, especially for its Committee on Civil Liberties, Justice and Home Affairs (LIBE). In fact, since the 1970s, the EP has been the clearest advocate for data protection issues among the EU institutions. Neither the Commission nor the Council had been particularly pressed to harmonize basic standards of data protection (De Hert et al., 2008, p. 127; Newman, 2008, p. 109) and remained inactive until pressures from the Single European Market and the Schengen Agreement revealed the necessity to legislate at the EU level (De Hert et al., 2008; Pearce and Platten, 1998).

The first attempt to regulate data protection for community matters (i.e. for the first pillar) was encapsulated in the Data Protection Directive (DPD) (European Parliament and Council of the European Union, 1995). The DPD introduced a specific EU model of data protection. The new model – strongly supported by the

EP – combined high standards of protection with the abolition of internal barriers to the free flow of personal data. Thus, it aimed to foster the internal market while ensuring that human rights were sufficiently protected (Pearce and Platten, 1998; Fromholz, 2000). However, there was no equivalent framework for data falling under the third pillar (police and judicial cooperation in criminal matters), so the EP continued to call for an all-embracing framework that would also cover third-pillar measures. A third-pillar text was eventually produced in 2008 (Council of the European Union, 2008) after much deliberation in the Council and several re-consultations with the EP (Guild et al., 2009; O'Neill, 2010).

The separation of data protection into two pillars was at the core of most EP-Council disagreements. For instance, the PNR Agreements with the US sparked intense criticism from the EP, which considered that the quantity and types of data transmitted to the US violated the DPD. However, the PNR case was also a clear demonstration of the limitations that the consultation procedure inflicted on the EP: It allowed Members of the European Parliament (MEPs) to bark, but not bite (Koesters et al., 2010). In this sense, Pawlak (2009, p. 38) has underlined that '[i]t is not difficult to conclude that the behaviour of the EP exhibits elements of a "turf war" for more power and influence'.

In fact, until the extension of the co-decision and consent procedures introduced by the Treaty of Lisbon, the EP had to develop strategies of contestation that did not involve legislative influence. Since the late 1990s, the LIBE committee has been very effective in making public new cases of data protection violations. The committee made use of public hearings and resolutions to shape its position[3] (e.g. Statewatch, 2003). Several resolutions on the fight against terrorism and especially on data-sharing with the US put the committee in the limelight and portrayed it as a major advocate of data protection issues.

Thus, the EP had been very consistent in its defence of data protection standards, especially since the events of 11 September 2001, when national and international pressures increased the potential conflicts between security measures and personal privacy. In view of this past behaviour, there was a general assumption that the EP would use an increase in its powers to fight for an overhaul of any internal security policies that affected data protection. This expectation was two-fold: It was assumed that the involvement of the EP would lead to greater parliamentary scrutiny – and thus narrow the democratic gap in the AFSJ (Maurer, 2001; Carrera and Geyer, 2007) – or that it would tip the balance towards a more rights-based approach (Grabbe, 2002; Guild and Carrera, 2005). However, these expectations have sometimes fallen short. After the extension of co-decision in 2005, the EP has been upgraded to the role of co-legislator in all internal security matters falling under the first pillar.[4] Despite now having full veto power that allows it to block legislation, the EP has not made use of this power to block legislation in the AFSJ. On the contrary, its behaviour has become more consensual, with clear impacts on policy outcomes (Ripoll Servent, 2011).

The Data Retention Directive (DRD) (European Parliament and Council of the European Union, 2006) is the clearest example of this change of behaviour. The proposal, which aims at retaining telecommunications data for the purpose of investigating and prosecuting serious crimes, was the first text linked to counter-terrorism to be negotiated under co-decision. The original proposal fell under the third pillar, but, ultimately, it was transferred to the first pillar, allowing the EP to co-legislate with the Council. Since the EP had been very critical of data retention since the early 2000s, it was expected that, under co-decision, it would fight for stricter data protection standards. However, after only three months of negotiations, the EP caved in and accepted a text characterized by high degrees of flexibility for member states, which undermined considerably the extent of the data protection (Peers, 2005).

The example of the DRD sets a good benchmark to compare the high expectations raised by the behaviour under consultation and its actual performance when forced to take responsibility for the outcome of legislation (Ripoll Servent, 2009). Therefore, it is important to analyse the performance of the EP in the negotiations on SWIFT to determine the extent to which it lived up to the expectations raised prior to the introduction of the Treaty of Lisbon.

2. Background to SWIFT

This second section situates the SWIFT Agreement within its historical context. SWIFT was not new in 2009, but had for years proven to be a highly contentious topic within the EP because of the data protection implications, demonstrated by the fact that the EP released three resolutions on SWIFT between 2006 and 2009 (European Parliament, 2006, 2007, 2009).

SWIFT is a Belgian company that facilitates international bank transfers. These transfers contain the personal data of both the payer and the payee (González Fuster et al., 2008). Since SWIFT is responsible for about 80 per cent of this market globally (Deutsche Welle, 2010), access to its data is of clear interest to the US security authorities. This potential was recognized in the aftermath of 11 September 2001 by the US Department of the Treasury (UST), which created a TFTP based on information provided by SWIFT. Because SWIFT had one of its mirrors in the US (Virginia),[5] it was obliged to cooperate with the US authorities, who requested data from SWIFT in the form of subpoenas (administrative requests).

The TFTP system remained secret until it was revealed on 23 June 2006 in *The New York Times*. This came as a surprise 'almost for everybody' (González Fuster et al., 2008, p. 194) and raised several questions about US processing of data and data protection. Among the first to denounce the system was the EP, which put pressure on the company to change the system. Consequently, SWIFT decided to migrate all intra-European data contained in the US server to a new server in Switzerland (Kaunert and Leonard, 2011). In practice, this meant that the US could no longer use subpoenas to request data on European transactions via the US server. This created a gap in the US system, since it also affected data exchanged between countries connected to the European zone, such as Pakistan, Iraq and Sudan.[6] The inability to access such crucial data sparked talks between the EU and the US to find an agreement that would allow the latter to access European data without having to resort to bilateral agreements on judicial cooperation (Occhipinti, 2010, p. 137), which were seen as too cumbersome.

Being a third-pillar agreement, the Swedish Presidency took the lead and, after intense negotiations, an interim agreement was finalized and agreed upon by the Council on 30 November 2009, one day before the EP would have to consent to the agreement. This decision sparked the fury of the EP and it continued to grow under the Spanish Presidency (which took over the reins of the Presidency in January 2010).[7] Matters were not improved when the US, fearing a negative vote from the EP, made an 'unprecedented' lobbying effort towards the EP (Monar, 2010, p. 145). Hillary Clinton, the US Secretary of State, and Timothy Geithner, the Treasury Secretary, contacted on repeated occasions EP leaders (Monar, 2010, p. 145; Geithner and Clinton, 2010) and the US even made threats about bypassing the EU and opening up bilateral agreements with specific member states were the EP to reject the agreement (Monar, 2010, p. 145).

In the end, the first SWIFT Agreement was rejected in plenary.[8] This situation left all sides at an impasse. After a few weeks of stalemate, the US decided to press on with an EU-US Agreement, recognizing that it had to cooperate and compromise with the EP for the sake of SWIFT and future EU-US agreements. After a second negotiation process in which the US gave into some of the EP's demands on data protection, the EP passed the Agreement on 8 July 2010.[9]

3. Resolutions and Results

In order to evaluate the different decisions of the EP regarding SWIFT (its rejection or support of the Agreement), it is important to examine what position it publicly supported as well as how this position compares with the eventual outcome of negotiations. Therefore, we first focus on the EP resolution, containing the main points of concern regarding SWIFT and compare it to the text of the permanent Agreement decided upon in Summer 2010.

The EP's Resolution of September 2009

This section examines the EP's 17 September 2009 resolution. We focus on this resolution because it was the most developed prior to the EP gaining consent under the new post-Lisbon rules. In addition, the EP released a fourth resolution on 5 May 2010 (European Parliament, 2010b), but this came after both the February vote and the introduction of the post-Lisbon rules.

The EP did not necessarily oppose an EU-US SWIFT Agreement (as demonstrated in all three resolutions), but MEPs were critical of the data protection issues raised by US use of such data. In the resolution of 17 September 2009, the EP took a firm stance towards the Agreement and raised a number of concerns that would be at the core of disagreements in the months to come. The EP's list of concerns consisted of several main points. First, it raised doubts about the necessity and proportionality of a SWIFT Agreement and about the purpose limitation of the definition of terrorism (Point 7.a.).[10] It insisted that the use of data outside of terrorism financing and transfer of data to third parties not connected with fighting terrorism should be prohibited (Point 7.f.) and that data reciprocity[11] must be strictly adhered to (Point 7.g.). Equally, the EP specified that batches and large files relating to the Single European Payments Area (SEPA) must fall outside the scope of the data to be transferred to the UST (Point 9). Second, there was generalized opposition towards the 'pull' system[12] (Point 7.b.) required by the transfer of 'bulk data'.[13] The EP preferred a 'push'[14] system instead or, at least, asked to introduce a judicial authorization for the transmission of 'bulk data' (Point 7.c). Third, the EP raised several points concerning the absence of a judicial review when the legality and proportionality of the transfers was questioned (Point 7.d.), requiring that transferred data be subject to the same judicial redress mechanisms as in the EU (Point 7.e.). Finally, the EP proposed that the Commission should evaluate the possibility of setting up a European TFTP (Point 12) (European Parliament, 2009).[15]

The greatest problem here was that some of these points would inevitably clash with the US' red lines and would thus be difficult to conciliate.[16] These points demonstrate that the EP's stance was in accordance with its long-term preferences on data protection. However, raising expectations to the point where the EP hoped to change the fundamentals of the US' TFTP system risked disappointing the proponents of data protection because there were some areas, such as 'bulk data', on which the US could not compromise. As it turned out, few of the EP's key concerns were integrated into the first Agreement, giving the EP a reason to vote against it. Given that the EP changed its position (from rejection to support) in a period of just five months, we now turn to the second Agreement to look at its contents in order to evaluate what changed that could explain such a U-turn in the EP's position.

The Results of the Permanent SWIFT Agreement

The first SWIFT Agreement was considered unacceptable by the EP particularly because of the 'pull system' and the 'transfer of bulk data'. The second Agreement maintains both, with no binding solutions to either concern. There are vague commitments to improve this situation, but these are subject to implementation. Although changes did boost data protection in the Agreement, we demonstrate that they are weak because the US is still able to make vague requests for data. Therefore, we start with the assumption that the second SWIFT Agreement was not significantly different from the first.

The second SWIFT Agreement did not deal with most of the EP's main concerns[17] On the one hand, there were several improvements. Peter Hustinx, the European Data Protection Supervisor (EDPS), and the Article 29 Working Party analysed the agreement and underlined that some elements had been strengthened in the new version (European Data Protection Supervisor, 2010; Kohnstamm and Pizzetti, 2010). These provided for a more restrictive definition of terrorism (Article 2) and the exclusion of data from SEPA, thus withholding internal Eurozone financial transactions from the scope of the agreement (Article 4.2.d). They were also positive on the stricter provisions set out regarding data subjects' rights (Articles 14–18), which, among others, strengthened the right to be informed and obtain redress, and simplified the right of access to, and the rectification of, one's data (European Data Protection Supervisor, 2010, p. 3).

The EDPS also welcomed the inclusion of an EU 'scrutineer' (Article 12), but warned that its benefits depended on how the tasks would be interpreted and implemented (European Data Protection Supervisor, 2010, p. 13). Also, the EP attempted to justify the absence of change with regard to 'bulk data' by inserting an EU-TFTP system into the agreement (Article 11). An EU TFTP system would ensure that data would be analysed and leads extracted on EU territory, and only then would they be 'pushed' towards the US when requested.[18] However, the creation and practical implementation of such a system remains unclear.

There are, however, significant caveats to these improvements. For instance, as one EU official remarked,[19] although data protection provisions were beefed up in the second Agreement, ultimately, there had been no change in the US legislation on data protection. Most importantly, the Agreement remains based on a 'bulk data' mechanism. In addition, the new compromise does not foresee any system of judicial oversight. The only prior control is now in the hands of Europol, which is a police cooperation agency, not a judicial authority (Article 4). Although some sources have expressed doubts about Europol's legal basis,[20] Hustinx underlined a potentially more damaging concern – that Article 10 allows Europol to request information obtained through the TFTP for investigating terrorism. Therefore, Europol will almost certainly be pressured to maintain good relations with the US in order to successfully obtain TFTP leads, compromising its effective review (European Data Protection Supervisor, 2010, p. 10). Finally, the new agreement mentions in its referrals that EU nationals have access to non-discriminatory treatment when seeking administrative or judicial redress. However, the TFTP Agreement remains an executive agreement and because of this, potential victims will not benefit from any kind of judicial review in the US (EDRI, 2010a).

In summary, although the new agreement enhanced some data protection provisions and restricted its scope, the main concerns raised by the EP in its previous reports were not substantially addressed. Certainly, the EP managed to insert an EU 'scrutineer' and a reference to a future EU-TFTP, but both measures remain subject to interpretation and implementation.[21] In addition, the EU-TFTP appears to be window-dressing, rather than a fundamental change in the system.

4. Legitimizing the Agreement through Other Means?

In the aftermath of the first vote on SWIFT, Martin Schulz, leader of the socialist group in the EP, justified the rejection on the following grounds:

> The US Administration may have wrongly thought they could deal with the European Parliament like Gulliver with the Lilliputians. Under the Swedish Presidency, European governments and the Council also made a mistake to believe it would be possible to force the European Parliament to give its consent on an unacceptable agreement based more on the US approach to security than on the EU's defence of citizens' fundamental rights (Euractiv, 2010b).

It is clear that the rejection of the interim Agreement had been based on three different (albeit interrelated) grounds: an inordinate amount of pressure from the US; resentment against the Commission and the Council for having ignored the EP at the precise moment when the Treaty of Lisbon was introduced; and concerns over data protection. These three grounds are also at the core of the different explanations for the U-turn in the position of the EP that eventually led to it accepting the permanent Agreement. We examine each of the three explanations in order to highlight the main reasons for the EP's acceptance of a text that did not match its high expectations.

Policy Preferences: The 'Twin-Track' Approach as a New Legitimizing Tool

As we have seen, the EP managed to introduce three main points in last-minute negotiations (namely, an EU 'scrutineer', an enhanced role for Europol and a mention of a future EU-TFTP system). These points were rebranded as a 'twin-track' approach that aimed to fill the gaps of the first interim Agreement. This approach emphasized the changes inserted in the Agreement at two different levels. First, EP negotiators highlighted the increase in controls over data transfers. In this sense, the increased data protection safeguards, the presence of an EU 'scrutineer', as well as the new role given to Europol as an 'authorising' figure should offer some guarantees to EU citizens. However, this ex ante control did not solve the issue of 'bulk data' transfers. This issue was to be addressed by the second level of the 'twin-track' approach, namely the development of an EU-TFTP.[22]

The efforts of the EP negotiators to achieve this balance of present improvements in data protection control and a future solution to the 'bulk data' issue provided enough arguments to the larger parties to legitimize their change of opinion. The 'twin-track' approach was especially promoted by those political groups that had already been more open to accepting the interim agreement back in February 2010. The right wing of the spectrum (with the European People's Party [EPP] at its core) was the main promoter of the change and pushed socialists and liberals (Alliance of Liberals and Democrats for Europe [ALDE]) to accept this solution and vote in favour of the permanent Agreement (European People's Party, 2010). As a consequence, socialists and liberals, who had been at the core of the winning coalition in February, presented this new approach as a solution to the necessity of transferring 'bulk data' to the US (Moraes in European Parliament, 2010a; ALDE Group, 2010).

However, the idea of the 'twin-track' approach is not without problems. For instance, the US has been able to circumvent the data protection controls of the SWIFT Agreement by sending Europol vague requests for data. Despite the changes gained by the EP, the first review of Europol's involvement in the SWIFT Agreement by Europol's Joint Supervisory Board (JSB) pointed out that:

> At the time of inspection, Europol had received four requests for SWIFT data. Those four requests are almost identical in nature and request – in abstract terms – broad types of data, also involving EU Member States data. Due to their abstract nature, proper verification of whether the requests are in line with the conditions of 4(2) of the TFTP Agreement – on the basis of the available documentation – is impossible. The JSB considers it likely that the information in the requests could be more specific (Europol, 2010).

These problems had already been foreseen by the EDPS and the left-wing groups of the EP (Greens and European United Left/Nordic Green Left [GUE/NGL]). The latter highlighted that the core principles of the Agreement (namely transfer of 'bulk data') had not been addressed and that it could enter into conflict with EU law (Greens/EFA, 2010; Tavares in European Parliament, 2010a).

In consequence, the EPP, socialists and liberals managed to introduce some additional safeguards into the permanent Agreement; more significantly, they rebranded the package deal in a way that legitimized the changes in the eyes of the voters. It seems, thus, that it was especially important for these groups to find agreement with the US, even if not all the data protection issues were addressed in this second text. The next two explanations address other alternative (or additional) grounds for accepting the new SWIFT Agreement.

External Factors: Keeping Peace with the US

The vote on 11 February 2010 left all sides at an impasse. The rejection in February had come as a surprise to the US Administration.[23] The pressure exerted by the US had not pushed the EP into accepting the Agreement, but had sparked more resentment. It was not until the end of February that the impasse ended, at which point the Commission was able to start to draft a mandate for a permanent Agreement (Euobserver, 2010).

This state of uncertainty put pressure on the EU institutions. On the one hand, the EU had more leverage in SWIFT than in previous EU-US agreements such as the PNR. There, the US was able to impose its will by putting private companies between a rock and a hard place: Either they complied with US demands for passenger data or they violated EU data protection legislation, as with the PNR (Argomaniz, 2009). SWIFT presented the opposite situation: The US was in a weaker position because they were asking for data on EU soil. Thus, the EU could ask the US to come closer to the position of the EU in order to speed up the process.

On the other hand, this objective leverage was attenuated by two factors based on perceptions internal to the EU. First, the EU negotiators were not sure about how patient the US would be. They knew that the US wanted an agreement as quickly as possible in order to reduce the amount of data lost due to the absence of the Agreement. Yet, they were also concerned that if it was made to wait too long, the US would bypass the EU venue and negotiate bilaterally with some specific member states (notably the Netherlands and Belgium).[24] Second, both a majority of member states in the Council and a large number of the MEPs did not want to disrupt transatlantic relations, especially in the field of counter-terrorism.[25] This was either because of traditional Atlanticism or because they wanted to continue outsourcing their security to the US (Aldrich, 2009; Argomaniz, 2009). In sum, most EU actors did not want to disrupt the EU-US partnership.

This reticence increased among the MEPs, especially after the efforts made by the US to listen to the EP. Rather than becoming more coercive, the behaviour of the US actually changed from pressure to encouragement. This reflected a major shift away from the way the Bush Administration had treated the EU,[26] and it was undoubtedly an effort to 'woo' the EP into accepting the Agreement. The US issued invitations to LIBE MEPs to visit the US (Euractiv, 2010a) and the US President or Vice-President, Joe Biden, visited the EP on 6 May 2010. It was the first visit by a US Vice-President since 1985 (European Parliament, 2010c) and, thus, it was a clear sign of respect towards the EP.[27] This softer US posture gave MEPs a sense of importance that they were not used to and convinced them that the US was going to listen to them.

Indeed, the US gave into a couple of the EP's demands: the 'scrutineer' and EU TFTP. These concessions were essential to change the position of the EP, first, because it strengthened the EU-US partnership (now creating a new dialogue with the EP) and, second, because (as seen previously) they made it possible to rebrand the Agreement as a new 'twin-track' system that engaged the US in a future EU-TFTP system.

Institutional Changes: Learning How to Use a New Institutional Tool

Finally, the change in decision-making procedures after the introduction of the Treaty of Lisbon played an extremely important role in the EP's U-turn on the SWIFT Agreement. The rejection of February 2010 can be understood largely as a vote of protest against the way the Council and Commission had treated the EP during the negotiations for a SWIFT interim agreement. The Council had proved unwilling to make any concessions towards the EP and that had irritated an EP leadership ready to use their increased powers. SWIFT was thus the perfect occasion for the EP to 'flex its muscles and show the power acquired under Lisbon'.[28]

However, the rejection also showed that the formal rules of the Treaty had important limitations. If used literally, the consent procedure was a potential 'nuclear' power (Smith, 1999, p. 76), since the EP could only accept or reject an agreement. Indeed, that proved to be fatal in the case of SWIFT. Although the negotiations were led without any formal hiccups (the EP was informed during the process), it was clear that – in order to be successful – the EP would have to be involved informally from the earliest stages of negotiations. As a consequence, the Commission (now in charge of negotiations), decided to tweak the rules of the game and adopt a slightly different interpretation of the Treaty rules.[29] Commissioners Malmström and Reding involved the EP from the beginning, providing information[30] and discussing the new mandate with key MEPs.[31] By doing so, the Commission effectively interpreted the obligation to *inform* the EP at all stages as being equivalent to *involving* the EP from the earliest stages of the procedure.

The Council also recognized that it needed to change its behaviour if it wanted to have an agreement before summer.[32] The change was particularly evident in the behaviour of the Spanish Presidency, which was more accommodating than during the first months of 2010. Notably, during the last stages of negotiations, the EP was still dissatisfied with some points and thus allied with the Spanish Presidency to modify Article 12.[33] In a certain way, the EP managed to turn the procedure upside down and informally transform the consent procedure into a *quasi*-co-decision.

However, the change towards a procedure that resembled co-decision had further consequences, since the EP also needed to change its behaviour and abandon past inter-institutional conflicts. It required a change of behaviour from the MEPs, who were asked to be *responsible* (i.e. to be cooperative and constructive) and use the new tool with care. Rejecting the agreement for a second time would have been seen as an irresponsible decision and would have seriously undermined future negotiations in which the EP's consent was required. Alexander Alvaro, ALDE rapporteur for the second Agreement, justified the change by pointing out that the EP had to engage in discussions in order to gain in responsibility and powers.[34] Similarly, Simon Busuttil, political coordinator for the EPP group in LIBE, reflected on the legacy of SWIFT for future consent cases, underlining that the experience was also a lesson for the EP. The MEPs had to realize that the increased power would have to be carried with responsibility.[35]

In the end, the necessity to behave *responsibly* meant that the EP had to settle for an agreement with fewer changes than those desired at the beginning. As we have seen previously, the final result did not fulfil the basic claims of the EP regarding 'bulk data' and judicial redress in the US. The red lines of the US were ultimately respected and the EP successfully inserted some provisions to justify a positive vote. Yet, ultimately, the EP had to sacrifice its policy preferences in order to be effective in the negotiations.

Conclusion

Despite its rapid growth in the last years, EU counter-terrorism literature has overlooked the role played by EU institutions, the EP in particular. However, given the increased role of the EP in counter-terrorism decision-making, it is essential to review its past positions and future potential. As we have seen, the EP's long-term preferences had been geared towards increasing the protection of data in the EU. Under consultation – with only the power to give its opinion – the EP grew to be a clear data protection champion. However, this absolute position might be starting to erode. With the gain in decision-making powers, the EP has abandoned its policy preferences and acquired a taste for consensus and more moderate views. The DRD is perhaps the best example of this: Despite being one of the first occasions for the EP to put its stamp on a co-decision dossier in the area of counter-terrorism, the result was all but a model of data protection. Interestingly, the EP seems to have followed a similar trend during the SWIFT negotiations. Before the changes introduced by the Treaty of Lisbon, the EP had consistently opposed EU-US agreements for being too damaging to data protection for European citizens. The EU-US PNR Agreement is probably the best example from the past. By opposing the PNR Agreement and showing resistance to the SWIFT Agreement, the EP led many to believe that it would stand in favour of data protection and would re-balance the EU-US relationship, which appears, for now, to have been mostly one-way traffic from the US.

In the case of SWIFT, the EP set out quite strongly its preferences in the resolutions leading up to the SWIFT Agreement. However, the increase in institutional power from the Treaty of Lisbon seems to have led the EP to abandon, or at least compromise on, its principles. Although the EP objected to fundamental parts of the US' TFTP (especially regarding 'bulk data') and also took issue with the weak data protection laws in the US, it gained nothing in these areas. Instead, the EP gained a few small compromises from the US; for example, the 'scrutineer', stronger data protection safeguards, and the suggestion of a future EU-TFTP. Even so, the latest revelations of the US circumventing the new data protection controls in the report by Europol's Joint Supervisory Board demonstrates that the EP gained little in the way of substantive changes to the second SWIFT Agreement. In future

EU-US agreements, these reports of abusing the system may well be used against the US, but that is for the future.

Instead, the EP justified its acceptance of the SWIFT Agreement on the basis of a 'twin-track' approach, its willingness to maintain good relationships with the US, and the need to be responsible after its increased role in negotiations. In this way, the most important gains for the EP were in the area of procedure, where it managed to get the Commission and Council to involve MEPs as early as possible in the second Agreement.

As a result, the EP has continued to act consistently with the most recent institutional trends, exhibiting consensual behaviour towards the Council. With increasing power, the EP is showing greater responsibility (i.e. more consensual behaviour) towards the member states. This trend, however, might worry proponents of data protection and civil liberties in Europe. Contrary to past expectations, the EP is not using its new veto powers to open up debate and raise the standards of civil liberties in the field of counter-terrorism. Instead, it is increasingly willing to compromise on its fundamental principles in order to be seen as an efficient and responsible actor in negotiations. Whether this will continue in the area of EU-US agreements in future, however, is yet to be seen.

Notes

[1] The EP will have the chance to vote on the PNR later in 2011.
[2] The dates of the SWIFT resolutions were as follows: 6 July 2006, 12 July 2007 (also on the PNR) and 17 September 2009.
[3] Interview with EP Official, January 2009. Semi-structured interviews were done during March and July 2010 with a variety of actors, mostly from the three main EU institutions. Some interviewees requested anonymity and we have therefore not used their names, only their function. Interviews are listed under references.
[4] Except for family law and legal immigration.
[5] Another mirror server was based in the Netherlands.
[6] Interview with Diplomatic Source A, March 2010.
[7] Ibid.
[8] The first Agreement was rejected by 378 votes to 196 and 31 abstentions (European Union, 2010).
[9] The second Agreement was accepted by 404 votes to 109 and 12 abstentions (Votewatch, 2010).
[10] Their preference was to use the EU definition as set out in Article 1 of the EU Council Framework Decision 2002/475/JHA of 13 June 2002 on combating terrorism. As well as this, the EP wished to restrict usage of the data to known and agreed individuals.
[11] Data reciprocity requires competent US authorities to transfer relevant messaging data to EU authorities when requested.
[12] A 'pull system' would mean that the US could have direct access to the data.
[13] 'Bulk data' means all the data from specified countries and banks over a certain period of time – i.e. millions of transactions (EDRI, 2010b).
[14] A 'push system' is one in which filtered and targeted data would be forwarded to US authorities.
[15] This was vaguely inserted into the first SWIFT Agreement (Art. 9) (Council of the European Union, 2009), but strangely, it was not in the EP's 5 May 2010 resolution. Even so, the second SWIFT Agreement had a more detailed article (Art. 11) on an EU-TFTP than the first Agreement.
[16] Interviews with EU Official and Commission Official A, March 2010.
[17] Interviews with Diplomatic Source B; Commission Official B and EU Official A, July 2010, and communication of Sophie in 't Veld, July 2010.
[18] Interviews with Alexander Alvaro, MEP; EU Official and Diplomatic Source A, July 2010.
[19] Interview with EU Official, July 2010.
[20] Interviews with Commission Officials B and C; Diplomatic Sources A and B, July 2010.

[21] The EU 'scrutineer' started work in the UST on 26 August 2010 (Council of the European Union, 2011).
[22] Interviews with Alexander Alvaro, MEP; EU Official; and Diplomatic Source A, July 2010.
[23] Interview with Commission Official B, July 2010.
[24] Interview with MEP, July 2010.
[25] Interview with EU Official, July 2010.
[26] Interview with MEP, July 2010.
[27] Interview with Commission Official B; MEP, July 2010.
[28] Interview with EU Official, March 2010.
[29] Interviews with Diplomatic Source A, March 2010, and Commission Official B, July 2010.
[30] Interview with Diplomatic Source A, March 2010.
[31] Interview with Commission Official A, March 2010.
[32] Interview with Alexander Alvaro, MEP, July 2010.
[33] Interviews with MEP; Diplomatic Source A; EU Official and Commission Official B, July 2010.
[34] Interview with Alexander Alvaro, MEP, July 2010.
[35] Interview with Simon Busuttil, MEP, March 2010.

Bibliography

ALDE Group, 2010. Parliament gives green light to new, improved data sharing agreement with USA [online]. Press Release. Available from: http://www.alde.eu/press/press-and-release-news/press-release/article/parliament-gives-green-light-to-new-improved-data-sharing-agreement-with-usa-33821/ [Accessed 16 February 2011].

Aldrich, R., 2009. US-European intelligence co-operation on counter-terrorism: Low politics and compulsion. *British journal of politics and international relations*, 11 (1), pp. 122–139.

Argomaniz, J., 2009. When the EU is the 'norm-taker': The Passenger Name Records Agreement and the EU's internalisation of US border security norms. *Journal of European integration*, 31 (1), pp. 119–136.

Brouwer, E., 2009. Towards a European PNR system? Questions on the added value and the protection of fundamental rights [online]. Available from: http://www.europarl.europa.eu/activities/committees/studies/download.do?language=en&file=30170#search=%20PNR [Accessed 18 March 2010].

Bures, O., 2006. EU Counter-Terrorism Policy: A 'paper tiger'? *Terrorism and political violence*, 18 (1), pp. 57–78.

Carrera, S., and Geyer, F., 2007. The Reform Treaty and justice and home affairs – Implications for the common area of freedom, security. *CEPS policy brief*, 141.

Council of the European Union, 2008. *Council Framework Decision of 27 November 2008 on the Protection of Personal Data Processed in the Framework of Police and Judicial Cooperation in Criminal Matters, 2008/977/JHA, Official Journal, L 350/60.*

Council of the European Union, 2009. *Council decision on the signing, on behalf of the European Union, of the Agreement between the European Union and the United States of America on the processing and transfer of financial messaging data from the European Union to the United States for purposes of the Terrorist Finance Tracking Program, 16110/09.*

Council of the European Union, 2011. *Europol's role in the framework of the EU-US TFTP Agreement 1 and state of play of operational and strategic agreements of Europol (specific focus: the agreement on exchange of personal data and related information that Europol has with the US) – EU information policy on the TFTP Agreement, 6266/11.*

De Hert, P., Papakonstantinou, V., and Riehle, C., 2008. Data protection in the third pillar: Cautious pessimism. *In*: M. Maik, ed. *Crime, rights and the EU: The future of police and judicial cooperation*. London: Justice, pp. 121–194.

Deutsche Welle, 2010. US accesses European bank data under controversial SWIFT Agreement [online]. Available from: http://www.dw-world.de/dw/article/0,,5855750,00.html [Accessed 11 August 2010].

EDRI, 2010a. FAQ 2.0 on SWIFT Agreement [online]. Available from: http://www.edri.org/faq-2-swift-agreement-edri [Accessed 28 October 2010].

EDRI, 2010b. New SWIFT Agreement as bad as the rejected one [online]. *EDRI-gram*, 8 (12). Available from: http://www.edri.org/edrigram/number8.12/new-switf-proposal-bad [Accessed 25 September 2010].

Edwards, G., and Meyer, C.O., 2008. Introduction: Charting a contested transformation. *Journal of common market studies*, 46 (1), pp. 1–25.

Euobserver, 2010. Ministers want to give EU-US bank data deal another try [online]. Available from: http://euobserver.com/9/29556 [Accessed 28 October 2010].

Euractiv, 2010a. EU, US re-assess SWIFT data-sharing deal [online]. Available from: http://www.euractiv.com/en/financial-services/meps-washington-collapsed-data-sharing-deal-news-355141 [Accessed 28 October 2010].

Euractiv, 2010b. MEPs say 'no' to SWIFT [online]. Available from: http://www.euractiv.com/en/justice/meps-say-no-swift [Accessed 28 October 2010].

European Data Protection Supervisor, 2010. *Opinion on a proposal for a Council decision on the conclusion of the Agreement between the European Union and the United States of America on the processing and transfer of financial messaging data from the European Union to the United States for purposes of the Terrorist Finance Tracking Program (TFTP II)*. [online]. Available from: http://www.edps.europa.eu/EDPSWEB/webdav/site/mySite/shared/Documents/Consultation/Opinions/2010/10-06-22_Opinion_TFTP_EN.pdf [Accessed 28 October 2010].

European Parliament, 2006. *Resolution of 6 July 2006 on the interception of bank transfer data from the SWIFT system by the US secret services, P6_TA(2006)0317*.

European Parliament, 2007. *Resolution of 14 February 2007 on SWIFT, the PNR Agreement and the transatlantic dialogue on these issues, P6_TA(2007)0039*.

European Parliament, 2009. *Resolution of 17 September 2009 on the envisaged international agreement to make available to the United States Treasury Department financial payment messaging data to prevent and combat terrorism and terrorist financing, P7_TA(2009)0016*.

European Parliament, 2010a. Debates – Tuesday, 6 July 2010 – SWIFT [online]. Available from: http://www.europarl.europa.eu/sides/getDoc.do?type=CRE&reference=20100706&secondRef=ITEM-005&language=EN&ring=A7-2010-0224 [Accessed 16 February 2011].

European Parliament, 2010b. *Resolution of 5 May 2010 on the recommendation from the Commission to the Council to authorise the opening of negotiations for an agreement between the European Union and the United States of America to make available to the United States Treasury Department financial messaging data to prevent and combat terrorism and terrorist financing, P7_TA-PROV(2010)0143*.

European Parliament, 2010c. Special edition: President Buzek news on the European Parliament and the United States [online]. Available from: http://www.europarl.europa.eu/president/ressource/static/newsletter/newsletter-7/newsletter.html [Accessed 25 September 2010].

European Parliament and Council of the European Union, 1995. *Directive of 24 October 1995 of the European Parliament and of the Council on the protection of individuals with regard to the processing of personal data and on the free movement of such data, 95/46/EC, Official Journal L 281/31*.

European Parliament and Council of the European Union, 2006. *Directive of 15 March 2006 on the retention of data generated or processed in connection with the provision of publicly available electronic communications services or of public communications networks and amending directive 2002/58/EC, 2006/24/EC, Official Journal, L 105/54*.

European People's Party, 2010. SWIFT: Agreement essential to fight terrorism [online]. Available from: http://www.eppgroup.eu/press/showpr.asp?PRContentID=16321&PRContentLG=en&PRControlDocTypeID=1&PRControlID=9530 [Accessed 16 February 2011].

European Union, 2010. *Minutes of the Sitting of 11 February 2010 Official Journal C 110/178*.

Europol, 2010. Report on the inspection of Europol's implementation of the TFTP Agreement, conducted in November 2010 by the Europol Joint Supervisory Body [online]. Available from: http://www.ip-rs.si/fileadmin/user_upload/Pdf/novice/Terrorist_Finance_Tracking_Program__TFTP__inspection_report_-_public_version.pdf [Accessed 15 April 2011].

Fromholz, J.M., 2000. The European Union data privacy directive. *Berkeley technology law journal*, 15, pp. 461–484.

Geithner, T.F., and Clinton, H.R., 2010. Letter from Timothy Geithner and Hillary Clinton to Jerzy Buzek [online]. Available from: http://www.statewatch.org/news/2010/feb/eu-usa-swift-letter.pdf [Accessed 25 September 2010].

González Fuster, G., De Hert, P., and Gutwirth, S., 2008. SWIFT and the vulnerability of transatlantic data transfers. *International review of law, computers and technology*, 22 (1), pp. 191–202.

Grabbe, H., 2002. Justice and home affairs: Faster decisions, secure rights [online]. *CER Policy Brief*. Available from: http://www.cer.org.uk/pdf/policybrief_jha.pdf [Accessed 19 February 2009].

Greens/EFA, 2010. SWIFT Agreement: A setback for international fundamental tights protection [online]. Available from: http://www.greens-efa.eu/cms/pressreleases/dok/347/347055.swift_agreement@en.htm [Accessed 16 February 2011].

Guild, E., and Brouwer, E., 2006. The political life of data: The ECJ decision on the PNR Agreement between the EU and the US [online]. CEPS Policy Brief (109). Available from: http://www.ceps.eu/system/files/book/1363.pdf [Accessed 30 September 2010].

Guild, E., and Carrera, S., 2005. No constitutional treaty? Implications for the Area of Freedom, Security and Justice [online]. CEPS Working Document (231). Available from: http://www.ceps.eu/book/no-constitutional-treaty-implications-area-freedom-security-and-justice [Accessed 18 March 2010].

Guild, E., Carrera, S., and Eggenschwiler, A., 2009. Informing the data protection debate [online]. CEPS Special Report. Available from: http://www.ceps.eu/book/informing-data-protection-debate [Accessed 25 September 2010].

Hailbronner, K., Papakonstantinou, V., and Kau, M., 2008. The agreement on passenger-data transfer (PNR) and the EU-US cooperation in data communication. *International migration*, 46 (2), pp. 187–197.

Kaunert, C., 2007. 'Without the power of purse or sword': The European Arrest Warrant and the role of the Commission. *Journal of European integration*, 29 (4), pp. 387–404.

Kaunert, C., 2010a. The Area of Freedom, Security and Justice in the Lisbon Treaty: Commission policy entrepreneurship? *European security*, 19 (2), pp. 169–189.

Kaunert, C., 2010b. The external dimension of EU counter-terrorism relations: Competences, interests, and institutions. *Terrorism and political violence*, 22 (1), pp. 41–61.

Kaunert, C., and Leonard, S., 2011. EU counterterrorism and the European Neighbourhood Policy: An appraisal of the southern dimension. *Terrorism and political violence*, 23 (2), pp. 286–309.

Keohane, D., 2005. *The EU and counter-terrorism* [online]. London: Centre for European Reform. Available from: http://www.cer.org.uk/pdf/wp629_terrorism_counter_keohane.pdf [Accessed 12 April 2011].

Keohane, D., 2008. The absent friend: EU foreign policy and counter-terrorism. *Journal of common market studies*, 46 (1), pp. 125–146.

Koesters, J., et al., 2010. Who cares about Strasbourg? The role of the European Parliament in the PNR Agreements [online]. *Maastricht European studies papers*, 1 (1). Available from: http://www.fdcw.unimaas.nl/mesp/Papers%20%282006%29/MESP_Koesters%20et%20al.%20_2010_.%20Role%20of%20EP%20in%20PNR%20Agreements_PUBLICATION.pdf [Accessed 25 September 2010].

Kohnstamm, J., and Pizzetti, F., 2010. Letter from the Article 29 Working Party to Juan Fernando López Aguilar [online]. Available from: http://ec.europa.eu/justice/policies/privacy/docs/wpdocs/others/2010_06_25_letter_to_libe_en.pdf [Accessed 28 October 2010].

MacKenzie, A., 2010. The European Union's increasing role in foreign policy counterterrorism. *Journal of contemporary European research*, 6 (2), pp. 148–164.

Maurer, A., 2001. Democratic governance in the European Union: The institutional terrain after Amsterdam. *In*: J. Monar and W. Wessels, eds. *The European Union after the Treaty of Amsterdam*. London: Continuum, pp. 96–124.

Monar, J., 2010. The rejection of the EU-US SWIFT interim Agreement by the European Parliament: A historic view and its implications. *European foreign affairs review*, 15 (2), pp. 143–151.

Newman, A.L., 2008. Building transnational civil liberties: Transgovernmental entrepreneurs and the European data privacy directive. *International organisation*, 62 (01), pp. 103–130.

Occhipinti, J., 2010. Partner or pushover? EU relations with the US on internal security. *In*: D.S. Hamilton, ed. *Shoulder to shoulder: Forging a strategic US-EU partnership*. Washington, DC: Johns Hopkins University Centre for Transatlantic Relations, pp. 121–138.

O'Neill, M., 2010. The issue of data protection and data security in the (pre-Lisbon) EU third pillar. *Journal of contemporary European research*, 6 (2), pp. 21–235.

Pawlak, P., 2009. The external dimension of the Area of Freedom, Security and Justice: Hijacker or hostage of cross-pillarisation? *Journal of European integration*, 31 (1), pp. 25–44.

Pearce, G., and Platten, N., 1998. Achieving personal data protection in the European Union. *Journal of common market studies*, 36 (4), pp. 529–547.

Peers, S., 2005. The European Parliament and data retention: Chronicle of a 'sell-out' foretold?[online]. *Statewatch Analysis*. Available from: http://www.statewatch.org/news/2005/dec/sp_dataret_dec05.pdf [Accessed 5 August 2010].

Rees, W., 2006. *Transatlantic counter-terrorism co-operation: The new imperative*. London: Routledge.

Rees, W., 2008. Inside out: The external face of EU Internal Security Policy. *Journal of European integration*, 30 (1), pp. 97–111.

Ripoll Servent, A., 2009. Setting priorities: Functional and substantive dimensions of irregular immigration and data protection under co-decision. *Journal of contemporary European research*, 5 (2), pp. 225–242.

Ripoll Servent, A., 2011. Playing the co-decision game? Rules' changes and institutional adaptation at the LIBE Committee. *Journal of European integration*. (online). Available from: http://dx.doi.org/10.1080/07036337.2011.566332, Accessed 4 May 2011

Smith, J., 1999. *Europe's elected parliament*. Sheffield Academic Press.

Statewatch, 2003. European Parliament – Data protection since 11 September 2001: What strategy for Europe? [online]. *Statewatch News Online*. Available from: http://www.statewatch.org/news/2003/mar/hearing-25-03.htm [Accessed 25 September 2010].

Votewatch, 2010. Roll-call vote – Agreement between the EU and the USA on the processing and transfer of financial messaging data from the EU to the USA for purposes of the terrorist finance tracking program [online]. Available from: http://www.votewatch.eu/cx_vote_details.php?id_act=843&lang=en [Accessed 1 November 2010].

Zimmermann, D., 2006. The European Union and post-9/11 counter-terrorism: A reappraisal. *Studies in conflict and terrorism*, 29 (2), pp. 123–145.

Interviews

Alexander Alvaro, MEP, July 2010
Commission Official A, March 2010
Commission Official B, July 2010
Commission Official C, July 2010
Communication of Sophie in 't Veld, July 2010
Diplomatic Source A, March 2010
Diplomatic Source A, July 2010
Diplomatic Source B, July 2010
EU Official, March 2010
EU Official, July 2010
EP Official, January 2009
MEP, July 2010
Simon Busuttil, MEP, March 2010

The EU Strategy in Tackling Organized Crime in the Framework of Multilateralism

DANIELA IRRERA

ABSTRACT *Transnational organized crime (TOC) is dramatically increasing its ability to perform at a global level. There is not yet, however, a common definition of organized crime, nor a common strategy to fight it. Even though it is currently included in the political agenda on a global level and often associated with transnational terrorism and security issues, organized crime is not an exclusive policy priority. The differences in position among the most important political actors – the US, the EU, the EU member states and the UN – are significant and confused. The EU, in particular, has developed an advanced strategy based either on single member states' experience or on shared principles and perceptions. The main assumption here is that in the broader context of multilateralism and by respecting the leading global actors' view (that of the UN and the US), the EU has built its own strategy, which constitutes an added value to the global struggle against TOC. In the first part of this article, TOC will be analysed as a global threat and towards other challenges as global terrorism, ethnic wars and failed states. In the second part, the EU strategy will be analysed and compared to the most important positions and strategies developed by the leading political actors. The most important changes introduced through the Lisbon Treaty will be stressed as well. The last part of the article presents some conclusions on the perceptions of organized crime within political agendas at the global level.*

Introduction

The management of global security is a collective concern and requires more responsibility and involvement from the international community. Major challenges deal with the ability of non state groups to play play a role in the international affairs. This can contribute to democratization and openness to civil society's needs; at the same time, it can strengthen 'uncivil' groups, as organized crime can be defined. Organized crime is progressively increasing its ability to perform at a global level (moving resources, activities and incomes), to combine forces with other seditious groups (terrorists, paramilitaries, etc.) and to establish its 'free areas' inside failed and weak states, marked by ethnic and/or religious conflicts. Nevertheless, there is no established common definition of organized crime, nor a common strategy to fight it. Even if it is part of the global political agenda and increasingly associated with transnational terrorism and security issues, organized crime is not a special policy priority. The differences among the most important political actors' positions – the United States (US), the European Union (EU), the EU member states and the United Nations (UN) – are significant. This can contribute dangerously to a lack of awareness about the problem and, consequently, to a lack of real global commitment. Even though the institutional discourse on transnational organized crime (TOC) is still very vague and hesitant, the transformations affecting the concept of global security are modifying governments' understanding, pushing them to include TOC more and more on the list of global threats. Therefore, there is a significant gap between the discourse and the perception of TOC within the international political system.

This paper aims at defining and discussing the relationship between TOC and global security in the broader context of multilateralism rules, by stressing the role played by the EU. Firstly, TOC will be analysed against the background of the rise of non-state actors, the crisis of state sovereignty and new threats, such as ethnic wars and failed states. Secondly, in order to describe how perceptions are changing while discourse tends to remain rigidly confused, the International Relations theories on global security will be used as a theoretical framework to analyse the documents produced by the leading political actors to express their strategies and positions. The main assumption is that any internationalization process of crime definition and crime control is the outcome of the export of domestic perceptions and definitions, which reflects the relations among political powers. Thus, these agendas are based essentially on the attempts of Western powers to export their domestic definitions, expressed in political, economic and moral terms. The US and EU security agenda – namely, their official documents – will be examined and compared. Their shifting perceptions of global threats, in which TOC is coming to be increasingly present, will be at the core of the analysis. These considerations will be used, thirdly, to provide some conclusions on the political implications as outcomes of the different perceptions within the political agendas at a global level. Even though TOC is still perceived as a national law enforcement issue, multilateral cooperation, defined as the conduct founded on universal principles, equal participation of states in collective mechanisms, and no discrimination in putting principles into action (Attinà, 2008, pp. 6), as shaped by the US and the EU, can be the only way to match perception to discourse as well as the only political framework within which a coherent and efficient counterstrategy can be conceived and developed.

Non-State Actors and Global Security

The Westphalian nation-state was the dominant political arrangement for centuries. In the period between the two world wars and, even later, during the cold war, the nation-state remained the most important actor within the international system, determining foreign policy and global decision-making (Roberts, 1991). In the 1960s and 1970s, however, states had to recognize that new and different actors were evolving, imposing their requirements in the international arena and demanding to be involved. Globalization processes contributed to the rise of these actors and required a collective approach to problem resolution. In this sense, globalization had a democratizing effect: The states started to govern as members of regional and/or international organizations and shifted their decision-making to a supranational level. In doing so, the states sought to guarantee several goods to their citizens, including a higher level of security, better living conditions and greater political stability. However, globalization did not produce only positive effects; it also instigated differences among states and among continents, which increased fragmentation, separatism and national struggles. States were not sufficiently prepared – especially after the fall of the Berlin Wall – to face these new issues (Gellner, 1994; Bartelson, 1998).

This affected sovereignty: Traditional political and normative powers were less effective, borders could be more easily crossed and more citizens wanted to be involved than in the past (Strange, 1996). The state, still important within the global system, is not disappearing. It continues to remain the most solid and implemented political management system, yet, it appears to be necessary to go beyond the traditional elements of the state in order to face modern challenges, in particular the rising of non-state actors.

International organizations, lobbies, corporations, NGOs and non-profit organizations can be considered to be the non-state actors that have posed these challenges. They have members and an internal management structure, but no territory. They are autonomous, but not sovereign. Through their stance and behaviour, since the 1950s and 1960s, they have been able to influence international policies (Galtung, 1987; Trentmann, 2000; Boyd and Oakeshott, 2004; Müller, 2006). Such organizations involve many people internationally and their major participation in decision-making has led some scholars to say that 'group policy' is no longer made *only* by sovereign states, but *also* with the help of such different types of actors (Bull and Watson, 1984).

One logical evolution from this globalization of issues and problems is that the traditional nation-state may retreat in the face of other actors, reducing, in small or large quantities, its sovereignty (Strange, 1996; Attinà, 1997). By working with 'positive' non-state actors, retreat as a mechanism fosters the accomplishment of major goals and contributes to introducing democracy and pluralism, but, with 'uncivil' actors, the results will necessarily be different. Criminal clans, terrorist groups and/or paramilitaries can be considered such non-state actors. They are usually based within the territory of a state, but they know no borders; yet, they do have an internal structure, they represent some interests, even if illegal or subversive, they are autonomous and, by pursuing their aims, they are able to influence the global system. The quality of their activities has, however, a very negative influence. Non-state actors must hold dialogues with national institutions in order to function, but at the same time, they challenge legal systems and rules (Rosenau, 1990).

In order to face the challenges posed by non-state actors, states have to struggle against organized crime. They can fight it through their national legislation and/or international conventions, as most states certainly do. States that have a long standing problem of criminal activity have developed several counter-attack means, including laws and regulations, police officer codes and specialized agencies. In some cases, organized crime is not opposed by the states, so it can interact with them. How it interacts depends on the 'strength' of the state as well as its vulnerability and this can produce different gradations of criminalization. Several analyses made on the wide range of possible cases can be summed up in the following taxonomy (Irrera, 2007):

- Weak states: In the first step in the criminalization process, criminal groups prey on state weaknesses when institutions are able to function, but in a less efficient way. For example, this occurred in the post-colonization period of the African states (Jackson, 1990).
- Fragile states: The political and institutional dimensions are absent, and the economic and financial ones are lacking, too, as, for example, in Central Europe after the fall of communism and in some Latin American countries (Sorensen, 1999).
- Kleptocratic states: Increased vulnerability to criminalization is evident where illegal activities produce the most significant or only economic resource and are necessary to guarantee services to citizens, as, for example, in Serbia and Kosovo (Grossman, 1999).
- De-structured states: In such a chaotic situation, the institutions in some sectors are not able to function at all and they retreat completely in the face of organized crime groups. In other words, they accept being replaced by criminals, as is happening in Russia and other former Soviet Republics such as Moldova.
- Captured states: Criminal overtaking increases further as institutions in some sectors are replaced by organized crime groups (Williams, 2001).
- Mafia states: With the merging of criminal elements with the corrupted state, a crime group is able to corrupt and manage political activity and combine with the political system, which has abandoned its legitimate functions.
- Failed states: With the total absence of legitimate state characteristics, institutions and public services are no longer existent and criminal organizations, in effect, replace the legitimate governance of the state.

Usually, public and private domains are clearly separated within a state. The two dimensions cannot be merged together and nobody who has a public charge can act for a personal or private benefit. But if the state retreats in the face of an illegal actor, on an illegal issue, this separation becomes increasingly blurred. The retreat can be gradual – beginning from the lower level (i.e., a public administrative officer illegally accepting money to do his/her job) to the middle level (i.e., a private company benefiting from public funds or engaging in vote-management in local political elections) to the upper level (i.e., politicians and party leaders involved in illicit deals) (Chiottolini, 1995).

Corruption is defined as the act of a public charge to gain a private benefit, and it is the mode used by organized crime to spread throughout the state and reach its apex. The most serious results are evident when every sector and every institution of a state have become corrupted. When regular productive capacity is reduced and competent national institutions are unable to manage resources on their own, the fiscal system becomes inefficient or nonexistent. In such a case, the most likely probability is an economy where any resource and activity, legal or illegal, will be accepted to ensure survival. This grave situation is often associated with total corruption (Gupta *et al.*, 1998; Rose-Ackerman, 1999).

In conclusion, fragmented political and economic contexts, with neither cohesion nor autonomy, represent the best route for an organized crime group to enter a state, gain a footing and conquer it. The retreat of the state and the rise of these actors produce detrimental effects, firstly on the state itself, and subsequently, on the whole international system. Even though the fact is rarely reported by the international media or discussed in debates, for several years, TOC has posited itself silently as a dangerous global threat. The consequences it is able to effect should be linked to the transformations occurring in the concept of global security (Migdal, 1988).

The traditional concept of security is associated with the state, the images of the enemy, and with military mobilization against the potential for violence. The technological improvements, the rising of non-state actors, the political innovations introduced during and after the cold war have all contributed to change this perception by changing the nature of contemporary civil conflicts as well as the importance of weak, collapsed and failed states. Institutional weakness, no rule of law and economic backwardness became the cause of *new* wars (Holsti, 1999). The most important trait frequently mentioned by scholars is the shift from the interstate to the intrastate war dimension. This distinction does not imply that the effects of conflict are contained within state borders. On the contrary, conflict normally spreads from a country to its neighbouring countries and region. An additional and important common feature of these wars is the active, and sometimes conditioning, presence of non-state actors. New wars are fought by a wide range of political and social groups that have different identities and alliance relations. Conflicting parties are sometimes inclined to easily change alliance alignments (Kaldor, 1999). In many cases, the state is not the aggressor and plays no role in the causes and development of conflict (Monteleone and Rossi, 2008). Lastly, in these wars, the clear distinction between civilians and combatants fades dramatically. Organized crime groups can join fighters effortlessly by filling the grey zones that rise dramatically in deprived conditions or by establishing stable relationship with terrorist groups or local paramilitaries. In doing so, the possibility of exerting a significant influence on the conflict is high. Thus, these kinds of new wars affect different levels of security, which cannot be reduced only to the military dimension and, consequently, require a more adequate global strategy.

Buzan started analysing security in agreement with Waltz (1958) by stressing the existence of three levels of analysis (individual, state and international system) as well as of a series of dimensions (political, economic, social), which are parallel to the military ones (Buzan, 1991). Later, he continued his analyses within the Copenhagen School. The concept of 'comprehensive security' became more diversified and enriched; a wide range of sectors (they identified security through its military, environmental, economic and political spheres) implies different actors involved as well as different actions. In weak states, security does not deal with the state, but mainly with the antagonist groups and individuals (Kaldor, 1999). At the same time, a diversified concept of security requires a proper set of actions; the Copenhagen School stressed on securitization, arguing that an issue is securitized when it is considered an actual threat and emergency measures are adopted to redress it (or prevent it). The following theoretical debate continued to take this concept into account and added new aspects and elements. Knight affirms that terms such as 'comprehensive security', 'common security' and 'human security' 'are being utilised to embrace the range of issues that are being placed on a revised security agenda of an emerging global polity' (Knight, 2001, p. 14). However, the concept of comprehensive security means not only protecting people from armed violence, it 'must change from an exclusive stress on national security to a much greater focus on people's security from security through armaments to security through human development, from territorial security to food, employment and environmental security'.

Human security is, therefore, perceived more and more as a multilevel dimension, both in a vertical sense (different threats shape the state by involving the individuals) and in a horizontal one (threats engage different sovereign states). Evidently, some securitization processes remain useless and inefficient if included only in the national political agendas. The dangerous potential conveyed by TOC is a very good example.

Crimes are defined and created by states through law. Thus, any internationalization process of crime definition and crime control is, first of all, the outcome of the export of domestic perceptions and definitions. In the aftermath of the cold war, this process occurred according to the same rules that dominated the relations among political powers. In other words, it was essentially the attempts of Western powers to export their domestic definitions, expressed in political, economic and moral terms.

This happened officially through the production of formal definitions and documents. At the same time, this procedure is based on the governments' understanding of organized crime itself. The notion of perception of organized crime is the basis of our analysis and it will be used to explore the different attitudes of the leading political actors.

The different policies produced by the US and the European states – as well as the EU member states – reflect their dissimilar perceptions of organized crime as well as their dissimilar approaches to security. However, the shifting perceptions of the security environment, together with the parallel transformation of the global system, have pushed the prominent states to change their attitudes and to strengthen multilateral cooperation to develop adequate responses to new threats. The events of 11 September 2001 (9/11) dramatically contributed to change the perception of threat. This happened more easily with some threats, such as terrorism; it is still occurring with organized crime.

The EU Security Agenda and TOC

The internationalization of European Community/EU crime control started at the beginning of the cold war, through the development of cross-border policing institutions and the extension of its own practices to its neighbours. The deepening and widening of the European integration contributed to the enlargement of this two-fold process.

As far as the first element is concerned, Didier Bigo observed that an 'internal security field' was emerging in Western Europe, dealing with a 'continuum' in which organized crime, terrorism and illegal migration were placed together, and underlining the need for more structured joint policies (as quoted in Andreas and Nadelmann, 2006, p. 178).

The nuclear deterrence strategy and arms control negotiations of the cold war and the subsequent détente era, the three decade long Helsinki process, and the formulation of national and multilateral defence policies in the 1990s in response to new security threats, such as new wars, the rising of civil conflicts and the proliferation of weapons of mass destruction (WMDs), contributed to the increasing willingness of the European countries to strengthen their cooperation in the key issue of drug trafficking (Shelley, 1995).

As affirmed by the European Monitoring Centre for Drugs and Drug Addiction, during the 1990s, the number of member countries that started to have national single documents and the trend to produce joint policies both increased.

The adoption of the EU Drug Strategy in December 2004 pointed to the existence of a larger political concern about drugs across the EU countries, beyond the different approaches of the member states. The successive EU Drugs Action Plans, including the latest one for the period, 2009–12, are based on the same set of basic principles: a balanced approach to reducing the supply and demand for drugs and the founding values of the EU, which are respect for human dignity, liberty, democracy, equality, solidarity, rule of law and human rights. The measures prescribed for establishing joint policies include the enhancement of judicial cooperation in the area of combating drug trafficking and law enforcement and the strengthening of the Europol, Eurojust and other EU structures.[1]

As far as the second element is concerned, the tradition of close cooperation with underdeveloped countries in the field of aid and relief offered an already in-use platform and expertise for improving cooperation with third countries and international organizations in the field of drugs through closer coordination of policies within the EU. In other words, the perception of organized crime within and outside EU borders cannot be in contrast with the set of principles at the base of integration and civil power.

The internationalization of the EU's organized crime control measures can also be seen in the document, *A secure Europe in a better world,* issued by the European Council in December 2003, in which the EU High Representative for Common Foreign and Security Policy, Javier Solana, points out the main elements that are required to build a strong and solid European Security Strategy (ESS). The abovementioned set of principles is used also for enlarging EU capabilities and contributions to global security. Therefore, this can be envisaged as a message to the world, aiming to explain how the EU would be able to face global challenges and threats, including that of TOC.

The ESS stresses European responsibility for global security, the need for effective multilateralism and the extension of the international rule of law, considering that 'the post Cold War environment is one of increasingly open borders in which the internal and external aspects of security are indissolubly linked' (Solana, J., 2003).

The ESS lists five key threats to Europe: terrorism, the proliferation of WMDs, regional conflicts, failed/failing states, and organized crime. This last one, in particular, is linked to the conditions that cause conflict, fear and hatred, a criminalized economy that profits from violent methods of controlling assets, weak illegitimate states, and the existence of warlords and paramilitary groups.

The US Security Agenda and TOC

Since the first articulated analysis made by the Kefauver Committee in 1951, the American perception of organized crime as a domestic issue has changed significantly. The alien conspiracy has turned into a larger involvement in illegal migration and border control issues, especially in the relationship with Mexico and other Central American countries (Bynum, 1987; Finckenauer, 2005).

However, drug trafficking and money laundering continue to be the most important targets. In the process, the US has developed an international strategy, which has been essentially based on the protection of American interests and the strengthening of law enforcement and information systems. As Anderson affirms: 'In America, the traditional Mafia has evolved into a relatively complex organisation which perpetuates selected feature[s] of the older peasant organisation but subordinates them to the requirements of bureaucracy' (Anderson, 1965, p. 310).

The Bureau of International Narcotics and Law Enforcement Affairs (INL) is part of the structures created by the Department of State to reinforce the international network of laws and conventions against the narcotics trade and corruption, Also, a wide range of bilateral, regional and international initiatives that aim to strengthen the law enforcement capabilities of foreign governments is provided.

In the aftermath of 9/11, US officials started to include counternarcotics in a broader security strategy focused on lawless zones. In March 2003, General James Hills described this change as follows:

> Today's foe is the terrorist, the narco-trafficker, the arms trafficker, the document forger, the international crime boss, and the money launderer. This threat is a weed that is planted, grown and nurtured in the fertile ground of ungoverned spaces such as coastlines, rivers and unpopulated border areas. This threat is watered and fertilised with money from drugs, illegal arms sales, and human trafficking. This threat respects neither geographical nor moral boundaries (as quoted in Andreas and Nadelmann, 2006, p. 198).

The US National Security Strategy (NSS), issued by President Bush in 2002, marked the formalization of this change and contributed to linking new global challenges, including organized crime activities, to the fertile ground that can be easily found in weak or failed states.

In the latest NSS, published in 2006, this affirmation is confirmed and globalization becomes the new force that is shaping national security more and more. However, any strategy against TOC and its consequences is still related to information system and transport control:

> Illicit trade, whether in drugs, human beings, or sex, exploits the modern era's greater ease of transport and exchange. Such traffic corrodes social order; bolsters crime and corruption; undermines effective governance; facilitates the illicit transfer of WMD and advanced conventional weapons technology; and compromises traditional security and law enforcement (White House, 2006).

Transatlantic Cooperation, Multilateralism, and the EU's Added Value

Even before 9/11, the transatlantic law enforcement infrastructure was working actively through several joint initiatives against money laundering and cybercrime. However, the terrorist attacks contributed to changing the characteristics of those initiatives because they modified the security dimension.

As already seen, in the aftermath of 9/11, the security strategies of both political powers presented some significant differences, but also some potential sources for cooperation. The ESS was formulated essentially in response to the challenges posed by the US to the EU's actorness in the sphere of security policies. The list of key security issues is basically identical in the two texts. They list terrorist threats, WMDs and state failures as key dangers. However, both documents use different tones to describe the same need for a more joint cooperation. The ESS argues that 'the best protection for our security is a world of well-governed democratic states', and for strengthening international order, 'spreading good governance, supporting social and political reform, dealing with corruption and abuse of power, establishing the rule of law and protecting human rights' are necessary (Solana, 2003, p. 10). The NSS affirms that 'the United States must start from the core beliefs and look outward for possibilities to expand liberty' (White House, 2002, p. 3). Moreover, while the US stresses the term, 'rogue states', the EU document refers to 'failed' or 'failing states' to indicate the fertile ground in which terrorism and organized crime can be nurtured. There are many 'enemies' in the NSS and many 'challenges' in the ESS. Finally, the EU explicitly includes regional conflicts and organized crime in its list.

As in the past, the US documents and declaration show a more authoritative language, and they take the lead, but, at the same time, require the US' allies to assume their own responsibilities. In the latest NSS, issued in 2006, national security is no more defined in traditional terms, but associated instead with the globalization of threats and with the need for greater cooperation.

This evident shift in language and approach is affecting the perception of TOC as well because it establishes new patterns of cooperation and a re-launch of multilateral structures.

According to Attinà, multilateralism is a step down the road of civilizing politics among states, if it is considered as the attitude of acting together of several states, and it sides with the political science view of multilateralism as conduct founded on universal principles, equal participation of states in collective mechanisms, and no discrimination in putting principles into action (Attinà, 2008, p. 6).

In doing so, multilateralism is firstly a 'commitment to common ways of working and agreed rules': Common rules and norms are commonly created for solving problems. Secondly, multilateralism means 'coordination', instead of rivalry or simply juxtaposition. If the human security approach is considered as the most efficient way to face global threats, then a greater coordination of policies in different fields, including external relations, trade, development and security is required (Keohane, 1990; Caporaso, 1993; Ruggie, 1993; Lake, 2006). These considerations throw up some important political implications.

The responses and new partnerships created for combating global threats and emergencies should be utilized first of all to solve a specific problem, but they can also simultaneously serve as catalysts for changing the existing political conditions to tackle other problems, for establishing new rules of conduct and, in the long run, for enforcing the rules themselves.

In mobilizing the Regional Core Group to respond to the tsunami of 2004, the US leadership contributed, for example, to creating a more structured international response to global emergencies. The efficacy of the response to the tsunami in Southeast Asia as well as the earthquake in Pakistan developed new channels of communication and cooperation at a local level, which have been exploited in other fields, too, namely, in the long-standing regional conflicts in Aceh and Kashmir (Koivusalo and Ollila, 1997).

Attempts to facilitate greater cooperation in crime control on an international level necessarily involve multilateral arrangements on a regional and global level. However, such arrangements are created also for promoting more communication, establishing guidelines and best practices, and regularizing cooperation (Hignett, 2008).

Even though the US played an important role in motivating and deepening new agreements in criminal law enforcement issues, the EU showed a different approach which, in the context of multilateralism, can be an added value. As the ESS clarifies, the rationale on which the fight against TOC is based is part of a broader security culture the European countries have founded in the early 1990s for avoiding international and internal wars in the region. This culture is based on shared principles and beliefs as well as on common actions and commitments (Attinà, 2007). Behind these policies was the conviction that the same security arrangement could be assembled in other parts of the world. Therefore, the EU has become a regional power, able to use its own principles and actions in a larger context. The constant use of common patterns of behaviour during these last few decades has contributed to the rise of a specific international image of the EU as a civilian power. The will to build long-term stabilization, to act through multilateralism, and to be inspired by norms and ideas are the main elements of the global actorness the EU has developed in the field of the promotion of democracy and security (Duchene, 1972). The more complex set of competencies the Treaty of Lisbon will give to the High Representative for Foreign Policy should strengthen even more the fight against TOC.

Therefore, a common perception of the threat passes through a multilateral process of building up joint policy initiatives and rational exploitation of international institutions, such as the United Nations, the World Bank and the International Monetary Fund, as well as regional ones.

Conclusions

In this chapter, we argued that TOC is still perceived as a national law enforcement issue. Some significant changes are, however, occurring within the international system. The shifting of the perception of TOC from a domestic public order issue to a global threat is due to some broader transformations affecting, firstly, the relations among states and, secondly, the concept of human security. The internationalization of crime control was essentially the export of law enforcement rules – namely, the domestic definition of security and of organized crime – from the Western powers to the rest of the system. Even though they tried to collaborate on various initiatives, since the cold war, the US and the EU have offered contrasting views of the threat and how it should be tackled. The EU was mainly focused on cross-border law enforcement and judicial cooperation, while US security power was based more on information systems and transport.

Both the US and the EU contributed to shape the international set of definitions and rules in the field of organized crime by using their different but leading roles. The globalization process, the rising of non-state actors and the consequent development of the human aspects of security, as well as the events of 9/11, pushed the main international political actors to change this composite structure of relations. The security agendas they produced were apparently divergent, but both focused on the need to strengthen regional and global cooperation and to re-launch transatlantic relations. The potential the EU has developed, in particular, can be considered as a fundamental basis for launching multilateral cooperation in security affairs.

In this framework, even TOC has started to be perceived as an increasing challenge, and even though it is not yet at the core of joint priorities, like terrorism is, the danger it represents for the whole system is being agreed upon more and more. The already significant gap between the discourse and the perception of TOC within the international political system is also increasing more and more. Multilateralism – defined as the conduct founded on universal principles, equal participation of states in collective mechanisms, and no discrimination in putting principles into action – can represent the only tool for filling this gap as well as the only political context within which a coherent and efficient global counterstrategy can be conceived and developed.

Note

[1] Council of the European Union, 2008. *EU drugs action plan for 2009–12*. OJEU C326/7, 20 December 2008.

References

Anderson R. T. (1965), *From Mafia to Cosa Nostra* in "American Journal of Sociology", vol. 71.
Andreas, P., and Nadelmann, E., 2006. *Policing the globe: Criminalisation and crime control in international relations*. Oxford University Press.
Attinà, F., 1997. Globalisation and crime: The emerging role of international institutions. Department of Political Studies, Jean Monnet Working Paper in Comparative and International Politics JMWP 07.97.
Attinà, F., 2007. Multilateral security and peace operations: The decentralisation turn. *Paper presented at the 21st Congress of the Italian Political Science Association*, 20–22 September 2007 Catania, Italy.
Attinà, F., 2008. Multilateralism and the emergence of minilateralism in EU peace operations. *Romanian journal of European affairs*, 8 (2), 5–24.
Bartelson, J., 1998. Second nature: Is the state identical with itself. *European journal of international relations*, 4 (3), 295–326.
Banks, M. and Shaw, M. eds, 1991. State and society in international relations. Exeter: Wheatsheaf.
Boyd, R., and Oakeshott, M., 2004. On civility, civil society and civil association. *Political studies*, 52 (3), 603–622.
Bull, H., and Watson, A., eds., 1984. *The expansion of international society*. Oxford: Clarendon Press.

Buzan, B., 1991. *People, states and fear*. Pearson: Longman.
Bynum, S. ed. Organised crime in America: Concepts and controversies. Monsey: Criminal Justice Press.
Caporaso, J., 1993. International relations theory and multilateralism: The search for foundations. In: J.G. Ruggie, ed. *Multilateralism matters. The theory and practice of an institutional form*. New York: Columbia University Press, 51–90.
Chiottolini, G., 1995. The 'private', the 'public', the 'state'. *The journal of modern history*, 67 (4), S34–S61.
Council of the European Union, 2008. EU drugs action plan for 2009–12. OJEU C326/7, 20 December pp.
Duchene, F., 1972. Europe's role in world peace. In: R. Mayne, ed. *Europe tomorrow: Sixteen Europeans look ahead*. London: Fontana, pp. 32–47.
Finckenauer, J., 2005. Problems of definition: What is organised crime? *Trends in organised crime*, 8 (3), 63–83.
Galtung, J., 1987. A new era for nongovernmental organisations in the UN? *Transnational associations*, 3, 183–186.
Gellner, E., 1994. *Conditions of liberty: Civil society and its rivals*. London: Hamish Hamilton.
Grossman, H.I., 1999. Rival kleptocrats: The mafia versus the state. In: G. Fiorentini and S. Zamagni, eds. *The economics of corruption and illegal markets*. Northampton: Edward Elgar, pp. 143–155.
Gupta, S., Davoody, H., and Alonso-Terme, R., eds., 1998. Does corruption affect income inequality and poverty? IMF Working Paper, WP/1998/76.
Hignett, K., 2008. Transnational crime and its impact on international security. In: M. Shanty, ed. *Organised crime: From trafficking to terrorism*. Santa Barbara: ABC-CLIO, 294–298.
Holsti, K., 1996. *The state, war, and the state of war*. Cambridge University Press.
Irrera, D., 2007. Organised crime, non-state actors and weak/failed states. In: M. Shanty, ed. *Organised crime: From trafficking to terrorism*. Santa Monica: ABC-CLIO, 357–363.
Jackson, R.H., 1990. *Quasi-states: Sovereignty, international relations and the Third World*. Cambridge University Press.
Kaldor, M., 1999. *New and old wars: Organised violence in a global era*. Cambridge: Polity Press.
Keohane, R., 1990. Multilateralism: An agenda for research. *International journal*, 45 (4), 731–764.
Knight, W.A., 2001. *Adapting the United Nations to a postmodern era: Lessons learned*. New York: Palgrave.
Koivusalo, M., and Ollila, E., 1997. *Making a healthy world: Agencies, actors and policies in international health*. Helsinki: Stakes.
Lake, A.D., 2006. American hegemony and the future of East-West relations. *International studies perspectives*, 7 (1), 23–30.
Migdal, J.S., 1988. *Strong societies and weak states*. Princeton University Press.
Monteleone, C., and Rossi, R., 2008. Security and global management: A global perspective. In: Geistlinger, M. et al. eds. *Security identity and the Southern Caucasus*. Wien: Verlag, 49–80.
Müller, K., 2006. The civil society-state relationship in contemporary discourse: A complementary account from Giddens' perspective. *British journal of politics and international relations*, 8 (2), 311–330.
Rose-Ackerman, S., 1999. *Corruption and government: Causes, consequences and reform*. Cambridge University Press.
Rosenau, J.N., 1990. *Turbulence in world politics: A theory of change and continuity*. New York: Harvester Wheatsheaf.
Ruggie, J.G., ed.,1993. *Multilateralism matters: The theory and practice of an institutional form*. New York: Columbia University Press.
Shelley, L., 1995. Transnational organised crime: An imminent threat to the nation-state? *Journal of international affairs*, 48 (2), 466–467.
Solana, J., 2003. *A secure Europe in a better world, European security strategy*. Brussels, 12 December.
Sorensen, G., Development in Fragile/Failed States. West Lafayette, Purdue University, 1999, 14p.
Strange, S., 1996. *The retreat of the state: The diffusion of power in the world economy*. Cambridge University Press.
Trentmann, F., 2000. *Paradoxes of civil society: New perspectives on modern German and British history*. New York: Berghan Books.

Waltz, Kenneth, 1958. *Man, the state, and war*. New York: Columbia University Press.
Williams, P., 2001. Transnational crime and corruption. In: B. White, R. Little and M. Smith, eds. *Issues in world politics*. New York: Palgrave, pp. 235–256.
White House, 2002. *The national security strategy of the United States of America*. September 2002.
White House, 2006. *The national security strategy of the United States of America*. March 2006.

The Transition of Egypt in 2011: A New Springtime for the European Neighbourhood Policy?

PATRICIA BAUER

ABSTRACT *As we have witnessed in the first few weeks of 2011, the Tunisian and the Egyptian people have promoted a fundamental change in government and leadership within their countries. In the case of Egypt, the direction and likeliness of a deep societal democratization process are still unclear. The role and ability of foreign actors such as the European Union (EU) and its member states to support this process have so far not been shaped into a new political strategy of the European Neighbourhood Policy (ENP). Before the Arab revolutions of 2011, the foreign policy of the EU towards the Mediterranean countries was often characterized by the dilemma between the EU's stability and democratization goals. The change from the EMP to the ENP was assumed to imply a reorientation of EU foreign policy goals from a normative long-term oriented democratization to a strategic short-term stabilization of authoritarian systems on the Southern shore of the Mediterranean Sea. This ambivalence of EU foreign policy is due to the environment of authoritarian rule and restrictions it has had to act within during the last few decades.*

The article will first give an empirical overview of the ENP policy towards Egypt. The empirical results show a multilayer policy of the EU, containing different goals and working with a combination of interest-based and normatively oriented tools. In this respect, the ENP towards Egypt mirrors the ambivalent objectives and ideas of the EU's role in the Southern Mediterranean. Secondly, the article will survey the first EU initiatives and actions after the revolution in Egypt. It will analyse the short-, medium- and long-term steps of the EU to support the starting process of democratic and economic transition and compare them with the existing ENP policies in order to identify commonalities and changes in the EU approach. The normative questions on the democratic power of the EU will be discussed in this context.

Introduction

As we have witnessed in the first few weeks of 2011, the Tunisian and the Egyptian people reached a fundamental change in government and leadership within their countries. This historical break that no political analyst had predicted is still open-ended and raises a number of questions for the role of the European Union (EU) in the future. In the case of Egypt, the direction and likeliness of a deep societal democratization process are still unclear. The role and ability of foreign actors such as the EU and its member states to support this process have so far not been shaped into a new political strategy of the European Neighbourhood Policy (ENP).

Before the Arab revolutions of 2011, the foreign policy of the EU towards the Mediterranean countries was often characterized by the dilemma between the EU's stability and democratization goals (Cavatora and Pace, 2010). The change from the EMP to the ENP was assumed to imply a reorientation of EU foreign policy goals from a normative long-term oriented democratization to a strategic short-term stabilization of authoritarian systems on the Southern shore of the Mediterranean Sea. In this context, we often had to bid farewell to the EU as a democratizing power.

And indeed, in the first days of the Egyptian revolution, the European political elite tread carefully on the subject of Hosni Mubarak stepping down, indicating this dilemma and referring to European interests touched by the changes in Egypt. On the other hand, after the completion of the revolution by the retreat of Mubarak and the takeover by the Supreme Council of the Armed Forces, the EU decidedly joined and supported the decision of the Egyptian people. This ambivalence of EU foreign policy is due to the environment of authoritarian rule and restrictions it has had to act within during the last few decades.

In general, the recent events shed new light on the discussion about the democratic power of the EU in its foreign relations:

- How much influence on democratization can the EU exercise towards countries with authoritarian rule?
- Is democratization from outside a normatively desirable policy goal? and
- How will the instruments and strategies of the European foreign policy be redefined after these events?

This article will first give an empirical overview of the ENP with regard to Egypt: The ENP's composition, strategies and tools present a variable picture of how the EU combines strategic and democratic intentions and tools of foreign policy. The empirical results show a multilayer policy of the EU, transporting different objectives and working with a combination of interest-based and normatively oriented tools. In this respect, the ENP towards Egypt mirrors the ambivalent objectives and ideas of the EU's role in the Southern Mediterranean.

Secondly, the article will survey the EU initiatives and actions after the revolution in Egypt. It will analyse the first steps of the EU to support the incipient transition process and compare them with the existing ENP policies in order to identify commonalities and changes in the EU approach. The question of the democratic power of the EU will be discussed in this context.

2. Analytical Framework

The present article tries to avoid characterizing the EU's foreign policy with a catchphrase, summarizing both significance and performance by terms such as 'superpower', 'normative power' or 'civilian power' (Bull, 1982; Galtung, 1973; Hill,

1990; Laïdi, 2008; Manners, 2002, 2010; McCormick, 2006; Reid, 2004; Schnabel, 2005; Smith, 2000; Telò, 2006). Rather, it approaches the subject from an empirical perspective, presenting what the EU's policy concept in the context of the ENP contains, what role the environment of authoritarian statehood (particularly in the case of Egypt) plays, and what is actually implemented by the EU under the given circumstances.

Hence, one central point for the understanding of the current shape, merits and challenges of the EU's EMP is to consider the institutional dimension of the interaction between two forms of organization – on the one hand, the EU with its complex forms of policy-making as well as sophisticated requirements of communication and organizational skills, and, on the other hand, the Mediterranean target countries, i.e. Egypt, and its hierarchical forms of top-down organization, requirements for subordination and limited space for self-organization within authoritarian rule.

The differences in these two systems, welded together by the ENP and its implementation, is a major source of ineffectiveness in all fields of the EMP.

This institutionalist perspective (March and Olsen, 1989; Scott, 1995; Pierson, 1996; Hall and Taylor, 1998) allows us to analyse the dialogue between the EU and the Mediterranean countries without simultaneously promoting a normative idea about democracy and human rights promotion (Pace, 2007; Grabbe, 2004). The recent events in Tunisia and Egypt show that the revolutions originated from inside the society, and the processes of transition under way are conflictual and open-ended. Although the general ideas of participation and democratic rule originating from the Western countries play a major role in this process, it might be an overestimation of the role of the EU and its member states to attribute a decisive influence to them.

With respect to EU-Egypt cooperation within the ENP, this article argues that the systemic differences of the two interacting systems led to a process of narrowing down of the content of ENP actions in a way that the action on the ground represents a common denominator of both cooperation partners. This might change in the future, but until now, we find only symbolic action from the EU side and practically no response from the Egyptian side, where the lower levels of the regime are still in office.

Egypt's political system and social structures, like many in the Arab world, have been described widely as authoritarian or neo-patrimonial (Weber, 1922).[1] The central structural features of these systems are: informal influence, bargaining and strong leaders (Pawelka, 1985). This societal organization, along with the family and patriarchal social structures, forms systems of high concentration of political power. In concrete terms, the Egyptian President, Hosni Mubarak, as the strong leader figure, was surrounded by a number of competing elite groups, like the military, police and businessmen, who received different forms of privileges, such as monopolies, credits, land deals or direct funding, directly and informally from the ruler. At the same time, the distance between the citizens and the elite was assured and kept up by strict control and complex and hierarchical bureaucracies (Kreitmeyer and Schlumberger, 2010, pp. 17 f.). The logic of the persistence of these systems was the suppression of alternative political movements or oppositions.[2]

Currently, this structure is under attack by the revolutionary protests, but it cannot be judged to be abolished yet because the logic of the system of hierarchical interaction and the personnel running this system have not changed, except from the top decision-making positions. It goes without saying that this organizational feature will not be changed overnight, and in this respect, it is still a major determinant of the EU-Egyptian interaction after the revolution.

On the other hand, the analysis of the EU policy towards Egypt should be approached in accordance with the findings on the logic of the EU system itself – as a mix of policy motives and interests that have developed incrementally within the process of the dialogue with the Mediterranean countries, which is subject to intergovernmental bargains as well as supranational policy management. In this respect, the EU's actual foreign policy is understood as the result of a preceding problem-solving and learning process within itself.

It is important for the design of the ENP that it fall within the competence of the European Commission, which organizes policy-making along the lines and experiences of preceding policy cycles. The ENP is an example for the growing influence of the Commission on the European Union's foreign policy. It is hence instructed by the Commission's experience of the Eastern enlargement policy in terms of organizational and policy-making structures. The central feature of the European Commission's policy-making is problem solving with the organizational tools that are available and that have evolved over the process of integration. This path dependency is characterized by incremental processes of adaptation and policy learning (Kelley, 2006, pp. 31 ff.), which are strongly influenced by the context of authoritarian statehood.

In other words, the problem the European Commission is facing in the Southern Mediterranean with special respect to Egypt is how to influence a reluctant environment. Here, several factors have a problematic impact on the results of the ENP:

- Egypt shows an enormous gap in democratic as well as economic development, marking a difficult starting position for the demanding tools of the ENP;
- Despite all rhetorical commitment, until now, Egypt has reacted in an extremely sensitive way to interference in its internal affairs, which, of course, is an integral part of the procedural approach of the ENP; and
- Finally, these obstacles cannot be overcome by any strong incentive, such as the membership option. Thus, the means for mitigation are limited financial help and economic preferences for common market access.

In this difficult context, the ENP provided a filtering system for policy implementation, extracting central objectives and concentrating efforts and funding in certain areas. Whereas the objectives are applied in limited sectors in Egypt, their configuration still tries to cover all aspects of the dialogue, reaching from democracy promotion to trade facilitation to ensuring sustainable development.

This concentration process within the framework of financial aid mirrors the problem-based approach of the Commission and the permanent adjusting of the measures to the various countries' conditions. At the same time, the ENP keeps affirming the importance and achievements of the Barcelona Process and its values, which allow conducting a permanent dialogue on democratization. In this respect, the ENP is a multifaceted policy, which is composed of different incrementally evolved layers.

Recently, Catherine Ashton published the Joint Communication, 'A partnership for democracy and shared prosperity with the Southern Mediterranean' (European Commission High Representative, 2011a), which might have the potential to revitalize the democratic and human rights content of the Barcelona Process. The role and position of this Partnership within the EMP is neither clearly specified nor fostered with concrete action at the moment of writing. There is some evidence that, notwithstanding potential new designations, the structural approach of the ENP will remain the main means of operationalization of the EU's policy towards Egypt.

3. The Background: From EMP to ENP

European-Mediterranean relations celebrated their 15th anniversary in 2010. Starting from the Barcelona Declaration on the European Mediterranean Partnership (EMP) in 1995, the EU took a broad approach in forging relations with the Southern Mediterranean countries (MENA). The basket structure of the Barcelona Process aimed to define three fundamental tasks and chose a comprehensive policy approach imitating the CSCE structure of the 1970s (Fenech, 1997; Marchetti, 2004):

- Political and stability basket: Creating a common area of peace and security through political and security dialogue;
- Economic and financial basket: Aiming at a zone of prosperity through an economic and financial partnership and the gradual establishment of a free trade area; and
- Social, cultural and human rights basket: Approaching people, aiming at understanding between cultures and civil society.

This ambitious idea was implemented with quite a complex structure of multilateral as well as bilateral negotiations. Due to the agenda-setting role of the EU through its funding, the Barcelona Process soon acquired the image of an 'asymmetric partnership' (Marquina, 2003), especially amongst Arab analysts.

After almost a decade, the idea of this Mediterranean CSCE was renounced because of meagre results in all dimensions:

- The political dialogue did not lead to the long-anticipated 'third wave' (Huntington, 1991) of democratization and rule of law in the Arab world;
- The conflict prevention and resolution objective was undermined by the perturbing influence of the Palestine conflict, in turn affecting the principle of multilateralism (Attinà, 2005, 2007); and
- The prosperity gap between the Northern and Southern partners was not bridged and the Southern free-trade area, the Agadir Agreement, which still has a torso of just Morocco, Tunisia, Egypt and Jordan, showed poor results (Wippel, 2005).

In addition, the EU's internal considerations induced a rearrangement of the relations with the Southern Mediterranean countries beginning 2003:

- The enlargement fatigue after 2004–07 led to the strategy of offering the neighbourhood countries a privileged partnership without entering a new

enlargement debate ('everything but membership'). This was intended to satisfy the neighbours' cooperation needs by creating a 'ring of friends' around the EU. At the same time, it promised to support EU interests in security as well as economic prosperity;
- It promised to balance the interests of Southern versus Central European EU member states by dealing with the Southern partners just as with the Eastern neighbours; and
- Through its technical approach, the ENP seemed to offer a much more organized framework for the continuation of the Barcelona Process.

Considering the general objectives and structures of the ENP, this argument was substantiated. The areas and objectives defined by the Commission (2007) show a concentration on 'vital aspects for the future development of the European integration process in a friendly environment' without offering a membership option. These aims are:

- Economic integration and market access;
- Conflict settlement;
- Sectoral reforms in energy, environment, transport, maritime policy, research and education, employment and social policy;
- Enhancing people-to-people contacts; and
- Political and regional cooperation.

The language and formulation of the objectives shows much more concreteness than the EMP and how the Commission introduced priority areas for reform.

Though the ENP for the Mediterranean region is allocated within the framework of the EMP, in Egypt, the new policy was approached with scepticism and reluctance. In the rhetoric of the Egyptian Foreign Ministry, the ENP was virtually disregarded between 2007 and 2010, or subsumed under the EMP, and as late as in early 2010, Foreign Ministry officials still considered the EMP to be the main context of Mediterranean politics in the sense that it provided a framework for human understanding and cultural dialogue.[3]

Only from 2010 on did the shift of European politics from the EMP to the ENP start being described by Egyptian Foreign Ministry officials as both fundamental and problematic: Whereas the EMP was assessed as a process of – albeit asymmetric – partnership, the ENP's general approach was seen as the EU's way of dealing with 'areas of risks', not partners or friends.[4] And the operational approach was regarded as a means to the 'Europeanisation of the Southern Mediterranean' by defining the EU as the force of gravity in the bilateral relations.[5] In particular, the concreteness and directness of the ENP approach was considered rather inconvenient due to the fact that they were requesting concrete action that was partly touching Egyptian 'internal affairs'.

In addition, the switch from a 'partnership' to a 'neighbourhood' relation was noticed as a degradation of the bilateral relations. The perception of Egypt as having a special and highlighted role as a leader in the Arab world, due to its population, location and cultural and military power, is of great import for the self-image of the Egyptian political elite.[6] Though the reasons and perceptions of the Egyptian foreign policy elite might be biased by the vision of the Egyptian role and interest configuration, there is some reason in it: The EU has modelled the ENP on the enlargement blueprint (Kelley, 2006), decreasing the context of interaction for Egypt with the Mediterranean region by abolishing multilateralism and applying procedures with the potential of impinging on the integrity of national authority.[7]

The general idea behind the ENP is to base any EU activity on an Action Plan for a partner country, which consists of central objectives for the exclusively bilaterally organized relations. They are formulated for three to five years and consist of a bilateral definition of the policy aims and main areas of reform. Action Plans are defined on the principle of 'joint ownership',[8] which offers the neighbourhood countries the option to negotiate their own interests and to lay them down in their Action Plans. Joint ownership is also an instrument to reach concrete resolutions that commit the partner country. The Action Plans are the basis for the annual Progress Reports, which report the progress or stagnation in all areas covered by the Action Plan.

The link between the Action Plan (European Union and Arab Republic of Egypt, 2007) and financial aid is provided by the Country Strategy Paper (European Union, 2007), which gives priority objectives for the National Indicative Programme (NIP). This, in turn, is formulated officially in accordance with the Egyptian national plans and instructs the allocation of the European Neighbourhood Policy Instrument (ENPI) funding. Currently, the active formulation of the policy objectives is done by the Commission officials, whereas the Egyptian side is falling behind due to lack of information or innovative concepts inside the Egyptian administration.[9]

In principle, the continuation of funding is conditional on the successful attainment of objectives or progress in a targeted field. Despite the widespread praise of this 'positive conditionality' introduced by the linkage between objectives and financial instruments, the problem is that countries might not be able or willing to follow the general lines of EU standards, be it in democratization or in economic liberalization. Less known is that even the field of economic liberalization, which is a high priority area for Egypt, raises fundamental problems in negotiations: The Commission's demands in trade affairs promote an economic model at odds with the Egyptian ideas of national economic planning and autonomy.[10]

This policy design raises a number of issues concerning the application of the ENP in the Southern Mediterranean, and in particular in the Egyptian, context: For the EU's bargaining position, copying the enlargement policy without the same perspective of accession lacks the core incentive for the partner countries to commit and comply with the objectives. The established procedures of Progress Reports and the linkage between progress and further funding lack deeper sense if the consequences are of minor relevance or sanctions are not exerted.

For the treatment of authoritarianism, it is important to keep in mind that Egypt has been extremely successful in balancing the survival of the central features of its system and assent to certain external requests for democratization and good governance. This creates a credibility problem for the EU (Kelley, 2006, p. 46), manifesting itself in the clash between the stability versus democracy orientation and the perceived 'double standard' of the EU Mediterranean Policy (Demmelhuber, 2009, pp. 282 ff.).

4. The EU-Egypt Neighbourhood Policy: Components and Instruments

The EU-Egypt Action Plan

The EU-Egypt Action Plan, adopted in March 2007, was the core document for all further actions in the bilateral relations between the EU and Egypt. The text describes the Action Plan as covering an 'ambitious field of issues' (European Union and Arab Republic of Egypt, 2007) concerning the deepening of economic integration as well as of political, cultural and social cooperation.

Its objectives encompass all relevant areas of the dialogue within the region in general, such as promotion of peace, stability, growth, development and prosperity, and the modernization of the Egyptian economy and society in particular. Its priorities of action cover political issues formulated in general terms as well as comparably specific economic cooperation and development issues (European Union and Arab Republic of Egypt, 2007, pp. 2 ff.).[11]

It is based on the core principles of the ENP: joint ownership, common interests, reciprocal commitments, differentiation, shared values and implementation of national plans and reform programmes, politically, economically, socially and institutionally. The formal adoption took place in the EU-Egypt Association Council in March 2007. The monitoring is carried out by joint bodies and through regular reports. The country reports provide the function of an annual review of the common objectives. The Action Plan contains a clause allowing review after two years following the adoption, giving opportunity for amendments. However, no review has taken place till now.

This document is significant and instructing in different perspectives, content-wise and procedurally. The content reflects the common denominators in the bilateral relations. Its priorities can be clearly traced back to the influence of both sides.[12] Interestingly, it still contains general ideas reflecting the achievements of the Barcelona Process. They keep the human rights and democratization rhetoric as well as the general idea of economic integration. It might be labelled 'Barcelona acquis' and is so general and so devoid of the threat of sanctions that both sides have no problem accepting it. Two other motives can be discerned – economic development, and political and security cooperation. Altogether, it shows the following content:

- A 'Barcelona acquis', covering human rights protection, political dialogue and conflict resolution, democratization, economic integration, improving macroeconomic governance, science and technology cooperation, and people-to-people contacts;
- A group of economic development fields in a developmental politics sense, with issues such as industrial development, regulatory approximation to EU standards and poverty reduction. The reformulation of the fields of economic action as development issues is clearly an expression of the main Egyptian interests in the ENP; and
- A group of political fields, encompassing central, recent EU interests in the cooperation with Egypt, such as the management of migration related issues, cooperation on organized crime and trafficking, and the enhancement of cooperation in the energy sector.

This mirrors the direction and development of the EU-Egyptian interest constellation by carrying the central ideas of the Barcelona Process into the ENP, while adding new or reformulated fields of interest. It is a document reflecting the bargaining structure between the EU and Egypt in a perfect way: The reformulation of the economic objectives as development issues is caused by the lasting and deep economic gap between the EU and Egypt. Economic development and access to the European market (especially for agricultural goods) are explicit Egyptian priorities. The development goals are garnished with ideas of sustainability and environmental compatibility.

The new prominence of soft security issues, such as migration, organized crime and energy, can be identified as recently emphasized security topics of the EU. Egypt is encouraged to cooperate with FRONTEX in order to control migration from sub-Saharan Africa (Demmelhuber, 2011). The preparation of an Egyptian energy strategy converging with the EU is due to the European struggle for diversification of energy sources. German organizations, in particular, are already pushing this topic through diverse projects in Egypt.[13] With regard to Egypt's active role in fighting organized crime, it seems that both sides intend to solve their own respective problems – the Europeans to fight drugs and arms trafficking as well as terrorism, while the Egyptians take this as an opportunity to acquire control over the Internet and electronic media to control the (critical) civil society in the name of 'national security'.[14] After the 'facebook revolution' of 25 January 2011 in Egypt, we know that this has been entirely unsuccessful, even though the government shut down the Internet completely for six days, starting the night of 27–28 January 2011.

The whole package of the EU-Egypt Action Plan reflects general and lasting problems in the bilateral relations: the enduring problematic constitution of the authoritarian Egyptian state, the need for an extensive breaching of the development gap and economic cooperation and the need for cooperation with a strategically important country in the region, and tackling recent and concrete problems with regard to the stable and peaceful regional environment of the EU.

From the procedural perspective, the ENP Action Plan confronts the Egyptian state with the full arsenal of typical forms of European governance: permanent monitoring and evaluation of binding agreements, steady consultation and publication of results, inclusion of competent and implementing institutional actors in negotiations, inclusion of non-state actors in the process of implementation and demands on public-private partnerships and cooperation.

This catches the Egyptian administration on the wrong foot. As a matter of principle, inside Egypt, the Foreign Ministry is pooling all contacts and knowledge about European politics. The EU-Egyptian relations are managed by a very small number of Ministry of Foreign Affairs officials, who oversee and control nearly every move in European politics in the country. Equal participation of other institutions and actors meets huge obstacles.[15] Consequently, the Egyptian administration is characterized as a strict hierarchical system. For European politics, the Foreign Ministry is at the top of this hierarchy, filtering all information and further action for other ministries and administrations. It is strongly connected to state-controlled NGOs and works as a distributor for the implementation tasks of the ENP. All the other ministries are downstream, resulting in uninformed or partly informed desk officers without a clear understanding of their task. Only a few political entrepreneurs were able to acquire an independent and fully informed position in the ENP landscape of Egypt.[16]

These are limiting circumstances for the unfolding of competent and appropriate treatment of European affairs. Even top officials in the Egyptian Foreign Ministry speak of a 'moving target' concerning the negotiations with the EU, signifying the limited competence – even at the top of the hierarchy – to catch up with the Commission's forms of coordination. Officials from other ministries frequently do not even know how and whom to contact on implementation questions.

Though the Egyptians have successfully protested against the existing regime and started a process of transition, the central features of authoritarian statehood, such as the hierarchical organization and strict subordination, the channelling and filtering of information and the poor space for independent action, will remain central features of the Egyptian system and only change in a long-term learning and emancipation process.

Progress Reports

The annual Progress Reports[17] represent the European concern for the full range of fields and objectives covered by the EU-Egypt Action Plan. This Commission document supervises the actions taken either by the EU or Egypt and is organized along the structure of the Action Plan of 2007. It gives a clear overview of all the fields of EU-Egypt relations and enumerates the recent developments and roadblocks. It qualifies fields of progress, of no progress or slight progress by describing the activities in detail.

The 2010 Report (Commission, 2010, p. 2) summarized as follows:

> Concerns remain on the pace of the implementation [of] reforms in the field of democratisation and human rights, although the Government seems increasingly convinced of the need to tackle governance issues as part of its domestic reform agenda.
> Egypt remained an important trading partner for the EU despite the slowdown of bilateral trade in 2009. With the free trade agreement in the field of agricultural products adopted in 2009, there are good prospects that the economy will move up quickly to take advantage of the new opportunities offered by this agreement. ...
> Overall progress on the implementation of the Action Plan in 2009 can be summarised as encouraging, with a strong commitment to social, economic and sector reforms, and to a lesser extent to political reform. Moving towards enhanced relations is a shared objective of both, Egypt and the EU. Continued and consolidated progress in areas related to human rights and democracy will be an important foundation for these.

The Progress Report is an instrument of permanent communication with the Egyptian authorities. It works as an evaluative tool and, at the same time, its function is the blaming and shaming of deficiencies and shortcomings. In particular, the role of the persisting state of emergency since 1981 is highlighted as a major 'cause of concern and disappointment' in the field of rule of law, human rights and fundamental freedoms (Commission, 2010, pp. 5 ff.).

It is the core instrument of the ENP to keep up broad discourse in all fields of bilateral relations, in addition to the more concentrated objectives of the EU's country strategy and financial aid. In this respect, it can be termed, on the one hand, as a repercussion of the Barcelona Process and, on the other, as an ENP implementation tool for fields not covered within the framework of the financial aid instruments. Its logic of influence derives mainly from the discursive power of the EU. Its weakness is the lack of sanctions, especially with the Egyptian authorities rhetorically tending to refuse any external interference in their domestic affairs. Its strength is the permanent evaluation and publication of the state of play in European-Egyptian relations and the sustaining of the communication.

Country Strategy Paper and National Indicative Programme

The Egypt Country Strategy Paper for 2007–13 is the central document instructing a 'strategic framework' for the whole period. It considers the explicit Egyptian policy aims in the context of an analysis of Egypt's situation and past financial assistance by the EU. It understands the ENP as a framework for supporting the modernization process in Egypt and aims to 'focus on a limited number of specific priorities'. Three key objectives representing the mix of political, economic and social problem-solving approach used by the EU are:

- Supporting Egypt's reforms in the areas of democracy, human rights, good governance and justice;
- Developing the competitiveness and productivity of the Egyptian economy; and
- Ensuring the sustainability of the development process with effective social, economic and environmental policies and better management of natural resources (European Union, 2007, pp. 19 f.).

Two main reasons for this reduction of the objectives, compared with the priorities mentioned in the Action Plan, are given by the Commission: On the one hand, the obviously limited capacity of the Egyptian institutions to implement the Action Plan agenda, and, on the other hand, the EU's consideration of areas where it has 'comparative advantage and where there are distinct possibilities to complement the work of other donors ...' (European Union, 2007, p. 19).

These objectives to be funded by the European Neighbourhood Policy Instrument (ENPI) are principally managed under the National Indicative Programmes for 2007–10 and 2011–13 (European Union 2007 and 2010; Table 1). It allocated 558 Million euros during 2007–10 (an annual average of 140 Million euros) and 449 Million euros for 2011–13 (an annual average of 150 Million euros). The objectives as well as the funding are confirmed by an ENPI Memorandum of Understanding between the EU and Egypt (European Union and Arab Republic of Egypt, 2010).

In general, two-thirds of all EU funding are applied as budget support, which can be identified as the larger amounts in Table 1.[18] The project-oriented, smaller parts of the EU support are applied for technical assistance, capacity building and twinning projects with the EU. The comparison between the two funding periods (Table 2) does not only show a slight overall increase in EU funding, but a rearrangement of funding objectives.

Table 1. National Indicative Programmes for Egypt, 2007–13: Financial resources

Priorities	2007	2008	2009	2010	Total NIP 2007–10	% Budget	Total NIP 2011–13	% Budget
I. Supporting Egypt's reforms in the areas of democracy, human rights, justice					**40**	**7.2%**	**50**	**10.8%**
1. Support for political development, decentralization and promotion of good governance	–	13	–	–	13	2.3%	5	1.1%
2. Promotion and protection of human rights	–	17	–	–	17	3.0%	15	3.2%
3. Support for modernization of administration of justice	–	–	–	10	10	1.8%	10	2.2%
4. Upgrading of regulatory, institutional and legislative environment							20	4.3%
II. Developing the competitiveness and productivity of the Egyptian economy					**220**	**39.4%**	**209**	**45.0%**
Support for implementation of the Action Plan Programme (SAPP)	17	80	20	103	220	39.4%		
Technical support	17	–	20	33	70	12.5%		
Targeted support for sector reforms	–	80	–	70	150	26.9%		
Transport sector reform							85	18.3%
Energy sector reform							64	14.3%
Trade enhancement							20	4.3%
III. Ensuring the sustainability of the development process with better management of human and natural resources					**298**	**53.4%**	**205**	**44.2%**
Support for reform of education	120	–	–	–	120	21.5%		
Support for public health reform	–	–	120	–	120	21.5%		
Support for investment in the transport, energy and environment sectors (interest-rate subsidies)	–	29	–	29	58	10.4%		
Education and TVET reform							105	22.5%
Water sector reform							50	10.8%
Solid waste management							20	4.3%
Local community development							10	2.2%
Demining (El Alamein)							10	2.2%
Family planning							10	2.2%
Total	**137**	**139**	**140**	**142**	**558**	**100%**	**464**	**100%**

Sources: European Union, 2007, 2010; Interview with Commission official, 16 March 2011.

In particular, the 'support for Egypt's reforms in democracy, human rights and justice' was raised. This is due to the introduction of an additional sub-priority concerning the regulatory, institutional and legislative environment, which explicitly ties funding to conformity with European standards. One shift in allocation concerns the reduced funding of decentralization, with some components rearranged and now funded by Priority III. This reallocation should not be considered a withdrawal from this issue by the EU, but as an acknowledgement of the strong presence of and funding by USAID in this field.

In the area of 'developing the competitiveness and productivity of the Egyptian economy', the mixture of a broad number of unspecified target fields (from customs to agriculture and technology to modernization of statistics) was abolished in favour of three core reform fields: transport, energy and trade liberalization.

Table 2. National Indicative Programmes for Egypt, 2007–13: Priorities and components

Sub-Priorities	Components 2007–10	Components 2011–13
Priority I: Supporting Egypt's reforms in the area of democracy, human rights and justice		
1. Support for political development, decentralization and promotion of good governance	• Reform of electoral system • Decentralization and modernization of local administration • Modernization of public services with respect to good governance	• Improved capacity of institutions responsible for the electoral process • Reform of local administration • Improved management of public finances
2. Promotion and protection of human rights	• Human rights • Women's and children's rights • Strengthen civil society and its role in environmental protection • Promotion of the right of assembly and freedom of expression	• Effectiveness of national institutions in defending human rights and fundamental freedoms • Improved awareness of rights amongst women and children • Strong culture of respect for human rights and fundamental freedoms • Enhanced dialogue between government and civil society organizations on human rights and fundamental freedoms • Greater freedom of the media • Application of international conventions and protocols related to human rights
3. Modernization of administration of justice and enhancement of security	• Combating organized crime • Money laundering, terrorism • Management of migration flows • Improvement of the conditions in prisons and places of detention	• Independent and effective administration of justice • Greater capacity in fight against drugs and human trafficking • Improved economic justice • Improved places of detention and prison conditions
4. Upgrading of regulatory, institutional and legislative environment	[New in 2011–13]	• Matching European and international best practices institutionally and legislatively • Technical assistance for implementation of cooperation projects
Priority II: Developing the competitiveness and productivity of the economy		
1. Support for implementation of the Action Plan Programme	• Trade facilitation and customs reform • Economic legislation and business environment • Enhancing the agricultural sector • Support for transport, energy and technology • Modernization of statistical system	[Discontinued]
1. (new) Transport sector reform	[New in 2011–13]	• Separation of transport administration • Private involvement in transport projects and services • Application of air, waterway and road safety measures

(continued)

Table 2. (*Continued*).

Sub-Priorities	Components 2007–10	Components 2011–13
2. Energy sector reform	[New in 2011–13]	• Convergence of Egyptian regulations with the European energy market • Development of energy interconnections with the EU and the region • Development of policies on energy demand, management, efficiency, saving and renewables • Adoption and consultation with the EU on a long-term energy strategy
3. Trade enhancement measures	[New in 2011–13]	• Gradual liberalization in services and industrial goods • Enhance Egypt's export potential to EU • Enhance Egypt's participation in regional and sub-regional trade arrangements
Priority III: Ensuring the sustainability of the development process		
1. Reform of education	• Support for Egypt's reforms	• Effective public spending • Better training and human resource administration • Increased civil society participation in education reform • Increased capacities in education planning • Cooperation between training facilities and employment services • Correlation between training curricula and labour market needs
2. Public health	• Support for Egypt's health sector reform	[Discontinued]
3. Support for investment in transport, energy and environment sectors	• Support for the EIB loans in the three sectors	[Discontinued]
2. (new) Water sector reform	[New in 2011–13]	• Better management of waste production, delivery and treatment • Sustainable and fiscally decentralized water services • Coordination with private sector and civil society
3. (new) Support for solid waste management	[New in 2011–13]	• Improvement in collection, recycling and disposal of waste • Sustainable waste management and institutional structures • Coordination with private sector and civil society
4. Local community development	[New in 2011–13]	• Activation of non-state actors for needs of the community • Capacity-building of public agencies to provide services for local communities

Sources: European Union, 2007, 2010.

The concentration on transport and energy is underscored by the fact that nearly 20 per cent of the total funding is allocated for each.

In the area of 'ensuring sustainability of the development process', the support for educational reform is continued with a detailed specification of the components, aiming at capacity building inside Egypt in administration, inclusiveness and awareness. Although the EU withdrew from health reform, support for investments in transport (which is now covered by Priority II), and energy and environment, it established three new fields: water sector reform, solid waste management and local community development. Local community development aims at 'software' for the decentralization agenda in Priority I by capacity building of public services and the activation of civil society at the local level. Waste management is a new sub-priority, which turned out to be one of the most pressing environmental protection issues. The new framing of Priority III takes over parts of the components of Priority I. In addition, the emphasis on education as a highlighted sector with the largest single share of funding (23 per cent), the water sector and waste management tackle the core needs of the population and the development process.

5. Recent Developments

After President Mubarak stepped down, all four heads of the EU dealing with the ENP, Catherine Ashton, José Barroso, Štefan Füle and Herman Van Rompuy, gave statements on the events in Egypt or North Africa. Though Van Rompuy's statement (President of the European Council, 2011) is very general in stating the need for adapting the ENP, Füle (European Commissioner for Enlargement and Neighbourhood Policy, 2011) emphasizes the already existing framework of cooperation and priority on democratic reform, good governance and human rights within the ENP, which might meet a friendlier environment in Egypt after the revolution. A conceptually new approach is mentioned by Barroso (President of the European Commission, 2011) and specified by Ashton (European Commission High Representative, 2011b), talking about a three-fold response of the EU to the developments in North Africa, emphasizing 'deep democracy', economic development and renewed people-to-people contacts, which should lead to 'sustainable stability' as the new central idea on the treatment of the Mediterranean Neighbourhood countries. The 'deep democracy' concept consists mainly of the explicit inclusion of civil society, and the 'more for more' extended positive conditionality offers the enhancement of the former ENP approach. The conceptual framework was also elaborated by Ashton (European Commission High Representative, 2011a) as the new 'Partnership for Democracy and Shared Prosperity', drafted in a Joint Communication of the Commission on 8 March 2011. Three elements are specified as the basis for this new partnership:

- Democratic transformation and institution building;
- Stronger partnership with the people; and
- Sustainable and inclusive growth and economic development.

Although the rhetoric turn in EU foreign policy towards the Mediterranean promotes the democratic transition with unprecedented emphasis, the substantial content and procedures are still relying on the ENP programmes and tools. The revision of the ENP towards the Mediterranean countries might rearrange the emphases of the current implementation round, concerning direct approaches to civil society organizations and encouraging bottom-up initiatives, which might be served by the first-ever application of the Instrument for Stability in the Mediterranean since March 2011.[19] On the other hand, until now, the further development of big parts of the EU policy in Egypt is determined by the network of agreements and tools already decided upon; in this respect, any new approach is path-dependent on the ENP and the tools created by it.

6. Conclusion

This article has raised a number of questions concerning the recent developments in the Arab countries and the influence of EU policy. It places the findings on the ENP implementation in Egypt within the context of the debate about democratization by the EU and assumes that the impact of the ENP depends crucially on the interaction between the EU and the Egyptian system.

First, the existing EU policy towards Egypt displays a number of layers: Based on the EMP dialogue, the framework of the ENP was formulated as a concretization of objectives, which, in turn, focussed on national objectives in the ENP Action Plan between the EU and Egypt. The National Indicative Programme is composed of specified priorities within the framework of the National Action Plan to concentrate financial support in a few strategic areas.

This formulation of nested layers was developed in a continuous process of interaction between the Commission and Egypt, composed of defining objectives, negotiations with Egyptian decision makers, and evaluating and refining objectives and priorities as per the experiences with the Egyptian implementation.

Two types of ENP implementation tools have evolved so far. The National Indicative Programme for Egypt, as the main funding line, shows exemplarily how the Commission has mainstreamed and narrowed funding along the lines of democracy promotion, economic development and adherence to sustainability. The partly fuzzy delimitations during the first funding period have been concentrated on limited sub-priorities with clear components and objectives. The details show the ambitious intentions to address the central problems of Egyptian development, to include civil society and private actors, to build networks between stakeholders and central decision makers and to further push the Egyptian administration and government towards active liberalization. In this respect, the ENP's National Indicative Programme shows all facets of the dialogue process in a concentrated form. The ENP also includes a permanent consultation and communication process, addressing the whole spectrum of problems and issues in the bilateral relations. The Progress Reports are a tool of continuous demand for improvement and permanent screening of the political situation in Egypt and of Egyptian politics by the EU.

Though the contents of the objectives have been concentrated (some might say, reduced), the fields covered represent the central objectives of the ENP Action Plan and are of strategic importance for the further development of Egypt. From the procedural perspective, the concentration implies a densification of the requests for innovation in the targeted priorities, increasing the potential for institutional change in strategic sectors.

The recent developments in Egypt indicate that there is virtually no demonstrable connection between the democratic movement and the EU policy. The protest and democracy movement was nourished by domestic factors such as the manipulation of elections by and the enduring corruption of the regime, and the Tunisian example as an external factor. After the revolution, the administrative environment might develop to be more open and friendly than before, offering the ENP better conditions for democratic as well as economic reform agendas.

This leads to the second question. Democratization from outside is a long-standing request directed at the 'normative power Europe' in the EU's Mediterranean Policy. The empirical results show that the approach of concentration and narrowing of the ENP objectives is developed along a rigid context of authoritarian organization, limiting the content of EU policies to a 'common denominator' of areas. This might change in the future, but the procedural restrictions of limited administrative abilities and flexibility will stay for the time being as a constant factor. Concentrated content as well as the demanding procedural approach were and are of limited impact on the political situation in the country. However, being a highly prominent object of EU foreign policy analysis, one must not overestimate its practical reform potential for Egypt. Even after the revolution in Egypt, the EU is not as important for the people or the political elite as it is assumed by analyses, which overlook Egypt's relations with the US, Saudi Arabia, the individual EU member states and even China, and the financially light weight of the EU activities.

Even the rearrangement and redefinition of the EU approach after the Egyptian revolution does not indicate a fully new attempt. Rather, it seems to follow the recent path, correcting only some parts of the strategy. Even though in its new approach, the EU makes variations on the proven recipes of the ENP, the open-ended process of transition in Egypt offers the EU new opportunities for a supportive role. More than the selected sectors of activity, the procedural modernizing dimension of the EU activities could serve as a trigger for the development of a post-authoritarian statehood. In this respect, the most important role for the EU is supporting the ENP countries to develop their own concepts of democracy.

Notes

[1] On the challenge of Arab authoritarianism for the EU policy, see Brumberg, 2002; Jung, 2006; Asseburg and Koepf, 2007; Mattes, 2008; Bicchi, 2009; Youngs, 2006; Zaki, 2008.

[2] This included a lack of democracy with conditions diverging intolerably from the European ideas of participative democracy, rule of law and protection of human rights (see Council of the European Union, 2008; Cairo Institute for Human Rights Studies, 2009; US Department of State, 2008; Amnesty International, 2006).

[3] Two presentations on Egyptian politics towards the EU given by officials of the Egyptian Foreign Ministry: 28 February and 2 March 2010.

[4] Interviews with six officials from the Egyptian Foreign Ministry between 16 May and 7 July 2010.

[5] Presentation by an official of the Egyptian Foreign Ministry on 11 December 2010.

[6] Interview with an official of the Egyptian Foreign Ministry on 13 December 2010.

[7] The amount of sensitivity and discomfort Egyptian officials showed concerning this shift could serve as an indicator for the right direction the EU policy is taking in terms of democratization and Europeanization.

[8] See the Commission's concept drafted in several documents: Commission (2004, pp. 6 ff; 2006, p. 3; 2007, p. 3)

[9] Two interviews with Commission officials in Egypt, 22 November and 6 December 2010.

[10] This was partly characterized as Egyptian negotiants' 'Nasserist attitude' by members of the EU delegation in Cairo (interview with EU delegation official on 8 December 2010).

[11] *Political Priorities:* Political dialogue and cooperation (including the work on the settlement of the Middle East conflict), disarmament and arms control, strengthening democracy and the rule of law, protection of human rights, cooperation on migration, organized crime and people-to-people contacts. *Economic Priorities:* Economic integration with the EU, reforming economic policies and the financial sector, industrial development, rapprochement with EU economic and technical legislation, reforming taxation and public finance management, promotion of South-South trade, poverty reduction, promoting an information society, developing transport capacities, convergence in the energy sector and environmentally sustainable development.

[12] The following statements are based on interview results with several decision makers from the EU and the Egyptian side, conducted between September 2009 and October 2010.

[13] The German KfW and GTZ/GIZ run projects on renewable energy for industry and wind energy production and heavily support ideas concerning solar energy, including the Desertec project. Specialists from GTZ realize that, currently, this is mainly a sector to satisfy German environmental and industrial ambitions without having a solid basis in Egyptian society or economy (interview with German experts on 12 December 2010).

[14] Interviews with academic experts on 2 June and 7 October 2010.

[15] This description is based on 14 interviews with Egyptian officials from the Foreign Ministry, the Ministry for Higher Education, the Ministry of Agriculture, the Ministry of Telecommunication, the Ministry of Family and Population, the Ministry for Industry, the National Council for Human Rights, the National Council for Women, and the National Council for Childhood and Motherhood between March 2008 and November 2010.

[16] These are the former Chairwomen of the National Council for Childhood and Motherhood and former Minister for Family and Population, Moushira Khatab (out of office after January 2011), and the national TEMPUS manager in the Ministry for Higher Education, Yasser El Shayeb. Both have extremely strong records in implementing the prestigious 'Children at Risk' programme, and TEMPUS and FP 6 and 7, respectively.

[17] Until today, three Progress Reports have been published by the Commission (2008, 2009, 2010).

[18] The financial allocations presented in Table 1 and analysed here are partly derived from a comparison of the two National Indicative Programmes and partly corrected by interviews with the Commission officials in charge of the implementation, on 16 March and 29 March 2011.

[19] Interview with Commission official in Egypt on 16 March 2011.

References

Amnesty International, EU Office, 2006. *EU-Egypt Association Council Meeting: Amnesty International's key human rights concerns.* Brussels, 13 June 2006.

Asseburg, M., and Koepf, T., eds., 2007. *Challenges for policy-oriented research on the Middle East: Changing actors, reform priorities, and security approaches.* Berlin: German Institute for International and Security Affairs.

Attinà, F., 2005. The Barcelona process, the role of the European Union and the lesson of the Western Mediterranean. *In:* M. Bonner, M. Reif and M. Tessler, eds. *Islam, democracy and the state in Algeria: Lessons for the Western Mediterranean and beyond.* London: Routledge, pp. 140–152.

Attinà, F., 2007. EU relations with the Southern Mediterranean neighbours. *Intereconomics*, 42 (4), 196–200.

Bicchi, F., 2009. Democracy assistance in the Mediterranean: An overview. *Mediterranean politics*, 14 (1), 61–78.

Brumberg, D., 2002. The trap of liberalised autocracy. *Journal of democracy*, 13 (4), 56–68.

Bull, H., 1982. Civilian power Europe: A contradiction in terms? *Journal of common market studies*, 21 (2), 149–164.

Cairo Institute for Human Rights Studies, 2009. *Bastion of impunity, mirage of reform: Human rights in the Arab region: Annual Report 2009*. Cairo: Cairo Institute for Human Rights Studies.

Cavatorta, F., and Pace, M., 2010. The post-normative turn in European Union (EU)-Middle East and North Africa (MENA) relations: An introduction. *European foreign affairs review*, 15 (5), 581–587.

Commission of the European Communities, 2004. *European Neighbourhood Policy Strategy Paper*. Communication from the Commission, COM(2004) 373 final. Brussels, 12 May.

Commission of the European Communities, 2006. *On strengthening the European Neighbourhood Policy*. Communication from the Commission to the Council and the European Parliament, COM(2006)726 final. Brussels, 4 December.

Commission of the European Communities, 2007. *A strong European Neighbourhood Policy*. Communication from the Commission, COM(2007) 774 final. Brussels, 5 December.

Commission of the European Communities, 2008. *Progress Report Egypt: Implementation of the European Neighbourhood Policy in 2007*. Commission Staff Working Document, SEC(2008)395. Brussels, 3 April.

Commission of the European Communities, 2009. *Progress Report Egypt: Implementation of the European Neighbourhood Policy in 2008*. Commission Staff Working Document, SEC(2009) 523/2. Brussels, 23 April.

Commission of the European Communities, 2010. *Progress Report Egypt: Implementation of the European Neighbourhood Policy in 2009*. Commission Staff Working Document, SEC(2010) 517. Brussels, 12 May.

Council of the European Union, 2008. *EU annual report on human rights 2008*. Report, 14146/2/08 REV 2; COHOM 105. Brussels, 27 November.

Demmelhuber, T., 2009. *EU-Mittelmeerpolitik und der Reformprozess in Ägypten: Von der Partnerschaft zur Nachbarschaft*. Baden-Baden: Nomos.

Demmelhuber, T., 2011. The trap of competing policy concepts: The European Union and illegal migration in the Southern Mediterranean. *International journal of human rights*, 15 (6), in press.

European Commissioner Responsible for Enlargement and European Neighbourhood Policy, 2011. *Statement by Commissioner Štefan Füle on Egypt*. SPEECH/11/111. Strasbourg: Plenary Session of the European Parliament, 16 February.

European Commission High Representative, 2011a. *A partnership for democracy and shared prosperity with the Southern Mediterranean: Joint communication to the European Council, the European Parliament, the Council, the European Economic and Social Committee and the Committee of the Regions*, COM(2011) 200 final. Brussels: Commission of the European Communities, 8 March.

European Commission High Representative, 2011b. *Remarks by the EU High Representative Catherine Ashton at the senior officials' meeting on Egypt and Tunisia*. Press, A 069/11. Brussels: European Union, 23 February.

European Union, 2007. *Egypt Country Strategy Paper 2007–13*. Brussels, 4 January.

European Union, 2010. *European Neighbourhood and Partnership Instrument: Arab Republic of Egypt National Indicative Programme 2011–13*. 3 February 2010.

European Union and Arab Republic of Egypt, 2007. *European Neighbourhood Policy: EU–Egypt Joint Action Plan*, adopted at the 3rd EU–Egypt Association Council. Brussels, 6 March 2007.

European Union and Arab Republic of Egypt, 2010. *European Neighbourhood and Partnership Instrument: Egypt: Memorandum of Understanding between the European Union and the Arab Republic of Egypt regarding the National Indicative Programme 2011–13*. Cairo, 11 October.

Fenech, D., 1997. The relevance of European security structures to the Mediterranean (and vice versa). *Mediterranean politics*, 2 (1), 149–176.

Galtung, J., 1973. *The European Community: A superpower in the making*. London: George Allen & Unwin.

Grabbe, H., 2004. *How the EU should help its neighbours*. Centre for European Reform Policy Brief. London: Centre for European Reform (CER), June.

Hall, P.A., and Taylor, R.C.R., 1998. Political science and the three new institutionalisms. *In:* K. Soltan, E.M. Uslaner and V. Haufler, eds. *Institutions and social order*. Ann Arbor: University of Michigan Press, 15–43.

Hill, C., 1990. European foreign policy: Power bloc, civilian model – or flop? *In:* R. Rummel, ed. *The evolution of an international actor: Western Europe's new assertiveness*. Boulder, CO: Westview Press, 31–55.

Huntington, S.P., 1991. *The third wave: Democratisation in the late twentieth century*. Norman: University of Oklahoma Press.

Jung, D., ed., 2006. *Democratisation and development: New political strategies for the Middle East.* New York: Palgrave Macmillan.

Kelley, J., 2006. New wine in old wineskins: Promoting political reforms through the new European Neighbourhood Policy. *Journal of common market studies*, 44 (1), 29–55.

Kreitmeyer, N., and Schlumberger, O., 2010. Autoritäre Herrschaft in der arabischen Welt. *Aus politik und Zeitgeschichte*, 24/2010, 16–22.

Laïdi, Z., ed., 2008. *EU foreign policy in a globalised world: Normative power and social preferences.* Routledge/GARNET Series: Europe in the World 1. London and New York: Routledge.

Manners, I., 2002. Normative power Europe: A contradiction in terms? *Journal of common market studies*, 40 (2), 235–258.

Manners, I., 2010. Global Europa: Mythology of the European Union in world politics. *Journal of common market studies*, 48 (1), 67–87.

Marchetti, A., ed., 2004. *The CSCE as a model to transform Western Relations with the Greater Middle East.* ZEI Discussion Paper C 137. Bonn: ZEI.

March, J.G., and Olsen, J.P., 1989. *Rediscovering institutions: The organisational basis of politics.* New York: Free Press.

Marquina, A., 2003. From cooperative security to security partnership in the Mediterranean. In: H.G. Brauch *et al.*, eds. *Security and environment in the Mediterranean: Conceptualising security and environmental conflicts.* Berlin: Springer, 309–317.

Mattes, Hanspeter, 2008. "We're in the Arab World, man. Forget democracy." Die schwierige Transformation autoritärer Regime in Nahost. GIGA focus Nahost No. 8/2008, Hamburg: GIGA, p. 8.

McCormick, J., 2006. *The European superpower.* London: Palgrave.

Pace, M., 2007. Norm shifting from EMP to ENP: The EU as a norm entrepreneur in the South? *Cambridge review of international affairs*, 20 (4), 659–675.

Pawelka, P., 1985. *Herrschaft und Entwicklung im Nahen Osten: Ägypten.* Heidelberg: Müller.

Pierson, P., 1996. The path to European integration: A historical institutionalist analysis. *Comparative political studies*, 29 (2), 123–163.

President of the European Commission, 2011. *Statement by President Barroso on the situation in North Africa.* SPEECH/11/137. Brussels: Commission of the European Communities, 2 March.

President of the European Council, 2011. *Statement by Herman Van Rompuy, President of the European Council, on the developments in the EU's Southern neighbourhood.* Press, PCE 048/11. Prague: European Council, 23 February.

Reid, T.R., 2004. *The United States of Europe: The new superpower and the end of American supremacy.* New York: Penguin.

Schnabel, R.A., 2005. *The next superpower? The rise of Europe and its challenge to the United States.* Lanham, MD: Rowman & Littlefield.

Scott, W.R., 1995. *Institutions and organisations.* Thousand Oaks, CA: Sage.

Smith, K.E., 2000. The end of civilian power EU: A welcome demise or cause for concern? *International spectator*, 35 (2), 11–28.

Telò, M., 2006. *Europe, a civilian power? European Union, global governance, world order.* Basingstoke, Hampshire: Palgrave Macmillan.

US Department of State, 2009. *2008 Human Rights Report: Egypt, 25 February 2009* [online]. Available from: http://www.state.gov/g/drl/rls/hrrpt/2008/nea/119114.htm [Accessed 23 January 2011].

Weber, M., 1922/1972. *Wirtschaft und Gesellschaft: Grundriß der verstehenden Soziologie*, 5th ed. Tübingen: Mohr.

Wippel, S., 2005. *The Agadir Agreement and open regionalism.* EuroMeSCo Paper, 45. Lisbon: EuroMeSCo, September.

Youngs, R., 2006. *Europe and the Middle East: In the shadow of September 11.* Boulder, CO: Rienner.

Zaki, M., ed., 2008. *Civil society and democratisation in the Arab world: Annual Report 2007.* Cairo: Ibn Khaldun Center for Development Studies.

From 'Villains' to the New Guardians of Security in Europe? Paradigm Shifts in EU Foreign Policy towards Libya and Belarus

GISELLE BOSSE

ABSTRACT *This article analyses the EU's relations with Libya and Belarus over the past few decades. It is argued that the EU's pursuit of its internal security interests has led to significant U-turns in its perceptions of and policies towards autocratic regimes in its neighbourhood. Both Libya and Belarus were largely ostracized by the EU and the majority of its member states because of their grave concerns over democratic conduct and repeated violations of human rights in those countries. However, their increasingly important role in EU security (and, in particular, border security and the 'flight' against 'illegal' migration) has changed their image in and leverage over the EU. This paper first maps the competing paradigms of democracy promotion and the pursuit of internal security in EU foreign policy, followed by an outline of the key instruments used by it to implement its policies towards its neighbouring states. In the empirical parts that follow, the article examines the complex interplay between the two paradigms in the EU's policy towards Belarus and Libya and assesses their implementation in the political practice of day-to-day relations between the EU and both countries. By way of conclusion, the article's findings are placed in the broader context of the EU's normative power and future role as a 'successful democratiser'.*

Introduction

'*Yes, we sometimes have to engage in dialogue with regimes with whom we would prefer not to have to do so but, always, the aim is to help the people of that country.*'[1]

Since its enlargement to Central and Eastern Europe in 2004 and 2007, the European Union (EU) has struggled to find an appropriate policy to address its neighbours to the East and the South. Its efforts to support political and economic reforms in Ukraine and Moldova through the European Neighbourhood Policy (ENP) have yielded little success, and hopes to repeat the EU's success story of transforming post-communist countries in Eastern Europe without offering the prospect of EU membership, were quickly shattered. Likewise, the EU's partners in the Mediterranean saw little progress towards enhanced economic integration through the framework of the Euro-Mediterranean Partnership (EMP), a reality that has changed little following the introduction of the ENP. The ENP's difficulties in achieving its goal – enhanced relations and deeper integration in 'everything but institutions' (Prodi, 2002) – have been well documented (e.g. Whitman and Wolf, 2010). Nevertheless, most scholarly studies have tended to focus on so-called 'most likely cases', such as case studies of all those ENP partners that have expressed an explicit will to reform and democratize, with some expectation in the longer term to eventually join the EU (i.e. Moldova and Ukraine, Morocco), or at least the clear intent to integrate with parts of the EU's legislative *acquis* (Association Agreements within the EMP framework).[2] Most contributions have, therefore, analysed the EU's relations with countries that have in principle accepted its governance and rule transfer as a condition to further integrate with its economic and political structure (Lavenex, 2004, 2008). As a result, few have questioned the legitimacy of the EU's engagement with the wider neighbourhood.[3]

Yet, not all of the EU's neighbours aspire to reform their economic and political system. Instead, some have officially refused the join the ENP or outright objected to any intervention in their domestic affairs. This article aims to analyse and explain the EU's policy towards these 'least likely' cases in its neighbourhood, towards countries which have not expressed the will to adopt the fundamental values of the EU or to engage in political and economic reforms. In the East, Belarus expressed no immediate preference for joining the EU and the regime led by President Lukashenka – often cited as the 'last dictatorship' in Europe – made no visible moves towards democratization. In the south, Libyan leader Muammar Gaddafi officially refused to join both the EMP and the ENP, and, after 40 years in power, Gaddafi had introduced few political reforms to improve the country's human rights record and its reputation as one of the most authoritarian regimes in the Arab world. In recent years, however, the EU has nevertheless increasingly sought to cooperate with both regimes, despite them constituting 'least likely' cases for sharing its democratic values.

Following the end of the cold war, the initial EU policy towards Belarus and Libya was to express clear and unequivocal disapproval of both regimes. A decade later, however, the EU appeared to have changed its mind, despite little indication that the two regimes had changed their policies significantly. With regard to Belarus, in October 2009, the Council concluded that

> since October 2008 (...) new possibilities have opened up for dialogue and deepened cooperation between the EU and Belarus. The Council welcomes the increased high-level EU-Belarus political dialogue, the establishment of a Human Rights Dialogue, the intensified technical cooperation and the participation of Belarus in the Eastern Partnership, as ways of building mutual understanding and creating opportunities to address issues of concern (Council of the European Union, 2009, p. 1).

At the same time, and after decades of having imposed sanctions on Libya, the EU also begun to re-engage with the Gaddafi regime. Throughout the 1980s and 1990s, the EU officially isolated the Libyan regime as a supporter of international terrorism. Since 2004, however, it has considerably revised its policy and offered to negotiate a new framework agreement with Libya outside the structures of the EMP. The new approach was summarized in a concept note issued by the Commission in late 2009, which contends that

> the main political objective of the framework agreement is to strengthen relations and cooperation between the EC and its member states, on the one hand, and Libya on the other hand, on the basis of (...) strong common interests (Commission, 2009, p. 1).

Given the authoritarian nature of the Libyan and Belarusian regimes, the EU's increased engagement with the two countries necessitates a close and careful analysis, which is missing in contemporary research on the EU's ENP. Better knowledge of the EU's engagement policy with the autocratic regimes in its geographic vicinity is all the more important following a number of disturbing events in late 2010 and early 2011, which raised significant questions marks over the impact of EU policy on the autocratic regimes in its neighbourhood: In December 2010, the Lukashenka regime cracked down violently on opposition protests after the fraudulent presidential election and Belarusian security services arrested more than 700 people, many of whom are facing long prison sentences. Later, in Spring 2011, Gaddafi declared 'war' on his own population, following the popular uprising against his regime. The heavy fighting between the regime and the opposition rebels led to hundreds of casualties and caused a humanitarian crisis among large parts of the population in the cities under siege.

This article aims to conceptualize and trace the shifts in the EU's relations with Libya and Belarus over the past decade. It is argued that the EU's increasingly dominant externalized internal security agenda has led to significant U-turns in the EU's images of and policies towards the autocratic regimes in its neighbourhood: from an emphasis on the undemocratic nature of the regimes and the requirement to base cooperation on 'shared values' and democracy promotion to the pursuit of the EU's internal security interests based on an engagement with 'strategic partners'. In the first part of this article, I conceptualize the paradigms of democracy promotion and the pursuit of internal security in EU foreign policy and outline the key instruments it used to implement its policies. In the empirical parts that follow, I examine the complex interplay between the two paradigms in the EU's policies towards Belarus and Libya immediately after the end of the cold war, in the European Neighbourhood Policy, and in the Eastern Partnership (EaP)/Union for the Mediterranean (UfM), respectively, and assess their implementation in the political practice of EU relations with both regimes. By way of conclusion, I place the empirical findings in the wider context of the future and the legitimacy of the EU's policy towards autocratic regimes elsewhere in the world.

Competing Paradigms in EU Foreign Policy: Democracy Promotion vs. the Pursuit of EU Internal Security

Under the Treaty of Maastricht, the EU adopted democracy promotion as a goal for its own foreign policy, specifically with the aim to give itself a 'new and special international profile' (Olsen, 2000, p. 143). During the 1990s, the EU allocated substantial resources to democracy and human rights projects and the so-called 'democracy clause' was introduced into agreements between the EU and third states, providing for the suspension of aid and trade provisions in response to violations of democratic principles and human rights. Democracy promotion featured prominently as a key pillar in the EU's enlargement policies (especially towards Eastern Europe), took central place in the EU's 2003 Security Strategy, and has been integrated into almost all of its recent foreign policy initiatives, especially the ENP.

At the same time, the EU gradually externalized its internal security agenda. The Area of Freedom, Security and Justice (AFSJ) has been the EU's fasted growing policy area, and many of the internal security issues on the EU agenda required external action (i.e. organized crime or terrorism). As a result, the EU externalized its internal security objectives into its external relations, 'transforming itself into an external actor in its own right on internal security issues' (Monar, 2010, p. 23). The Amsterdam Treaty strengthened the EU's external action capabilities on international crime networks, terrorist activities and illegal immigration and, in 1999, the Tampere European Council decided that all EU external instruments could be used for the development of the AFSJ. In 2005, the Council adopted the Strategy for the External Dimension of the Area of Freedom, Security and Justice, which further institutionalized the EU's internal security goals in its external relations.

Democracy promotion and the pursuit of internal security, therefore, constitute two very different approaches informing EU foreign policy. They are distinct policy paradigms that advocate very different political aims. To depict these paradigms and their interplay in a concrete policy such as towards Belarus and Libya, I briefly sketch the different aims of the two paradigms and outline the main instruments used by the EU to achieve these divergent goals.

Democracy Promotion

In his recent analysis of EU democracy promotion, Richard Lappin (2010) concludes that there is a 'fundamental deficit in our thinking about what type of democracy we are assisting and how we should assist it' (p. 194). And indeed, the literature on EU democratization and democracy promotion efforts is remarkably silent on what type of democracy it aims to promote. This is perhaps less surprising taking into account the fact that the EU itself has chosen to define its understanding of democracy in only very vague terms. Lappin takes a more pragmatic angle on the question and distinguishes between the minimalist and maximalist definitions of democracy. Whereas the minimalist definition, based on the writings of Schumpeter (1947), refers to an electoral-based approach pertaining to the competitive struggle for people's votes, the maximalist definition (Held, 1996, pp.1–34) embraces the normative underpinnings of democracy and underlines the importance of participation, citizenship and participatory democracy (Lappin, 2010, p. 193). In theory, the

EU has incorporated the broader definition of democracy promotion in a variety of its foreign and aid policies (Youngs, 2003). In practice, the EU's human rights policies seem to resemble the minimalist definition. They exhibit a 'gradualist philosophy' and support gradual or 'controlled change' in third states. This particular approach tends to result in support for 'top-heavy political structures to manage reform processes' and institution building programmes, often at the expense of developing bottom-up civil society initiatives (Youngs, 2004, pp. 421–422). Both minimalist and maximalist definitions of democracy are, therefore, likely to feature in the EU's policies towards Belarus and Libya.

The Pursuit of Internal Security

Compared to democracy promotion, the goals pertaining to the paradigm of the pursuit of the EU's internal security are defined in a clearer manner. According to the Treaty on the Functioning of the European Union (TFEU), a 'high level of security' is one of the main objectives of the AFSJ (Article 67.3). The pursuit of national (internal) security interests continues to be deeply engrained in the structure of the European state system and, specifically, the traditional statist value of privileging the security and welfare of one's own citizens within national borders over and above the security of human beings in other states (Hoffman, 1997/98; Gelb and Rosenthal, 2003). Although the EU is often seen as a postmodern *sui generis* polity, beyond realpolitik, it is unreasonable to assume that the 27 member state governments will find it easy to privilege non-EU citizens over and above the security concerns of their citizens (and electorates) at home. Internal security concerns underpin the EU's externalized border and immigration policies towards third countries (e.g. Lavenex, 2001). EU border and immigration policies have focused on limitation of access to common territory through the strengthening of external borders, tight visa policies and the allocation of exclusive responsibility for the expulsion of illegal immigrants (Guild and Niessen, 1996). At the same time, and in the words of Hyde-Price, 'the EU as a collective actor seeks to shape its regional milieu in ways conducive to [its] economic, political and security interests' (Hyde-Price, 2004, p. 12). The latter goal is likely to play a role in the EU's policy towards Belarus and Libya, in particular regarding the EU's interest in securing its Eastern and Southern borders and ensuring the security of energy supply.

The instruments that the EU deploys to exert influence over third countries have been defined in a number of ways (Lappin, 2010; Schimmelfennig, 2007), though many build on Paul Kubicek's distinction between contagion, convergence and conditionality as the means for international actors to shape the processes of democratization (Kubicek, 2003, 2005). Contagion occurs when 'events or systems in one country or group of countries, to the extent that they are seen as attractive or achievable, can spread across borders' (Kubicek, 2003, p. 5). Convergence follows contagion and refers to the gradual movement towards system conformity and the internalization of EU norms by both the elite and the public in the targeted states. The EU has clearly attempted to use both contagion and convergence as 'passive leverage' over third countries to support democratization (Vachudova, 2005, p. 65), but also to pursue internal security interests (Wichmann, 2007, p. 7; Jones and Emerson, 2005, pp. 18–19). Conditionality, on the other hand, is a tool to exert direct leverage over a target country by linking 'perceived benefits (...) to the fulfillment of a certain program, advancement of democratic principles and institutions' and employing 'carrots and sticks' to 'persuade, induce, and at time coerce states into adopting the desired policy' (Kubicek, 2005, p. 273). Perceived benefits can be of a material (such as trade liberalization) or social (such as praise or recognition) nature (Schimmelfennig, 2007, p. 127). Conditionality is generally seen as one of the preferred tools of the EU in its relations with third countries (Portela, 2008).

In the empirical parts that follow, I will (1) examine the contours and interplay between the democracy promotion and internal security paradigms in the EU's policies towards Belarus and Libya over the past decades, and (2) assess their implantation in the political practices of the EU's relations with both regimes.

1. EU Relations with Belarus and Libya after the End of the Cold War: Isolating the 'Villains'

There were literally no relations between the EU and Libya after the end of the cold war until the turn of the millennium.[4] The Global Mediterranean Policy of the EU (1976–90) did not include Libya. The country was kept out as a supporter of international terrorism, accused of being involved in various terrorist attacks in Western Europe during the cold war, including the bombing of the La Belle disco in Berlin in April 1986 and the Lockerbie bombings in December 1988, which killed hundreds of civilians. In 1992, the heads of state and government of the European Community agreed to subject Libya to severe trade sanctions.[5] No agreements were negotiated or signed between the EC and Libya. Later, in the 1990s, as Gaddafi's revolutionary committee lost some of its power, largely because of the decline of the USSR, the country's leader sought to rebuild its international profile. In 2003, Gaddafi announced the discontinuation of Libya's efforts to develop and produce weapons of mass destruction and the payment of major compensation to the victims of the terrorist bomb attacks in which the Libyan secret services had been proven to be involved.

In contrast, relations between the EU and Belarus looked very promising just after the end of the cold war. The EC recognized Belarus' independence in December 1991 and, until 1994, their relations were based on the Trade and Cooperation Agreement (TCA) concluded with the USSR in 1989. In 1995, the EC and Belarus signed a Partnership and Cooperation Agreement (PCA) as well as an Interim Trade Agreement to bridge the time until the PCA's final ratification by all the member states. Between 1994 and 1997, however, the positive trend in EU-Belarus relations came to an end, following President Lukashenka's attempt to extend his presidential mandate in a referendum in 1996 by changing the constitution, and the increasing repression in Belarus of the opposition, independent media and judiciary. These developments prompted the European Council in 1997 to suspend the process of ratification of the PCA and to freeze the Interim Agreement. Since then, EU relations with Belarus remain covered by the 1989 TCA, which does not include any provisions for regulatory approximation to the EU's trade related *acquis*. The 1997 Council decision also restricted all political contacts with Belarus to below ministerial level. The only other legal instrument binding the EU and Belarus is the 1993 bilateral agreement on trade in textile products (Piontek, 2006).

Taking into account the fact that the EU had not fully developed its democracy promotion strategy in the first years preceding the end of the cold war, it used economic and trade sanctions to coerce the Lukashenka regime into democratic reforms. Relations with Libya, on the other hand, were suspended due to the EU's internal security concerns about Gaddafi's support for international terrorism.

2. The European Neighbourhood: Different Rhetoric for 'Different Dictators'

In 2002–03, the EU began to develop what was then called the Wider Europe – New Neighbourhood Strategy. Though initially designed as a response to the challenges and opportunities arising from the EU's new Eastern border, the policy soon also included countries of the Euro-Mediterranean Partnership due to pressure from the EU's Southern member states. As the ENP developed, Libya and Belarus were addressed in rather different terms.

Libya was included in the first framework documents of the ENP, although it had, like Belarus, no contractual relations with the country. In its Communication of March 2003, the Commission recalled that the EU had suspended sanctions against Libya and lifted restrictions on its diplomats and consular personnel. It also highlighted that Libya regularly observed the meetings of foreign ministers and senior officials within the framework of the EMP.

Despite Libya's refusal to accept the Barcelona *acquis*, the Communication proposed that

> The EU should therefore give consideration to how it could incorporate Libya into the neighbourhood policy. In order to send a coherent message, further engagement needs to be pursued within a conditional framework and a clear understanding of the benefits of making progress towards cooperation based on the respect for shared values (Commission, 2003, p. 17).

In the 2004 Strategy Paper on the ENP, the Commission repeats the conditionality attached to the EU's engagement with Libya based on its 'entry into the Barcelona Process on the basis of Libya's full acceptance of the Barcelona *acquis* and the resolution of outstanding bilateral issues' (Commission, 2004, p. 4). Only then could the EU anticipate 'pav[ing] the way to the establishment of normal relations so that Libya will be able to benefit from the European Neighbourhood Policy' and 'full integration into the Barcelona process is the first step towards new relations with the EU, which include the negotiation of an Association Agreement' (Commission, 2004, pp. 4, 12)

The Council of Ministers confirmed the conditional engagement with Libya later in 2004 and reiterated that

> on the basis of acceptance of the Barcelona acquis, resolution of all outstanding bilateral issues, including the 'La Belle' case and that of the Bulgarian medical workers, with EU member states and negotiating candidate counties, and the subsequent development of contractual relations with the EU, Libya would be eligible to participate in the ENP (General Affairs and External Relations Council, 2004a, p. 13).

The reconciliatory tone of the EU vis-à-vis the Libyan regime was a clear sign that the EU's short-term internal security concerns had started to override the long-term goal of democracy promotion. Libya increasingly gained importance in the context of the EU's immigration policy. The Foreign Ministers had already recognized Libya as a strategic partner in the 'fight' against illegal immigration back in 2003. They agreed that 'an expert mission should examine the situation and report back to the Council, which would then evaluate the situation in the light of technical and political criteria' (General Affairs and External Relations Council, 2003, p. 20). Already, in late 2005, the heads of state and government of the EU put pressure on the Commission to 'conclude the work to agree [on] the EU-Libya Action Plan on migration as early as possible in 2006 (...) and implement projects as soon as possible thereafter (Presidency Conclusions, 2005, p. 13).

Yet, despite the 'urgency' of cooperation with Libya on immigration, the member states reemphasized the EU's 'wish to see Libya become a full member of the Barcelona Process (...). Participation in the process, and subsequent progression towards the conclusion of an Association Agreement, would require Libya to accept the Declaration and Barcelona acquis in full (Presidency Conclusions, 2005, p. 23).

Thereafter, Libya hardly features in the official documents relating to the ENP. However, the Regional Strategy Paper 2007–13, in which the Commission outlines its strategic objectives with the Southern neighbourhood region under the European Neighbourhood and Partnership Instrument (ENPI), does not repeat the conditionality of engagement used in previous communications. It refers to Libya once, under the heading of 'concrete actions for energy', where it proposes the 'progressive integration of Libyan energy markets with neighbouring countries (Regional Strategy Paper, 2007–13, p. 8).

In addition, the European Parliament (EP) was initially rather keen on including Libya within the orbit of the ENP. In its Napolitano Report of 2003, the EP called for 'relations with the Mediterranean region to take account not only of those countries which are already members of the Euro-Mediterranean partnership but also of Libya', which had observer status and which was also, above all, a member of the 'embryonic Arab Maghreb Union' (Napolitano Report, 2003, p. 8).

Overall, the partial inclusion of Libya into the ENP clearly reflects the increasing role of the EU's internal security concerns vis-à-vis the country and a change in policy as concerns the instruments with which to pursue its goals. Rather than sanctions, Libya was now regarded as a 'partner' subject to a light conditionality vaguely tied to signing the Barcelona Declaration and adopting the EU acquis in the area of migration as part of the Action Plan.

In contrast, the ENP on Belarus was rather ambiguous initially. Belarus was considered a partner or 'subject' of a new neighbourhood policy right from the start. Yet, the Commission and High Representative initially highlighted an 'upgrading of the PCA relations with Ukraine and Moldova', with Belarus being a 'different partner', yet still a central focus of the EU's efforts to 'engage more actively in resolving problems' on its 'doorstep' (Patten and Solana, 2002, pp. 3–4). In November 2002, the Foreign Ministers in the Council even stated their intent to develop enhanced relations with Ukraine, Belarus and Moldova (General Affairs and External Relations Council, 2002, p. 1). The 2003 Commission Communication on the Wider Europe – New Neighbourhood Strategy did not, however, present a clear strategy for engagement with Belarus. It stated that:

> The EU faces a choice over Belarus: either to leave things to drift – a policy for which the people of Belarus may pay dear and one which presents the EU from pursuing increased cooperation on issues of mutual interest – or to engage, and risk sending a signal of support for policies which do not conform to EU values (Commission, 2003, p. 15).

Between 2004 and 2006, the EU started drafting Country Reports as well as Action Plans for the implementation of the ENP with most partner states, including the Mediterranean and South Caucasus, excluding Belarus. The 2006 Commission Communication on *Strengthening the ENP* makes no mention of Belarus (Commission, 2006a). Instead, the Commission issued a *Non-Paper* in December 2006, which essentially contains a list of democratization measures 'reflecting a principled, non-compromising approach'. It states that 'the EU cannot offer to deepen its relations with a regime which denies its citizens their fundamental democratic rights' and demands 'political, economic and administrative reforms' (Commission, 2006b). The *Non-Paper* is an expression of the EU's top-down approach to democratization: participation in the neighbourhood policy of the Belarusian government in return for democratic reforms. The EU's strict conditionality has, however, had no measurable effect on the Lukashenka government, not least because the conditions set out in the *Non-Paper* threatened the very existence of Lukashenka. The conditionality of the EU vis-à-vis the Belarusian regime was not feasible and too general. As George Dura (2008, p. 6) notes, 'Lukashenka would have to democratise Belarusian politics and society, thereby seriously jeopardising his future as Belarus' president.'

In addition to the promotion of democracy and human rights through coercive conditionality, the EU also used contagion to 'win the hearts and minds' of the Belarusian population as expressed in the 2004 Commission Strategy Paper:

> More can be done [...], in particular to support civil society, democratisation, independent media, the alleviation of problems in the areas affected by the Chernobyl disaster, humanitarian assistance as well as regional cooperation (Commission, 2004, pp. 4, 12).

In its official rhetoric, the EU has, therefore, drawn a rather clear distinction between the two authoritarian regimes. Belarus is addressed with the goal of democracy promotion and regarded as a 'villain', who must adopt full-fledged political and economic reforms before any engagement with the EU is deemed possible. The coercive conditionality towards Lukashenka was coupled with a strategy to exert passive leverage over the Belarusian population. By contrast, Libya was asked to adopt the Barcelona *acquis*, though references to its democratic credentials were very rare, which suggest a light conditionality approach on behalf of the EU.[6] Already, back in 2003, the EU had highlighted the strategic importance of Libya, a discourse that was entirely absent from its policy towards Belarus at the time. An engagement was sought in areas linked to the EU's internal security interests, as, for example, on illegal immigration or energy.

In the next section, I examine the extent to which the EU translated its coercive conditionality towards Belarus and its light conditionality approach towards Libya into practice.

3. Neighbourhood Relations in Practice: Turning 'Villains' into 'Partners'?

The Failure of the EU's Passive Leverage over Belarus

Support for civil society and NGOs is financed through the Neighbourhood Programmes (2005–06) and the European Neighbourhood and Partnership Instrument (ENPI) (2007–13). In 2005-06, assistance totalled €10 million (€8 million committed) and focused on (1) support for institutional, legal and administrative reform and (2) support in addressing the social consequences of transition, including support to civil society and democratization, education and training and support to the alignment with international conventions (Country Strategy Paper, 2005–06). Additional assistance was also provided via the European Instrument for Democracy and Human Rights (EIDHR) (€5 million in total, €2 million from the TACIS budget) (Country Strategy Paper, 2005–06). The ENPI is a new EC assistance tool and comprises national, regional, cross-border and thematic components. Belarus is receiving assistance for projects under the thematic programmes, Democracy and Human Rights and Non-State Actors and Local Authorities Development, the national component (€5 million per annum), including actions to alleviate the consequences of the Chernobyl catastrophe and democratic development and good governance (Country Strategy Paper, 2007–13).

The approval and implementation of projects for civil society in Belarus started very slowly. Most projects that have been funded through TACIS since 2005 aim at improving border management. A mere €130,000 was allocated to micro projects (human rights/ democracy). €2 million went into awareness raising TV/radio programmes for Belarus, but the funds only supported projects and project partners outside Belarus, i.e. a radio station for Belarus broadcasting from Poland (Commission-EuropeAid, 2008). One specific problem that frequently occurred in the funding of 'grass-roots' organizations and NGOs is the lengthy registration process for projects, which effectively gave the Belarusian authorities a veto on proposed projects. According to a Commission official, projects under the Annual Programs, which had already been agreed upon in partnership with the relevant mid-level authorities, often got rejected by the central authority, which refused to register them.[7] The very strict auditing rules and regulations of the TACIS instrument are also to blame for the difficulties in allocating funding to unregistered NGOs. The rules of the ENPI contain even stricter criteria that organizations participating in projects have to meet. This is one of the reasons why, even within the European Commission, the ENPI is not considered a useful tool to fund bottom-up/ civil society projects, especially in countries that do not welcome such support.[8] Because of their greater flexibility and direct funding channels (which also do not require prior agreement by national authorities), the EIDHR and the Non-State Actors Programmes are designed to finance the majority of civil society projects in the future (Bosse, 2008, pp. 52–53). The suitability of the ENP/ENPI as a tool to exert passive pressure and to raise the level of attractiveness of the EU in the eyes of the Belarusian population is therefore questionable.

Coercive Conditionality vs. Pragmatic Engagement in EU Policy towards Belarus

In contrast to the principled values-based approach in the EU's official rhetoric on Belarus, technical or expert cooperation in areas of mutual interest to the EU and Belarus has already been a relatively consistent feature of cross-border/ regional cooperation under the TACIS instrument. Belarusian Oblast (regions) participate in three of the EU's cross-border cooperation (CBC) programmes: Latvia-Lithuania-Belarus, Poland-Belarus-Ukraine and the Baltic Sea Programme. All three projects continue to be financed under the ENPI. Belarus has hosted several meetings of project selection committees, and cooperation in areas such as border crossing/ service issues is generally regarded as very constructive.[9]

The Commission has also moved towards an approach of technical engagement with Belarus in other policy areas. The 2004 ENP Strategy Paper confirmed that

> [...] if significant positive developments take place in democratisation in Belarus, there is scope for more active engagement with the Belarusian authorities at political level. Contacts between officials at technical level could be intensified and meetings at senior level, such as the Regional Directors' Troika resumed (Commission, 2004, p. 11).

Contrary to the coercive conditionality approach of its 12-point *Non-Paper*, the Commission's interpretation in practice of a 'significant positive development' was measured against fairly small political steps taken by the Belarusian authorities. In January 2008 and following the release of three political prisoners, experts from the Commission met their Belarusian counterparts in Minsk to discuss 'technical matters relating to the energy and transport situation in the EU and Belarus' and an additional meeting took place in early February on environmental issues (Commission, 2008a). The areas discussed in these technical meetings ranged from the identification of joint interests and possible projects, such as the improvement of safety of trucks, to investment plans and Russia's North and South Stream Projects.[10] On the part of the EU, officials from the Directorate General (DG), External Relations (RELEX), and the relevant line DGs participated, together with experts at or below the deputy ministerial level. According to one Commission official, democratic values were mentioned in technical meetings with Belarusian officials, but only if so requested by the Council and then usually with the 'understanding' that 'we put our lines', suggesting that the political issue of Democracy was of little relevance for the experts.[11] As a result, the Belarusian side was always very well prepared, professional and committed to not exploiting the meetings for media propaganda.[12] These observations suggest that some form of 'convergence' had taken place among the officials from the Commission and those involved from the Belarusian side. And the convergence of views seems to have occurred on both sides towards pursuing mutual interests, rather than 'socialising' the Belarusian officials towards internalizing the EU's democratic values or standards (see also Bosse and Korosteleva, 2009).

EU energy security concerns have also been driving the European Commission to develop ever closer ties with the Lukashenka regime. In the past couple of years, the EU's growing dependence on Russian energy, coupled with Belarus' role as a major transit country for Russian oil and gas, has clearly alerted the Commission. In 2007, for example, the Russian state operator, Transneft, cut off oil supplies transiting through Belarus via the Druzbha pipeline, which is one of Russia's principal oil arteries to Western Europe. Shortly afterwards, also in response to the Russia-Ukraine gas row in January 2006, the Commission published its proposals for the first comprehensive package of measures to establish a new Energy Policy for Europe with the aim of boosting the EU's energy security. In 2009, the Commission already anticipated the 'finalisation of a European Commission-Belarus declaration on energy, as a basis for further development of energy cooperation' (Commission, 2008b, p. 9).

Belarusian experts are also included in technical meetings and training events to address the issues of strengthening and reinforcing asylum, migration and border management standards and capacities within the framework of the Söderköping Process. This comprises an annual senior-level review meeting and working-level cluster meetings for migration service and border guard officials as well as non-governmental organizations (Country Strategy Paper, 2007–13, pp. 14–15).

In contrast to the coercive conditional approach emphasized in the EU's official rhetoric towards Belarus, the political practice under the ENP followed a different policy paradigm based on mutual interests with almost no conditionality attached. The Commission fostered (or at least consented to) the convergence of the Belarusian officials' views to the pursuit of cooperation with the EU based on mutual interests rather than democratic values. The EU's strategy of exerting passive leverage over the Belarusian population and to stimulate democratic reforms 'from within', however, had very little impact in practice due to the limited reach of financial assistance.

Implementing Light Conditionality in the EU's Relations with Libya

The EU started to engage with Libya in 2004, despite the absence of a bilateral or regional legal framework governing these relations. Already, back in 2002, the Council had stressed that it was 'essential to initiate cooperation with Libya' in the field of migration management (Council, 2002, p. 6). In 2003, the Commission conducted an exploratory mission to assess the willingness of the Libyan authorities to cooperate with the EU in the field of illegal migration and 'found Libya ready and willing to cooperate in this area' (Hamood, 2006, p. 72). Shortly afterwards, in April 2004, Gaddafi was invited to Brussels; this marked his first official visit to the EU in 15 years. In October of the same year, the Council decided to reinforce its cooperation with the Libyan regime as part of a new 'policy of engagement' and decided to lift all economic sanctions, including the arms embargo against the regime (General Affairs and External Relations Council, 2004b, p. 8). Throughout 2004 and 2005, several heads of government of the EU member states as well as Commission officials visited Gaddafi in Tripoli.

In the absence of formal legal relations, the EU then embarked on technical ad hoc cooperation with the Libyan government. A technical mission was sent out in 2004 to establish the grounds for cooperation between the EU and Libya on institution building, training, asylum issues and border control. The first projects were launched in June 2005. Two years later, in June 2007, FRONTEX, the EU's newly formed border control agency, sent another technical mission to the country to invite Libya to join its maritime operations to stop illegal immigration along Libya's cost. The mission praised the Libyan authorities for their 'great efforts to provide the necessary detailed logistical support' for the mission and invited the Libyan government to draft a list of technical hardware that it required from the EU. The list included, *inter alia*, surveillance radar, night vision devices, fingerprint and image recognition systems, satellite-based communication, navigation devices, trucks ('for desert intruders displacing') as well as patrol boats (FRONTEX, 2007, Annex 7, pp. 1–5).

The lifting of the arms embargo against Libya did indeed enable the EU to export military equipment to Libya within the framework of its projects in the area of migration. The use of that equipment was justified on the grounds that it was designed to help Libya to strengthen its border and immigration controls. Nevertheless, it is widely known that Libya had regularly violated the human rights of the irregular migrants entering and transiting through the country. Those found guilty of attempting to leave Libya suffered the worst mistreatment. The cooperation between the EU and Libya in the area of migration might, therefore, very well have conflicted with the EU's Code of Conduct on Arms Exports, which stipulates that EU countries should refrain from supplying weapons to countries committing human rights violations.[13] Nevertheless, the EU went ahead with the intensification of its technical ad hoc cooperation with the Libyan regime in the pursuit of its internal security interests, including the setting up of a joint EU-Libya committee to discuss joint training on external border management and a further 'inventory of technical requirements' (Hamood, 2006, p. 75).

In late 2004, the EU also began to offer limited financial assistance to Libya. Although it financed projects in the health sector (under the Action Plan for the Benghazi Children's hospital), the main focus of financial assistance was placed on the management of illegal immigration (EuropeAid, 2004). In addition, Libya received substantial financial support for the 'Prevention of irregular migration' at its Southern borders (€2 million) and the 'Management of irregular migration pressures (€3.5 million) under the 2008 Annual Action Programme for the EU's thematic programme on migration and asylum (Strategy Paper Libya, 2011–13, p. 43).[14]

Libya has also become the EU's third most important source of oil supply (since 2006) after Russia and Norway. Equally, gas imports from Libya to the EU have increased significantly over the past five years. In addition, only 25 per cent of the country is currently covered by exploration agreements, which makes Libya very attractive for major European energy companies. Nevertheless, as Joffé and Paoletti (2010, p. 28) note, the EU's security preoccupations do clearly prevail over questions of economic or commercial engagement, a trend that was already visible by mid-2010, when the EU prepared for the negotiations for a new Framework Agreement with Libya.

The political practice of the EU's neighbourhood policy towards Libya reveals that the EU has stuck to its ad hoc engagement approach and invested heavily in the pursuit of its internal security interests in cooperation with the Libyan regime. Nevertheless, the EU has struggled to implement even the 'lightest' conditionality (in the pursuit of its interests as well as in democracy promotion) vis-à-vis the Gaddafi regime and made significant financial concessions to keep the regime on the negotiating table. In contrast, the EU's ad hoc cooperation with Belarus clearly contradicted its 'principled' rhetoric. However, the EU appeared to be more successful in reaching a convergence of interests with its Belarusian counterparts, without having to make substantial financial concessions.

4. EaP and UfM: Institutionalizing Partnership

Belarus in the Eastern Partnership

The Eastern Partnership (EaP) was officially launched in Prague on 7 May 2009 at a joint summit between the EU member states and the six partner countries in the East: Ukraine, Moldova, Belarus, as well as Georgia, Azerbaijan and Armenia in the South Caucasus. The Belarusian government, too, was invited to the summit. Already one year earlier, in May 2008, the Polish and Swedish governments had lobbied for the inclusion of Belarus in the EaP and held consultations on the initiative with Belarusian government officials.[15] The Joint Declaration of the Prague Eastern Partnership Summit, signed *inter alia* by the Belarusian government, no longer adopted the strong language-based coercive conditionality. Instead, it highlighted that the EaP was a 'more ambitious partnership' between the EU and Belarus and 'founded on mutual interests and commitments as well as on shared ownership and responsibility' (Council of the European Union, 2009: p. 5).

In practice, the EaP foresees strengthened bilateral and multilateral cooperation between the EU and its Eastern partners. On the bilateral level, in November, the External Relations Council agreed to extend the suspension of the application of travel restrictions imposed on certain officials in Belarus until October 2010 and said it might decide to 'lift travel restrictions at any time'. Belarus is also included in the multilateral track of the EaP and its four platforms.[16] The State Border Committee of Belarus participated in a working session on Integrated Border Management in Odessa in mid-October 2009 (with Ukraine, Lithuania and Poland), which is one of the so-called 'flagship initiatives' within the framework of the platform, Democracy, Good Governance and Stability. The parties agreed to establish a permanent exchange of information between the border management units and to improve the infrastructure at their common borders within the EaP (BelTA, 2009, p. 1).

It is clear from the above that the tone and the proposed mode of engagement of the EU vis-à-vis Belarus changed quite significantly as compared to the coercive conditionality expressed in the 2006 Commission *Non-Paper*. The ad hoc engagement based on mutual interests and the EU's pursuit of its (internal) security concerns had been institutionalized in the EaP.

The EU's first responses to the fraudulent presidential elections on 19 December 2010 and the brutal crackdown of opposition protests appear to mark a continuation of its engagement policy, accompanied by some conditionality with respect to democracy and human rights. In January 2010, the Commissioner for Enlargement and Neighbourhood Policy, Štefan Füle, emphasized that 'regarding ENPI assistance to Belarus, I am clear that this should not be blocked' and 'I strongly believe that Belarus should continue to participate in the multilateral track of the Eastern Partnership' (Füle, 2011, p. 1). On 31 January, the Foreign Affairs Council decided to reinstate (and impose new) travel restrictions and an asset freeze against more than 150 Belarusian government officials (including Lukashenka), but reiterated that the 'EU remains committed to its policy of critical engagement, including through dialogue and the Eastern Partnership, and (...) that the EU has consistently offered to deepen its relationship with Belarus' (Council of the European Union, 2011, p. 2). In other words, the paradigm of prioritizing the pursuit of internal EU interests in relations with Belarus continues to inform EU policy, despite the events in the aftermath of the fraudulent presidential election in December 2010.

Libya and the Union for the Mediterranean

The Union for the Mediterranean (UfM) was launched in October 2008 and was largely seen as a response to addressing the limited success of the ENP in the region. The UfM was designed to include not only all the partners of the Barcelona Process (plus Libya), but also the wider Arab region. Yet, although Libya was invited to join the UfM, Gaddafi declined the offer officially because of his fears that the UfM would divide the African Union and the Arab League, of which Libya was a recognized and important member (Zoubir, 2009, p. 406). In essence, however, Gaddafi's move marked the continuation of a policy that sought to avoid being subjected to any of the EU rules or conditionalities (Joffé, 2001, p. 89).

The new Framework Agreement with Libya, for which negotiations were officially launched in November 2008, was not a full-fledged Association Agreement under the EMP. Rather, it prepared the ground for the formalization of already existing cooperation, especially in the areas of migration and energy, and paved the way towards a Free Trade Area. Libya's agreement to enter into negotiations on the new agreement opened up the opportunity for the country to receive financial assistance under the ENPI from 2011 onwards. The Commission prepared a Strategy Paper and a National Indicative Programme (NIP) for the implementation of the ENPI prior to concluding any contractual relations with Libya. That step is unprecedented in the EU's relations with its neighbours.

Moreover, the NIP explicitly excludes projects on democracy or human rights from the agenda in 2011–13:

> Mutual knowledge and trust need to be strengthened before (...) cooperation dealing with very sensitive issues, in particular in the governance area, can be envisaged. In the meantime, actions should be envisaged in sectors where there are clear and urgent priorities (Strategy Paper Libya, 2011–13, p. 15).

One priority sector is energy, in which 'improved cooperation with external partners and neighbours like Libya has gained new importance', especially in the context of the EU's interest to diversify the sources of its energy supply. The second priority sector is migration, which 'underpins the cooperation with Libya' (Strategy Paper Libya, 2011–13, p. 15). Later on in the NIP, the Commission highlights that

> [t]he EC's response strategy does not deliberately aim to deal directly with other important issues, such as for example those directly related to governance, human rights, education or environment. (Strategy Paper Libya, 2011–13: 18).

In June 2010, the Commission and Libya agreed on a Memorandum of Understanding providing for EU technical assistance and cooperation for the period, 2011–13. Approximately €60 million have been earmarked by the Commission to support projects in two priority areas (improving the quality of human capital and economic and social development). A third priority concerns 'addressing jointly the challenges of managing migration'. According to the indicative budget, this priority may indeed take precedence over the other two priorities as

> it is understood that if and when an agreement is reached between Libya and the EC on the scope of a possible project in this domain, resources should be mobilised under this NIP through a reallocation of the budget among the priorities (...)' (Strategy Paper Libya, 2011–13, p. 21).

The ad hoc cooperation in the field of migration was formalized by the signing of the Migration Cooperation Agenda by Commissioners Malmström (Home Affairs) and Füle (External Relations and Neighbourhood Policy) with the Libyan government in early October 2010. The agenda included concrete steps on a border surveillance system, mobility-related issues, smuggling and trafficking in human beings (Commission, 2010, p. 1). The cooperation was formalized despite a serious incident in September 2010, when a Libyan patrol boat (with Libyan personnel and Italian Guardia di Finanza officers on board) accidentally opened fire on an Italian fishing trawler, which they mistook for a boat with irregular migrants. According to Human Rights Watch, the 'bullet-riddled boat' showed a 'reckless use of potentially lethal force' (Human Rights Watch, 2010, p. 1).

By 2010, the negotiations for the Framework Agreement had entered the seventh round, largely due to Gaddafi's demands to receive a very large financial 'reimbursement' to avoid what he called a 'black Europe' (EUbusiness.com, 2010, p. 1). The Commission eventually agreed to contribute €20 million in extra financial assistance, despite the fact that Libya had ordered the officials of the United Nations High Commissioner for Refugees (UNHCR) to leave the country earlier in June 2010. It seemed that the Commission had almost completely abandoned any form of conditionality at that point in time. As Michele Cercone, spokesman for Commissioner Malmström, conceded in response to the closure of the UNHCR office in Tripoli, even if Libya was 'not the easiest with which to hold such talks', the EU would have 'no choice' (quoted in Kopp, 2010, p. 13).

The EU's policy of engagement with the Libyan regime ended abruptly following the increasingly brutal response of Gaddafi to the uprising against his regime throughout February and March 2011 and the UN Resolution authorizing military action to protect the Libyan civilian population. EU leaders held a special summit on Libya and North Africa on 11 March 2011 in order to reach a joint position on a political response to the unfolding crisis. However, the summit revealed severe divisions among the member states and its conclusions were effectively sidelined by the (unilateral) decision of French President Nicolas Sarkozy to recognize the Libyan opposition one day prior to the summit. The EU eventually agreed to extend the sanctions on the Gaddafi regime and to offer humanitarian assistance. The member states clearly prioritized democracy and human rights in the Declaration adopted by the Extraordinary European Council on 22 March 2011. They agreed to 'firmly condemn the violent repression the Libyan regime applies against its citizens and the gross and systematic violation of human rights', that 'the safety of the people must be ensured by all necessary means' and that 'Colonel Khadafi must relinquish power immediately' as 'his regime has lost all legitimacy and is no longer an interlocutor for the EU' (European Council, 2011, pp. 2–3). It seems evident that the EU has begun to rethink its engagement policy with the autocratic regimes in the Middle East and North Africa following the revolutions across the region throughout the Spring of 2011. Nevertheless, at the time of writing,[17] it is too early to predict the future course of EU policy in the region.

Conclusion

In this article, I have analysed the EU's relations with two of the 'villains' in its neighbourhood, Belarus and Libya. I evaluated the relations of the EU with the two regimes in the light of two contending paradigms at the heart of EU foreign policy: democracy promotion and the pursuit of the EU's internal security interests. I then assessed the implementation of the two paradigms in the political practice of the EU's relations with both countries.

First and foremost, EU relations with both countries differed right after the end of the cold war. Whereas relations with Belarus resulted in the conclusion of a PCA, relations with Libya were non-existent due to the country's involvement in international terrorist activities and the development of weapons of mass destruction. In 1992, the EU responded with coercive conditionality vis-à-vis the Libyan regime (economic sanctions, arms embargo) to protect its internal security. By contrast, the EU subjected Belarus to sanctions in 1997, in order to coerce the regime into democratic reforms.

The European Neighbourhood Policy did not include either Belarus or Libya as full members. Whereas Belarus was fully excluded from participation in the ENP in official discourse because of its undemocratic credentials, Libya was initially invited to join the ENP because of its strategic importance as a partner in the areas of migration and energy. Libya, however, declined the offer to join the ENP (as it had declined the offer to participate in the EMP) to avoid any political or economic conditionality from the EU. In its official rhetoric, the Commission insisted on a very coercive conditionality subject to democratic reforms, which the Belarusian government would have to implement before an engagement with the country was possible under the ENP. In contrast, the EU immediately addressed the Libyan regime as a 'strategic partner' in its pursuit of internal security concerns, subject only to a very light conditionality. The EU also appealed to 'winning the hearts and minds' of the Belarusian population by pledging its support for grass-root democracy and human rights – rhetoric that was almost entirely absent from the EU's rhetoric vis-à-vis Libya.

In practice, neither the approach of coercive conditionality vis-à-vis Lukashenka, nor that of passive leverage over the population, had any significant impacts on the political landscape in Belarus. Only the EU's pursuit of its internal security concerns proved relatively successful. The Commission started to engage with Belarusian officials below the ministerial level in order to enable a convergence of views on issues of common interest, in particular in the areas of border management, environment and energy.

In practice, the EU applied almost no conditionality towards the Libyan regime (neither with respect to democracy, nor in the pursuit of EU interests) and even made considerable financial concessions to the Gaddafi regime, including the delivery of significant amounts of military hardware, which potentially brought the EU in breach of its own and international human rights laws. And whereas the financial assistance for Belarus remains formally linked to the 'frozen' PCA (which contains some political and economic conditionality), the EU's offer to include Libya in the ENPI in the absence of any legal framework for bilateral cooperation effectively prevented it from subjecting Gaddafi to any further conditionality.

In conclusion, the EU's approach towards Libya has predominantly been linked to the paradigm pertaining to the pursuit of its own internal security interests (first via coercive conditionality and later with very light conditionality). The EU's policy towards Belarus has followed the democracy promotion paradigm for many years (via coercive conditionality and passive leverage). When the democracy promotion policy vis-à-vis Belarus failed, the EU slowly reverted to the same paradigm that it had successfully used in its relations with Libya – cooperation based on mutual interests with little or no conditionality attached. And although the EU's policy of engagement has suffered significant setbacks following the violent crackdown of opposition protests after the 2010 presidential election in Belarus, its initial response towards the regime suggests a continuation of a policy based on its internal security interests. In contrast, the EU's very clear condemnation of the Gaddafi regime following its brutal response to the uprising of the Libyan population in early 2011, and its call for Gaddafi to step down from power, suggest a rethink among EU officials and EU member states and a possible reemphasis of 'values' and democratic principles in the EU policy towards North Africa and the Middle East.

This paper has raised two major issues that concern EU external relations as a whole as much as its engagement with the 'wider Europe'. The first issue relates to the overall credibility of the EU's international engagement. The EU has applied a much lighter conditionality (and, in the case of Libya, no conditionality at all) in its relations with autocratic regimes than with those that are 'most likely' cases – countries that are willing to further integrate with the EU. The EU's foreign policies have, therefore, indirectly rewarded those countries that are not willing to adopt its rules and norms, and especially its democratic standards.

The second issue is of a more normative nature. If the EU aims to project itself as a normative power in international relations, then the emphasis on democracy promotion in official rhetoric alone (and in very select cases like Belarus) surely does not suffice. Ousting Belarus as the 'last dictatorship' on the European continent in official rhetoric might have superficially convinced some that Europe is indeed a normative power. Yet, already, the comparison of the EU's policy towards authoritarian regimes elsewhere highlights the double standards and thus the volatility of the imagery of a 'normative power' Europe. This article has shown that, regardless of the official rhetoric, the political practice of the EU's relations with autocratic regimes has increasingly been based on the pursuit of internal security interests. That surely demands a revision of the vision of a 'normative power' Europe, which has provided a significant source of legitimacy to EU foreign policy.

A 'normative power' EU would have few questions to answer about the violent crackdown of the opposition in the aftermath of the presidential election in Belarus in 2010. Nor would it have to respond to questions about the brutality of the Gaddafi regime against its own population following the uprising in early 2011. But an EU that has institutionalized interest-based cooperation with both regimes is obliged to answer these questions.

'We were very wise, now we are a safe country (...) we are trading now with our ex-enemies, we just have friends, no enemies anymore, no embargo, no sanctions, no threat.[18]

Notes

[1] Catherine Ashton, Address to the European Parliament, 22 March 2011, quoted in Banks, 2011.
[2] List countries in the e.g. Lavenex 2004, 2008, Whitman and Wolf 2010 EMP.
[3] If the legitimacy of the EU's engagement has been questioned, it was linked to the asymmetric nature of the rule transfer (Bosse and Korosteleva, 2009).
[4] Some of the member states maintained relations with Libya during and after the end of the cold war, for example, with France (arms and energy), Germany (chemical sector) and Germany, Spain and Italy (oil exports).
[5] OJ 1992 L 101/53.
[6] On the use of the similar, but slightly different concept of 'conditionality-lite', see Sasse, 2007.
[7] Interview with Commission Official, Brussels, 6 March 2008.
[8] Ibid.
[9] Interview with Commission Official, Brussels, 6 March 2008.
[10] Ibid.
[11] Interview with Commission Official, Brussels, 6 March 2008.
[12] Ibid.
[13] See Lutterbeck (2009) for a detailed discussion.
[14] The two programmes aimed at assisting the Libyan law enforcement authorities to improve their overall capacity and at reforming their system for preventing irregular migration.
[15] Interview with the Permanent Representation of an EU member state to the EU,
[16] The platforms are (1) Democracy, good governance and stability, (2) Economic integration and convergence with EU policies, (3) Energy security and (4) Contacts between people.
[17] April 2011.
[18] Saif al Islam, son of Gaddafi, quoted in BBC News, 2010, p. 3.

References

Banks, M., 2011. Ashton denies EU has 'lagged behind' in its response to Libyan crisis [online]. *The Parliament magazine,* 22 March, Brussels, Available from: http://www.theparliament.com/policy-focus/justice/justice-article/newsarticle/ashton-denies-eu-has-lagged-behind-in-its-response-to-libyan-crisis (Accessed 3 April 2011).

BBC News, 2010. Shrewd Gaddafi plays host to Rice [online]. 5 September. Available from: http://news.bbc.co.uk/2/hi/africa/7599479.stm (Accessed 8 October 2010).

BelTA, 2009. Belarus' Border Committee to partake in EU Integrated Border Management program [online]. Belarusian Telegraph Agency, Minsk, 21 October. Available from: http://news.belta.by/en/news/politics/?id=437239 (Accessed 8 October 2010).

Bosse, G., 2008. Justifying the European Neighbourhood Policy based on 'shared values': Can rhetoric match reality? In: E. Tulmets, and L. Delcour, eds. *Pioneer Europe? EU foreign policy in the neighbourhood*. Baden-Baden: Nomos, 43–54.

Bosse, G., and Korosteleva, E., 2009. Changing Belarus? The limits of EU governance in Eastern Europe. *Cooperation and conflict*, 44 (2), 143–165.

Commission of the European Communities, 2003. Wider Europe neighbourhood: A new framework for relations with our Eastern and Southern neighbours. Communication, 11 March, COM (2003) 104 final.

Commission of the European Communities, 2004. European Neighbourhood Policy – Strategy Paper, Communication, 12 May, COM (2004) 373 final.

Commission of the European Communities, 2006a. What the European Union could bring to Belarus, Non-Paper, December.

Commission of the European Communities, 2006b. Strengthening the European Neighbourhood Policy, Communication, 4 December, COM (2006) 726 final.

Commission of the European Communities, 2008a. Strengthening the European Neighbourhood Policy, Belarus: Commission experts in Minsk for technical talks on energy, transport and environment. Press Release, Brussels, 28 January, IP/08/95.

Commission of the European Communities, 2008b. Eastern Partnership, Communication, Brussels, 3 December, COM (2008) 823 final.

Commission of the European Communities, 2009. Concept Note - Libya: Country Strategy Paper and National Indicative Programme 2011–2013, Brussels, 16 April.

Commission of the European Communities, 2010. European Commission and Libya agree a migration cooperation agenda during high level visit to boost EU-Libya relations, Brussels, 5 October: MEMO/10/472.

Commission of the European Communities – EuropeAid, 2008. Project database [online]. Available from: http://ec.europa.eu/europeaid/cgi/frame12.pl (Accessed 5 October 2010).

Commission of the European Communities, 2010. Concept Note Libya, Country Strategy Paper and National Indicative Programme 2011–13. Brussels.

Council of the European Union, 2002. Draft Council conclusions on intensified cooperation on the management of migration flows with third world countries, "A" Item Note, 14 November, Brussels, 13894/02

Council of the European Union, 2009. Council conclusions on Belarus, 2974th External Relations Council Meeting, Brussels, 17 November.

Council of the European Union, 2011. Council conclusions on Belarus, 3065th Foreign Affairs Council Meeting, Brussels, 31 January.

Country Strategy Paper/ National Indicative Programme (Belarus) 2005–06. Brussels, 2004.

Country Strategy Paper/ National Indicative Programme (Belarus) 2007–13 – European Neighbourhood and Partnership Instrument. Brussels, 2006.

Dura, G., 2008. The EU's limited response to Belarus' pseudo 'new foreign policy'. *CEPS foreign policy brief*, No. 151, February.

EUbusiness.com, 2010. EU brushes aside Kadhafi immigration price tag [online]. 1 September. Available from: http://www.eubusiness.com/news-eu/migration-libya.5yg/?searchterm=black%20europe%20libya (Accessed 4 April 2011).

EuropAid, 2004. Aeneas programme for financial and technical assistance to third countries in the area of migration and asylum: Overview of projects funded 2004–06. Brussels: European Commission.

European Council, 2011. Extraordinary European Council, 11 March, Brussels, EUCO 7/11.

FRONTEX, 2007. Report on the Frontex-led EU Illegal Immigration Technical Mission to Libya, 28 May–5 June, Warsaw: European Agency for the Management of Operational Cooperation at the External Borders of the Member States of the European Union.

Füle, Š., 2011. Address at the extraordinary meeting of the AFET on Belarus, 12 January, Brussels, SPEECH /11/12.

Gelb, L.H., and Rosenthal, J.A., 2003. The rise of ethics in foreign policy: Reaching a value consensus. *Foreign affairs*, 82 (3), 2–7.
General Affairs and External Relations Council, 2002. 18 November, Brussels, 14183/02.
General Affairs and External Relations Council, 2003. 14 April, Luxembourg, 8220/03.
General Affairs and External Relations Council, 2004a. 14 June, Luxembourg, 10189/04.
General Affairs and External Relations Council, 2004b. 11 October, Luxembourg, 12770/04.
Guild, E., and Niessen, J., eds., 1996. *The developing immigration and asylum policies of the European Union: Adopted conventions, resolutions, recommendations, decisions and conclusions*. The Hague: Kluwer Law International.
Hamood, S., 2006. African transit migration through Libya to Europe: The human cost, forced migration and refugee studies. Cairo: The American University.
Held, D., 1996. *Models of democracy*. 2nd ed. Cambridge: Polity Press.
Hoffmann, S., 1977. The hell of good intentions. *Foreign policy*, 29 (Winter 1977/78), 3–26.
Human Rights Watch, 2010. Libya: End live fire against suspected boat migrants [online]. 16 September. Available from: http://www.hrw.org/en/news/2010/09/16/libya-end-live-fire-against-suspected-boat-migrants (Accessed 4 April 2011).
Hyde Price, A., 2004. The EU, power and coercion: From 'civilian' to 'civilising' power. Paper presented at the CIDEL Workshop, Oslo, 22–23 October.
Joffé, G., 2001. Libya and Europe. *The journal of North African studies*, 6 (4), 75–92.
Joffé, G., and Paoletti, E., 2010. Libya's foreign policy: Drivers and objectives. *Mediterranean Paper Series 2010*. Washington, DC: The German Marshall Fund of the United States.
Jones, S., and Emerson, M., 2005. European Neighbourhood Policy in the Mashreq countries enhancing project for reform. *CEPS Working Document*, 292. Brussels: Centre for European Policy Studies.
Kopp, J., 2010. Fatal alliance: EU-Libya cooperation on the prevention of illegal immigration. Förderverein PRO ASYL, September, Frankfurt.
Kubicek, P., 2003. International norms, the European Union, and democratization: Tentative theory and evidence. In: P. Kubicek, ed. *The European Union and democratization*. London: Routledge, 1–29.
Kubicek, P., 2005. The European Union and democratization in Ukraine. *Communist and post-communist studies*, 38 (2), 269–292.
Lappin, R., 2010. What we talk about when we talk about democracy assistance: The problem of definition in post-conflict approaches to democratisation. *Central European journal of international and security studies*, 4 (1), 183–198.
Lavenex, S., 2001. Migration and the EU's new eastern border: Between realism and liberalism. *Journal of European public policy*, 8 (1), 24–42.
Lavenex, S., 2004. EU external governance in 'wider Europe'. *Journal of European public policy*, 11 (4), 680–700.
Lavenex, S., 2008. A governance perspective on the European Neighbourhood Policy: Integration beyond conditionality? *Journal of European public policy*, 15 (6), 938–955.
Lutterbeck, D., 2009. Migrants, weapons and oil: Europe and Libya after the sanctions. *The journal of North African studies*, 14 (2), 169–184.
Monar, J., 2010. The EU's externalisation of internal security objectives: Perspectives after Lisbon and Stockholm. *The international spectator*, 54 (2), 23–39.
Napolitano Report, 2003. *Wider Europe – Neighbourhood: A new framework for relations with our Eastern and Southern neighbours:* 2003/2018. Draft report of the Committee on Foreign Affairs of the European Parliament [Rapporteur Pasqualina Napolitano].
Olsen, G.R., 2000. Promotion of democracy as a foreign policy instrument of 'Europe': Limits of international idealism. *Democratization*, 7 (2), 142–167.
Patten, C., and Solana, J., 2002. Letter to the Danish Presidency. Brussels, September.
Piontek, E., 2006. Belaru'. In: S. Blockmans and A. Lazowski, eds. *The European Union and its neighbours*. The Hague, TMC Asser Press, 531–547.
Portela, C., 2008. Sanctions against Belarus: Normative unintended. In: N. Tocci, ed. *The European Union as a normative policy actor*. CEPS Working Document, No. 281, 5–9.
Presidency Conclusions, 2005. Brussels European Council, 15–16 December, 15914/1/05.
Prodi, R., 2002. A wider Europe – A proximity policy as the key to stability. Speech, 6th ECSA-World Conference, Brussels, 5–6 December, SPEECH/02/619.

Regional Strategy Paper 2007–13 for the Euro-Mediterranean Partnership, European Neighbourhood and Partnership Instrument, Brussels, 2006.

Sasse, G., 2007. Conditionality-lite: The European Neighbourhood Policy and the EU's Eastern neighbours. In: C. Musu and N. Casarini, eds. *The road to convergence: European foreign policy in an evolving international system*. Basingstoke: Palgrave, 163–180.

Schimmelfennig, F., 2007. European regional organizations, political conditionality, and democratic transformation in Eastern Europe. *East European politics and societies*, 21 (1), 126–141.

Schumpeter, J.A., 1947. The creative response in economic history. *Journal of economic history*, 7 (2), 149–159.

Strategy Paper and National Indicative Programme Libya 2011–13, Brussels, 2010.

Vachudova, A.M., 2005. *Europe undivided: Democracy leverage and integration after communism*. Oxford University Press.

Wichmann, N., 2007. *The intersection between justice and home affairs and the European Neighbourhood Policy: Taking stock of the logic, objectives and practices*. CEPS Working Document, No. 275. Brussels: Centre for European Policy Studies.

Whitman, R., and Wolff, S., eds., 2010. *The European Neighbourhood Policy in perspective: Context, implementation and impact*. Basingstoke: Palgrave Macmillan.

Youngs, R., 2003. European approaches to democracy assistance: Learning the right lessons? *Third world quarterly*, 24 (1), 127–138.

Youngs, R., 2004. Normative dynamics and strategic interests in the EU's external identity. *Journal of common market studies*, 42 (2), 415–35.

Zoubir, Y., 2009. Libya and Europe: Economic realism at the rescue of the Qaddafi authoritarian regime. *Journal of contemporary European studies*, 17 (3), 401–415.

Reconceptualizing 'Cooperation' in EU-Russia Relations

CRISTIAN NITOIU

ABSTRACT *This paper argues that although the EU is yet to develop a common policy towards Russia, 'cooperation' with Russia stems from a pattern of enhanced bilateral relations with Moscow that most member states have sought to develop. These enhanced relations have been characterized by strong economic and energy security ties modelled on the approaches of big EU players such as Germany and France. Moreover, such approaches have impeded any solid practical promotion of the EU's norms and values both in Russia and its Eastern Neighbourhood – or any coherent CSDP actions, for that matter. This has happened although, rhetorically, states such as France and Germany present a highly normative discourse about the EU's role in its Eastern Neighbourhood. A second goal of this paper is to evaluate the way this pattern of 'cooperation' impacts on the EU's policy towards its Eastern Neighbourhood and on the geopolitics of the region. Consequently, the paper suggests that the practice of developing enhanced relations with Russia opens the way for Moscow to be viewed by the EU's Eastern neighbours as a power that can offer short-term solutions to pressing problems. At the same time, the shared framework for 'cooperation', which seems to inform the behaviour of most EU member states, de facto legitimizes Russia's bid to have the Eastern Neighbourhood under its sphere of influence.*

Introduction

Considerable scholarship has argued over the last few years that the relations between the European Union (EU) and Russia have been characterized by conflict (Averre, 2009; Ganzle, 2007; Haukkala, 2007, 2008a, 2008b, 2009, 2010; Hogenauer and Friedel, 2008; Leonard and Grant, 2007; Kux, 2005; Medvedev, 2008; Timmins, 2005; Rynning and Jensen, 2010; Rahr, 2007; Popescu and Wilson, 2009). However, this assessment is only half valid. Conflict between the EU and Russia has been most evident in relation to the modes of governance in the EU's Eastern Neighbourhood. Economical and political divergences have also appeared between Moscow and the various EU member states, but the development of enhanced bilateral relations has meant that their incidence and scope has decreased visibly.

This paper argues that although the EU is yet to develop a common policy towards Russia, 'cooperation' with Russia stems from a pattern of enhanced bilateral relations with Moscow that most EU member states have sought to develop. These enhanced relations have been characterized by strong economic and energy security ties modelled on the approaches of big EU players such as Germany and France. Moreover, these approaches have impeded any solid practical promotion of the EU's norms and values both in Russia and its Eastern Neighbourhood – or any coherent CSDP actions, for that matter. This has happened although, rhetorically, states such as France and Germany present a highly normative discourse about the EU's role in its Eastern Neighbourhood. A second goal of this paper is to evaluate the way this pattern of 'cooperation' impacts on the EU's policy towards its Eastern Neighbourhood and on the geopolitics of the region. Consequently, the paper suggests that the practice of developing enhanced relations with Russia opens the way for Moscow to be viewed by the Eastern neighbours of the EU as a power that can offer short-term solutions to pressing problems. At the same time, the shared framework for 'cooperation', which seems to inform the behaviour of most EU member states, de facto legitimizes Russia's bid to have the Eastern Neighbourhood under its sphere of influence.

The first section of the paper highlights the nature of the enhanced bilateral relations that most EU member states have sought to construct with Russia. Germany and France are considered to have developed the blueprint that other member states have applied in their enhanced relations. Nonetheless, Russia has not viewed its ties with Germany or France as being more important than those with other countries, applying an instrumental approach that has permitted it to advance its political and economical interests. The next section of the paper highlights the fact Russia has been more attractive in the EU's Eastern Neighbourhood due to the EU's lack of capacity to articulate a unified and coherent policy that could deliver practical solutions to the post-Soviet states. The paper concludes by exploring the consequences that the framework of enhanced bilateral relations has had on the EU's approach to its Eastern Neighbourhood. Many states from the region have criticized the EU for the dissonance between its rhetorical and practical commitments. This attitude is captured in the words of a Transniestrian commentator: '[T]he EU is doing nothing to make itself liked here, (…) even a micro-project, such as an EU-funded scheme to take care of the many stray dogs in Bender, could make a difference.'[1]

A Common Framework of Enhanced Bilateral Relations?

EU-Russia relations have been characterized by the dichotomy between conflict and cooperation (Averre, 2009; Ganzle, 2007; Lynch, 2005), translated into the fact that although, as a whole, the EU is inclined to accept and establish common rules and norms with Russia, at the national level, leaders are more prone to seek individualistic solutions – enhanced relations – involving Moscow. In the end, this seriously undermines the EU's normative endeavour. The main cause of the conflict between the EU and Russia lies in the incompatibilities that arise from clashes between the two identities. Incompatibility is the leitmotif found in the studies concerning EU-Russia relations: '[L]ike two galaxies, Russia and Europe are invariably bound to orbit on mutually diverging or converging paths' (Kononenko, 2008, p. 199). Russia's international actions point to an internal desire to regain its old great-power posture (Medvedev, 2008). For this reason, both scholars and politicians have been inclined to argue that Russia's foreign policy is still conducted in a realist paradigm driven by a zero-sum thinking, which opposes the normative approach of the EU (Hogenauer and Friedel, 2008; Haukkala, 2010; Light, 2008; Lukyanov, 2008; Nichol, 2009).

Cooperation here stems from the convergence of Moscow's economic interests with those of the important EU member states. The big EU member states and Russia see their relationship as a strategic partnership (Leonard and Popescu, 2008; Leonard and Grant, 2007; Timmins, 2005; Tardieu, 2009). Contrary to Lukyanov's (2008, p. 1118) views, politics doesn't dominate over economics in these enhanced relations. It is more that a high level of political credibility ensured by states such as Germany and France complement their strong economic ties with Russia. Moscow's preference for engaging in bilateral relations with individual EU member states is not an expression of a divide and rule approach towards them. Although that might have been the overruling logic in Yelstin's leadership (Rahr, 2005), Putin or Medvedev's close ties with other European leaders are more an expression of a rational, economically focused way of projecting Russia's interests. For example, Germany became, during Putin's leadership, Russia's most important trade partner and a close supporter of its energy policy. At the same time, Spain, France and Italy have developed similar strong ties with Russia in such areas as trade, energy and tourism.

At the EU level, the European Investment Bank and the European Bank for Reconstruction have been engaged in financing controversial energy and transport infrastructure in Russia.[2] This policy has been backed by big member states, such as France and Germany, which have been keen to block any effort by the Commission to withdraw support for the project due to Russia's stagnating human rights situation. Nonetheless, the official EU rhetoric has underlined that its contribution has helped to increase public accountability, participation and transparency in Russia. According to the High Representative for Foreign Affairs and Security Policy, Catherine Ashton, such issue-based approaches, where the EU abstains from publicly criticizing Russia, enhance Brussels' leverage to drive incremental progress on human rights.[3]

The big EU states have focused more on economic cooperation and Big Power bilateral relations towards Russia. France, Germany and Italy have shaped their policy towards Russia over the last years in order to construct a special relationship with Moscow. Moreover, such approaches have impeded any solid practical promotion of the EU's norms and values both in Russia and its Eastern Neighbourhood. This has happened although, rhetorically, states such as France and Germany still present a highly normative discourse about the EU's role in its Eastern Neighbourhood (Rahr, 2007, p. 141). In practice, they were successful in undermining the EU's possible stabilizing actions in countries such as Ukraine, Georgia and Moldova. Timmins (2005, p. 6) has suggested that because of the competition within the EU member states to establish a special relationship with Moscow, no coherent EU policy towards Russia has been achieved, division being the best term to characterize the EU's approach toward Russia on issues such as democracy promotion, rule of law and human rights. At the same time, a bilateral framework for developing enhanced relations with Russia has become the single similar rationale that the big EU players seem to use in their interactions with Moscow. According to Weaver (2010, p. 67), the EU as a whole has suffered in consistency and coherence as most member states have developed their enhanced relations with Russia overlooking the interests of their partners in the EU. Individual member states are thus more prone to seek their own agenda in their ties with Russia, leaving the institutions crippled and unable to put into practice any of their more ambitious policies in the Eastern Neighbourhood, which would conflict with Moscow's interests. The Commission and the European Parliament are only left with the power of responding rhetorically to Russia. Even though on some occasions, they have found support for their initiatives and policies from states such as Sweden, as in the case of inserting a membership perspective within the Eastern Partnership (EaP), Germany and France opposed it decisively.

Germany's relationship with Russia is arguably the most complex and special. Berlin is Russia's most important trading partner with an impressive total figure of almost US $70 billion in 2008. The strongest partnership between the two countries is in the energy sector, where Russia supplies 42 per cent of Germany's gas needs.[4] Former Chancellor Schroeder's involvement in the development of the North pushed the competition for a special relationship with Russia to a higher stake point. When completed, the pipeline will make Germany the chief distributor of Russian gas in Europe. Besides the German energy companies that have fostered special energy ties with Gazprom, other German businesses, too, have invested extensively in Russia over the last few years, the total amount going up to almost $5 billion in 2005 (Leonard and Popescu, 2008).

This special relationship was coupled with a strong political partnership that awarded international credibility to the regime in Moscow. Within the EU, Germany pushed a 'Russia-first policy' when dealing with the Eastern Neighbourhood. Simultaneously, France has also often persuaded other member states more critical of Moscow's intentions and international behaviour to not disrupt the EU's Russia-first policy. In practice, this translated into stopping all practical normative expressions of EU foreign policy towards the states in the region. Chancellor Merkel rightly feared that an ambitious normative agenda towards the former Soviet states would impede not just Germany's economical cooperation with Russia, but more broadly, Moscow's support of Western attitudes towards Afghanistan, Iran or the Middle East. Germany's special relationship with Russia holds the recipe for the ties that the other EU members have constructed with Russia. Be it energy, trade or tourism, almost all the big EU players (France, Germany, Italy and Spain) have sought a place in the sun alongside Russia. None of them have engaged in applying an instrumentalist approach by supporting the EU's possible normative actions, although all of them were overtly outspoken in favour of promoting the EU's norms and values in Russia and its Eastern neighbours.

It should be understood that Russia encourages special relations with all the EU countries because this is in its self-interest. Although Germany has the closest bilateral relations with Russia, it is no more special than Moscow's ties with the other EU member states. France follows suit as it has recently reinforced its enhanced relations with Moscow by selling it two warships and acquiring stakes in the North Stream gas project.[5] Moreover, the accession of the Central and Eastern

European (CEE) countries has toned down Germany's assumed leadership in framing the EU's normative policy towards Russia as Chancellor Merkel has shown reluctance in acting over the heads of the countries in the Eastern Neighbourhood.

Within the framework of enhanced bilateral relations, the Russian-Georgian war of 2008 represents a crucial moment (Rynning and Jensen, 2010, p. 142; Agh, 2010; Baun and Marek, 2010; Christou, 2010; Biscop, 2010; Cichocki, 2010; Haukkala, 2009, 2010; Najšlová, 2010; Sammut, 2010; Wolczuk, 2010; Weaver, 2010; Vasilyan, 2010). Firstly, it relinquished all doubts about Russia's desire to become a hegemon in the post-Soviet space. It showed that in times of crisis, it was willing to deal a swift and deadly blow with its military power in order to protect its interests. The presence of Russians in all the countries of the Eastern Neighbourhood has made their safety a matter of national interest for Moscow. Although the 2008 August war was a public display of Russian 'hard power' might, Moscow was also engaged in a more silent attack in the background. Since 2004, many non-Russian nationals from ENP countries have been awarded Russian passports, giving Moscow the legitimate right to protect them; it is estimated that at the time of the war, around 170,000 people in Georgia held Russian passports (Popescu and Wilson, 2009, p. 42). Nonetheless, Russia gave the West an important signal and managed to put its bid for leadership across to the EU (Sammut, 2010, p. 84). Conversely, France, Germany and Italy were instrumental in tempering the EU's official reaction to Russia's 2008 intervention in Georgia. Their views were backed by almost all the other member states, excluding the Baltics and the United Kingdom, which proposed suspending any form of cooperation with Russia and issuing hostile public statements.[6] Consequently, the EU's joint response to the 2008 war was more the concerted action of the big EU member states – excluding Britain – which, building on their enhanced relations with Moscow, pushed for a more Russia-friendly settlement.

EU-Russia Relations in Perspective: Cooperation through Bilateral Relations

Since Putin came to power in the early 2000s, Russia has tried to assert itself as a leader in the post-Soviet space and rebuild its sphere of influence (Popescu and Wilson, 2009; Pavliuk, 2005; Nichol, 2009; Najšlová, 2010). Moscow has successfully resisted the EU's attempts to incorporate it in the ENP. More than once, Russian leaders have pointed out that the EU's approach towards its neighbours is a scheme intended to promote by force a certain type of democracy in an attempt to globalize the region (Haukkala, 2010, p. 162). This type of Russian rhetoric has added legitimacy to its claims of leadership in this area (Cichocki, 2010, p. 12). Nonetheless, its discourse has also been translated into practice, as it has served as a point of attraction for the states in the region by delivering various incentives quietly and continuously. It has offered to its neighbours cheap gas and energy deals in exchange for control of energy infrastructure or other political or symbolical advantages, like placing individuals with Russian sympathies in high-level positions (Agh, 2010; Delcour, 2010; Haukkala, 2009; Sammut, 2010). Nonetheless, the Russian carrots have not come cheap; most times, the states have had to sign off their resources, making them highly dependent on Russian influence.[7]

Not at all surprisingly, this approach stems from the fact that Russia tends to view the Eastern Neighbourhood in competitive terms. Such a view is also prevalent in the post-Soviet space: Transnistrian leader Igor Smirnov argued that 'people understand that the EU and Russia are competing here, so if you choose Russia as a strategic partner, you perceive the EU as a threat'.[8] According to Christou (2010, p. 424), this behaviour can be explained by Moscow's attachment to a narrow Westphalian interpretation of sovereignty, in which there is no place for discourses about governance and multilateralism. In the case of multilateralism, Russians have argued that cooperation can be effective only if states and international organizations respect a positive interpretation of international law, in which the interests of the nation state – the powerful ones – come first. Although in dealing with Russia, most countries in the Eastern Neighbourhood acknowledge its fairly one-sided approach, recent years – after the global economic crisis – have shown that they are willing to overcome their doubts in order to benefit from Moscow's short-term solutions. On a smaller scale, their attitude resembles that of many African countries towards the Chinese power horse. This might prove to be very dangerous for such countries in the end, as Russia has showed its readiness to reconfigure political stability at its own will in the region (Popescu and Wilson, 2009, p. 17; Rahr, 2007; Delcour, 2010; Kononenko, 2008; Kux, 2005; Leonard and Grant, 2007; Leonard and Popescu, 2008). Moscow's campaign against Georgia is a prime example of how it disregarded the interests of a whole array of states in the Eastern Neighbourhood; for example, it disrupted the energy security of states such as Azerbaijan and Armenia, which were highly dependent on the infrastructure in Georgia, and it used the Black Sea fleet without consent on Ukraine's territory.

Russia's attraction in the Eastern Neighbourhood has also derived from the existence of a historical and cultural identity based on the pervasiveness of the Russian language, the large number of Russian minorities living in the area and the coagulating character of the Orthodox Church. However, these same identity components have historically separated it from the West. The clash with Western values has led Russian leaders to argue that the EU is only a self-asserting, normative, postmodern power whose intentions are more than questionable (Haukkala, 2009, 2010, p. 167; Averre, 2009; Aalto, 2011; Leonard and Popescu, 2008; Tardieu, 2009; Wolczuk, 2010; Cichocki, 2010; Christou, 2010). Various opinion polls in Russian speaking communities all around the ENP countries have shown that only a small minority desires integration with the West, thus reinforcing these claims (Popescu and Wilson, 2009). Conversely, the intrusion of Western modes of governance has often been securitized in Russian discourse as a threat against the common identity of the post-Soviet space.

On the other hand, the EU has continuously tried to persuade Russia that their relations are not competitive in nature and must not be viewed thus. Statements from the European Commission and other EU institutions have underscored that not only do Europe and Russia share a common set of values and historical experiences, but also many economical and security concerns that make their cooperation within the present context of the international scene imperative (Krok-Paszkowska and Zielonka, 2005, p. 163; Averre, 2009; Baun and Marek, 2010; Biscop, 2010; Cichocki, 2010; Clement-Noguier, 2005; Sammut, 2010). This study takes on board the official EU view that it shares a common past with Russia and posits that the relations between them and their identities have to be seen as historically constructed by their interactions. These identities have a dynamic character and have been shaped by the various instances of divergence or cooperation that have characterized the interactions between the EU and Russia. An important example of the track record of cooperation between the two actors is the EU's support for Russia's bid for WTO membership in exchange for Moscow ratifying the Kyoto Treaty. The EU's concern for cooperation with Russia stems from its acknowledgement that Moscow cannot in any way be bypassed when trying to promote democracy in the post-Soviet space (Rynning and Jensen, 2010, p. 146). Thus, in dealing with its Eastern Neighbourhood, the EU has developed a Russia-first policy (Biscop, 2010, p. 84). This has meant that the EU has had to keep a low profile where Russia had overt interests in order to maintain good relations. Simultaneously, the EU's cooperation with Moscow has been tailored so as to not upset the latter's domestic order.

In literature, the EU has been labelled as a postmodern actor, which, in opposition to Russia, does not rely on hard politics in its international relations (Emerson, 2001, 2006; Haukkala, 2007; Ganzle, 2007; Light, 2008; Christou, 2010; Weaver, 2010; Tonra, 2010; Manners, 2010). Such behaviour has created a degree of conflict in relation to the types of governance promoted in the Eastern Neighbourhood. But Russia also prefers a weak 'hard power' EU that does not have the capabilities to intervene in security issues: 'Russia is stronger and faster... In every conflict situation, it comes out better' (Popescu and Wilson, 2009, p. 39). Each time the EU has seemed to be flexing its muscles and talked of the CSDP missions in the Eastern Neighbourhood, Russia has openly expressed its criticism (Rahr, 2005, p. 223; Biscop, 2010; Emerson, 2001; Delcour, 2010; Haukkala, 2010). Consequently, Russia accepts the EU's *sui generis* identity uneasily as long as it gives it a free hand to exert its hard power.

In practice, Russia has not hesitated in using its hard power in the Eastern Neighbourhood. The presence of its troops in many of these countries has put a lot of strain on their decision makers. For example, Ukraine harbours around 15,000 troops, Armenia, 5,000, and Azerbaijan and Moldova, around 1,000 (Popescu and Wilson, 2009). On its part, the EU has managed to set up monitoring and border missions that have been highly constrained by the limitation of the CSDP budget – €300 million as compared to the more than €10 billion spent by Russia on defence (Vasilyan, 2010, p. 89). Moscow has also made use of the differentiated energy prices and gas and oil embargoes to project its hard power, while the EU has only managed to impose travel bans in cases where the ENP countries were steering in the wrong direction (Cichocki, 2010; Biscop, 2010; Hogenauer and Friedel, 2008).

Although the EU seems to be a champion of soft power, Russia's lure should not be underestimated. In a comparative assessment of the soft approach of Russia and the EU, Popescu and Wilson (2009, p. 3) show that both actors display similar degrees of attractiveness in relations with the Eastern Neighbourhood countries. Russia's investments in such strategic areas as energy infrastructure seem to weigh more than the EU's efforts to promote trade liberalization and democracy. Nonetheless, while Russian appeals to a common identity can spur considerable support, it is the promise of EU membership that drives the policy approaches of the states in the area, although the EaP has considerably dimmed the possibility of future accession. The carrot of membership still remains important as countries from the Eastern Neighbourhood tend to accept the EU's conditionalities even though

Russia offers the possibility of economic benefits without asking for any political reforms and provides bureaucracy free agreements, too.

The perspective of trans-Atlanticism has always loomed over EU-Russia relations. Moscow has tried to play Europe and the US against each other in order to assert itself as a hegemon in the post-Soviet space (Rahr, 2005, 2007, p. 178; Pavliuk, 2005; Nichol, 2009; Najšlová, 2010; Trenin, 2005; Kux, 2005; Kononenko, 2008). Nonetheless, in the EU-US-Russia security triangle, Moscow has tried to woo Europeans in various arrangements that would marginalize the Americans (Rynning and Jensen, 2010, p. 142). This approach has its roots in the Iraq war, when France and Germany were backed by Russia in their opposition to the intervention of the US-led coalition. With its war in Georgia, Russia showed that it was keener than the US to recognize the EU as a major international actor. Russia felt that all the major leaders in the EU (the President of the European Commission, the High Representative on Security and Foreign Policy, and the then President of the Council of the EU) had to be present in order to legitimize the important decision that was to come for the EU.[9] Russian attitudes towards the EU as a global actor have been contrasted with US perceptions of the EU. Although the foreign policy of the EU may be tagged as being normative, it does not fit into the more or less Machiavellian or missionary power framework developed by the US in its foreign policy. From this standpoint, Brussels brings an overt challenge to the American way of dealing in world politics. Over the last two decades, since the fall of the Communist regimes in Europe, US leaderships have perceived this radical engagement of the EU with world politics as being based on soft power, a type of power that has no real influence if it is not backed by strong military capabilities. Behind the American discourse lingers the threat that the new normative path that the EU has adopted might become more rigidly prevalent in the near future. On the other hand, the Russian leaders see the EU's stance in world politics as being both compliant and conflictual with their values and interests. Actually, all the relations between Moscow and Brussels have been influenced by the dichotomy of conflict and collaboration. Rhetorically, the Russian portrayal of world politics attributes an important role to the EU.

EU in the Eastern Neighbourhood

The normative narrative of the EU in the international system can only be sustained if it establishes various cooperative initiatives with its neighbours in order to integrate them in a space dominated by its democratic norms and values.[10] External sources of legitimacy are paramount for the EU's normative leadership both in its neighbourhood and globally (Manners, 2010, p. 38). The ENP has been created along the lines of this normative self-image of the EU. But this narrative has brought closer to the EU the problems and conflicts associated with the weak states in neighbourhood. After acknowledging the duty of spreading its norms in the post-Soviet space, the EU became highly sensitive to the developments in the region as Benita Ferrero-Waldner stressed in her speech on the EaP in 2009, 'When Russia cuts gas supplies to Ukraine... EU households suffered. The EU found its quality of life directly affected ... by the political and commercial landscape in its eastern neighbourhood', going on to project that, in this context, 'it is important... we have partners whose governance provides respect for the rule of law' (cited in Christou, 2010, p. 418). However, many have doubted whether the EU has either the practical capabilities or the normative ability to live up to its commitment in the Eastern Neighbourhood (Biscop, 2010, p. 79; Averre, 2009; Agh, 2010; Cichocki, 2010; Dangerfield, 2009; Clement-Noguier, 2005; Emerson, 2001, 2006; Ganzle, 2007; Hopf, 2008; Light, 2008; Lynch, 2005; Rynning and Jensen, 2010; Weaver, 2010; Vasilyan, 2010; Wolczuk, 2010). In hard power terms, it lacks the capacity and willingness to get involved in frozen conflicts. Secondly, the goals behind the EU's normative engagement in the Eastern Neighbourhood seem to be one-sided (Tonra, 2010, p. 66), depicting the ENP as an instrument that helps the EU to achieve control over its borders. Using this logic, stability, which could ensure the sustainability of the EU's economic interests, is valued against effective political and social reform. The promotion of human rights gets torn apart between the democratic ideal and a tendency to promote regional stability.

Both theoretically and practically, the ENP, at least in its Eastern concerns, isn't as complete or stable as officials in the Commission portray it. Christou (2010, p. 148) has posited that the ENP is the result of a double narrative that is detrimental to the development of a sustainable security environment in the region and of the economies of the EU's Eastern neighbours and their citizens' welfare. On the one hand, the EU portrays itself as a 'force for good' that promotes its norms for the well-being of other peoples. However, it was underlined above that there are various contradictions that plague the EU's normative approach and have the potential of determining its failure. On the other hand, another hidden and more malign narrative can be identified in the EU's policy in the Eastern Neighbourhood. Asymmetrical bilateral relations are the primary mode of interaction preferred by the EU in the ENP (Haukkala, 2010, p. 162). Europe's norms – be they democratic or liberal – gain pre-eminence over the culture and the values of the *other*. Tolerance for diversity in approaches to governance and security is considered to be secondary to the goal of asserting the EU as a global normative power whose norms have become universal.[11] The asymmetric policies of the EU are legitimized through the use of Europe as a discursive entity constructed in contradiction to the un-universal values of its non-European neighbours.

Over the last few years, there have been many disagreements between the member states over the role that the EU should play in its Eastern Neighbourhood and in the resolution of regional conflicts. Very few contributions to this debate have tried to portray a role for the EU that would oppose Russia's interest (Weaver, 2010, p. 73). After their accession, the CEE countries were very vociferous in articulating and promoting their national interests in opposition to Moscow. At the time, in 2005, the Commission encouraged the new member states to engage in the Eastern Neighbourhood in ways that would not unsettle the region (Pavliuk, 2005, p. 203). Since their accession, the CEE member states have drawn on the Commission's advice on their approach towards the big EU players, with important consequences. If, initially, the acceded CEE countries shared highly antagonistic views on Russia and an unwillingness to moderate their national preferences towards the East, adopting a framework of enhanced relations with Moscow not only toned down the CEE countries' preference for strong practical measures in the region, but also transformed their highly antagonistic discourse into one of mutual normative cooperation along the lines that the Commission had proposed in 2005. French President Sarkozy has praised Warsaw and other Central and Eastern European new member states for moderating their critical attitude towards Russia and proposing more feasible initiatives. Karol Karski, Law and Justice MP, has observed that it looks like although 'France, Germany and Russia make deals among themselves, Poland (and others) are 'now being allowed in to the group'[12].

Although, according to Wolczuk (2010, p. 48), the EU has sought to counterbalance Russia's influence in the post-Soviet area, it has done this less than half-heartedly. Stability in the region has been achieved only when Moscow's interests weren't harmed. Most EU member states have acknowledged this and drafted the EaP as a step towards cooperation with Moscow. Simultaneously, the EaP has been influenced by the lack of coherence in the EU's approach towards Russia created by the series of enhanced bilateral relations that most member states have constructed with it (Manners, 2010; Tonra, 2010; Weaver, 2010; Timmins, 2005; Rynning and Jensen, 2010). Russia complained overtly that the earlier EU initiatives had unsettled the region to its east because the countries there still expected that they would have an eventual chance at membership once they had adopted the norms from the Partnership and Cooperation Agreements (PCAs), European Neighbourhood Project (ENP) or Black Sea Synergy. What the EaP did, in the way framed by Poland and Sweden and negotiated by France and Germany, was that it replaced any direct or indirect promise of membership with the concept of enhanced cooperation. While the ENP countries were more than dissatisfied with this development, Russia agreed with the EU's new foreign policy instrument (Schimmelfennig and Scholtz, 2008). Even more, the EaP has given Moscow a free hand to pursue its activism in the region by appealing to the common identity Orthodox or Russian-speaking people and its willingness to provide strong short-term financial incentives. Russia's de facto acceptance of the EaP is echoed by its choice to not exclude itself publicly from the programme, as in the case of the other ENP initiatives. Nonetheless, the EU's mode of governance comes into direct clash with Moscow's own normative discourse about the Eastern Neighbourhood, which might affect its security interests in the long run. Consequently, for any future regional EU initiatives in the Eastern Neighbourhood to be successful, a different mode of governance that accommodates Russia's approaches must be constructed.

Since the launch of the ENP, the neighbourhood states have tried to persuade the EU to make a clear differentiation between their needs in drawing its policies (Cichocki, 2010, p. 11). Within the ENP, they have frequently asked for tailor-made approaches that suit each country's particularities. Picking from the EU's menu of regulations has been a privilege that the neighbourhood countries could better afford than the accession countries of the 1990s and early 2000s. The distant prospect of membership and the influence of Russia have made them more open to a gamble in adopting the EU's *acquis*. The ENP has been viewed in the post-Soviet space as a one-way street, where Europe imposes its normative agenda without incorporating any of the *other's* values (Haukkala, 2010, p. 164). Tonra (2010, p. 67) has pointed out that this has led to a dichotomous construction of the EU's image in the Eastern Neighbourhood. On the one hand, the EU has represented a common space that offered the possibility of joining if specific norms and values were present. Leaders in neighbourhood states have tried to model their rhetoric on this vision of the EU, arguing along the same lines as the post-communist Central and East European states about their duty to return to Europe. However, such discourses were manufactured; there was no pervasive myth of a common European destiny existing in these countries. Public support for integration is also low, with the neighbourhood countries averaging around 30 per cent; Moldova is an outlier here, with more than 70 per cent, due to its close links with Romania (Popescu and Wilson, 2009, p. 16). On the other hand, the EU is seen as an exclusive club that can create prosperity and, consequently, possesses considerable power of attraction for third parties, resembling a 'citadel' or 'metropolis' (Beland, 2009; Clement-Noguier, 2005; Dangerfield, 2009). This image is confirmed in reality by trade patterns where the European Union covers between 40–50 per cent of all neighbourhood states' trade.[13]

In 2008, the EaP promised to address all the concerns voiced by the neighbourhood countries. By proposing a tailor-made model, which enhanced cooperation, the EaP has allowed each state to develop links with the EU at its own pace. Paying attention to the specific characteristics of each country has made regionalization more effective under the EaP. However, what the EaP lacked, in the eyes of the post-Soviet states, was a clear commitment towards the resolution of regional conflicts (Weaver, 2010, p. 72). Governments here are left dealing with conflicts on their own, while the EU reassures them that internalizing its norms and values is the first step towards creating stability – promotion of good governance is preferred to intervening directly in frozen conflicts (Vasilyan, 2010, p. 48).

To conclude, it has become common place in scholarship to argue that the ENP has registered very few tangible successes over the years (Averre, 2009, p. 47; Cichocki, 2010; Delcour, 2010; Haukkala, 2008a, 2009, 2010; Nichol, 2009; Najšlová, 2010; Medvedev, 2008; Wolczuk, 2010; Weaver, 2010; Tonra, 2010; Vasilyan, 2010). Besides the contradictions within the EU's foreign policy narratives towards its Eastern Neighbourhood and the way they have been put into practice – as was outlined above – the complex institutional web in which the ENP is developed has contributed to its lack of coherence. The European Commission, and especially the Directorates General, External Relations (DG Relex) and Enlargement, the EU High Representative, the member states within the Council and foreign policy officials within the Council Secretariat have been the most important actors involved in designing and projecting foreign policy narratives and initiatives in the post-Soviet space. Consequently, the inter-institutional dynamic between the Council and the Commission is crucial for understanding the way the ENP/EaP was drafted. Due to its underfunding, the Commission could not implement its ambitious plans, which were watered down within the Council, where member states' representatives acted upon their enhanced bilateral relations with Russia (Cichocki, 2010, p. 421; Delcour, 2010; Leonard and Grant, 2007; Krok-Paszkowska and Zielonka, 2005; Kononenko, 2008; Hopf, 2008). The influence of the European Parliament was moderate to low in the drawing of the EU's policy towards Moscow, although it set up countless committees to deal with it and other related security issues.

Conclusion

Cooperation between the EU and Russia has been a priority for both actors over the last decade. Nonetheless, their views on how the cooperation should be carried out have been based on slightly different assumptions. Russian discourse has often stressed the need for relations between EU and Moscow to be developed bearing in mind a 'viable balance between cooperation and competition'.[14] It has recognized that Europe is a space that can offer Russia a myriad political and economical opportunities, making cooperation with the big member states a priority. The EU's view on cooperation has been shaped by the interaction between the common goal of engaging Russia in multilateralism and the more individualistic approach of most member states, which have sought to develop enhanced bilateral relations with Moscow. The EU's Russia-first policy seems also to be strengthened by the educational background of two of its Commissioners. Štefan Füle, the Czech Commissioner for Enlargement and European Neighbourhood Policy, and Maroš Šefcovic, the Slovak Commissioner for inter-institutional relations and administration, two crucial chains in the development of EU policy, are both graduates of the illustrious Moscow State Institute of International Relations.[15] According to the former, relations with Moscow can be developed only if Russia can be persuaded to adopt a multilateral approach to international politics, binding itself to the international legal order, 'because transparency and predictability are the key to good economic and political relations'.[16] Simultaneously, the Commission has tried to link Russian progress on human rights or multilateralism with the visa regime, highlighting that poor technical standards concerning visa and border security could be overlooked if Moscow were to improve its human rights track record and engage in multilateral agreements.

On the other hand, the paper has underscored that most member states have tried to construct enhanced bilateral relations with Moscow based on close economic and energy ties. Over the years, Germany, France and Italy have competed to forge more developed relations with Russia. The logic of this competition was the single practical approach towards Moscow that the EU members shared. Of course, on an ideational level, they were outspoken in expressing their commitment to a normative Europe that would include Russia. Yet, their discourses were not backed by practical EU engagements in Russia or the Eastern Neighbourhood. Moreover, on several occasions, they were instrumental in undermining the Commission's practical initiatives in the region. The dissonance between the EU's approach to Russia and the member states' tendency to forge enhanced bilateral relations with Moscow kept the ENP from being a success story. Consequently, this leads to the conclusion that in terms of the foreign policy narrative constructed by the EU towards its Eastern Neighbourhood, the EU's normative goal of promoting various norms imposes an asymmetric set of relations with its neighbours. Correlated with the practice of developing special relations with Russia, the normative narrative opens the way for Moscow to be viewed by the EU's Eastern neighbours as a power that can offer short-term solutions to pressing problems. At the same time, this pattern of practices, which seems to inform the behaviour of most EU member states, de facto legitimizes Russia's bid to bring the Eastern Neighbourhood under its sphere of influence.

Notes

[1] Transniestrian people stake their future on Russia, not EU. *EUObserver.com* [online], 24 January 2011. Available from: http://euobserver.com/9/31684 [Accessed 15 February 2011].

[2] Money talks in EU-Russia relations. *EUObserver.com* [online], 4 March 2011. Available from: http://euobserver.com/24/31920 [Accessed 15 March 2011].
[3] EU and Russia to sign trade memo amid US mockery. *EUObserver.com* [online], 7 December 2010. Available from: http://euobserver.com/9/31442 [Accessed 10 December 2010].
[4] Available from: http://tonto.eia.doe.gov/country/country_energy_data.cfm?fips=GM [Accessed 15 September 2010].
[5] Cablegate: France bullied Poland over Georgia war. *EUObserver.com* [online], 8 March 2011. Available from: http://euobserver.com/891/31941 [Accessed 15 March 2011].
[6] US cables shed light on EU 'Friends of Russia' in Georgia war. *EUObserver.com* [online], 1 December 2010. Available from: http://euobserver.com/9/31400 [Accessed 10 February 2011].
[7] EU neighbors are 'mafia states', US cables indicate. *EUObserver.com* [online], 2 December 2010. Available from: http://euobserver.com/9/31406 [Accessed 5 March 2011].
[8] Transniestrian people stake their future on Russia, not EU. *EUObserver.com* [online], 24 January 2011. Available from: http://euobserver.com/9/31684 [Accessed 15 February 2011].
[9] Europe behind Georgia but on its own terms. *The Messenger Online* [online], 3 September 2008. Available from: http://www.messenger.com.ge/issues/1682_september_3_2008/1682_summit.html [Accessed 10 December 2009].
[10] On the other hand, some scholars have argued that the Lisbon Treaty might drive the EU's policy in the Eastern Neighbourhood towards a more realist approach due to the creation of the External Action Service, which might try to impose its own organizational logic (Cichocki, 2010, p. 13). While this argument has a degree of legitimacy, it is hard to believe that the EU's newly formed diplomatic system would stray too much from the Commission's normative approach.
[11] Recently, norms have been conceptualized as 'universable' only when the relevant community for moral action is (constructed as) humanity at large' (De Zutter, 2010, p. 1117). Here, norms are not universal in their own selves; it is the inherent recognition by other actors in the international system that provides them that quality.
[12] Russia-EU relations: What's new? *European Voice* [online], 24 February 2011. Available from: http://www.europeanvoice.com/article/2011/february/russia-eu-relations-what-s-new-/70375 [Accessed 15 March 2011].
[13] Data from the World Trade Organization. Available from: http://www.wto.org/ [Accessed].
[14] Russia-EU relations: What's new? *European Voice* [online], 24 February 2011. Available from: http://www.europeanvoice.com/article/2011/february/russia-eu-relations-what-s-new-/70375 [Accessed 20 March 2011].
[15] From Russia with love. *European Voice* [online], 23 September 2010. Available from: http://www.europeanvoice.com/article/imported/from-russia-with-love-/68958.aspx [Accessed 10 February 2011].
[16] EU and Russia to sign trade memo amid US mockery. *EUObserver.com* [online], 7 December 2010. Available from: http://euobserver.com/9/31442 [Accessed 10 December 2010].

References

Aalto, P., 2011. *European Union and the making of a wider Northern Europe*. London: Routledge.
Agh, A., 2010. Regionalisation as a driving force of EU widening: Recovering from the EU 'carrot crisis' in the 'East'. *Europe-Asia studies*, 62 (8), 1239–1266.
Averre, D., 2009. Competing rationalities: Russia, the EU and the 'shared neighbourhood'. *Europe-Asia studies*, 61 (10),1689–1713.
Baun, M., and Marek, D., 2010. Czech foreign policy and EU integration: European and domestic sources. *Perspectives on European politics and society*, 11 (1), 2–21.
Beland, D., 2009. Ideas, institutions, and policy change. *Journal of European public policy*, 16 (5), 701–718.
Biscop, S., 2010. The ENP, security and democracy in the context of the European Security Strategy. In: R. G. Whitman and S. Wolff, eds. *The European Neighbourhood Policy in perspective: Context, implementation and impact*. London: Palgrave Macmillan, pp. 73–88.
Christou, G., 2010. European Union security logics to the east: The European Neighbourhood Policy and the Eastern Partnership. *European security*, 19 (3), 413–430.
Cichocki, M., 2010. European Neighbourhood Policy or neighbourhood policies? In: K. Henderson and C. Weaver, eds. *The Black Sea region and EU policy: The challenge of divergent agendas*. Surrey: Ashgate, 9–28.

Clement-Noguier, S., 2005. Russia, the European Union, and NATO after September 11: Challenges and limits of a new entanglement. In: A. J. Motyl and B. A. Ruble, eds. *Russia's engagement with the West: Transformation and integration in the twenty-first century*. London: M.E. Sharp, pp. 238–259.

Dangerfield, M., 2009. The contribution of the Visegrad Group to the European Union's 'Eastern' policy: Rhetoric or reality? *Europe-Asia studies*, 61 (10), 1735–1755.

De Zutter, E., 2010. Normative power spotting: An ontological and methodological appraisal. *Journal of European public policy*, 17 (8), 1106–1127.

Delcour, L., 2010. The European Union, a security provider in the eastern neighbourhood? *European security*, 19 (4), 535–549.

Emerson, M., 2001. *The Elephant and the Bear: The European Union, Russia and their near abroad*. Brussels: CEPS.

Emerson, M., 2006. Introduction. In: M. Emerson, ed. *The Elephant and the Bear try again: Options for a new agreement between the EU and Russia*. Brussels: CEPS, pp. 1–18.

Ganzle, S., 2007. The EU's policy toward Russia: Extending governance beyond borders? In: J. DeBardeleben, ed. *The boundaries of EU enlargement: Finding a place for neighbours*. New York: Palgrave Macmillan, 53–69.

Haukkala, H., 2007. The European Neighborhood Policy. In: S. Biscop and J. Lembke, eds. *EU enlargement and the Transatlantic Alliance: A security relationship in flux*. London: Lynne Rienner Publishers, 159–172.

Haukkala, H., 2008a. A norm-maker or a norm-taker? The changing normative parameters of Russia's place in Europe. In: T. Hopf, ed. *Russia's European choice*. New York: Palgrave Macmillan, 35–36.

Haukkala, H., 2008b. The European Union as a regional normative hegemon: The case of European Neighbourhood Policy. *Europe-Asia studies*, 60 (9), 1601–1622.

Haukkala, H., 2009. Lost in translation? Why the EU has failed to influence Russia's development. *Europe-Asia studies*, 61 (10), 1757–1775.

Haukkala, H., 2010. Explaining Russian reactions to the European Neighbourhood Policy. In: R. G. Whitman and S. Wolff, eds. *The European Neighbourhood Policy in perspective: Context, implementation and impact*. London: Palgrave Macmillan, 161–179.

Hogenauer, A.-L., and Friedel, M., 2008. The EU and Russia: Strategic or short-sighted partnership. In: D. Mahncke and S. Gstöhl, eds. *Europe's near abroad: Promises and Prospects of the EU's Neighbourhood Policy*. Brussels: College of Europe, 257–277.

Hopf, T., ed., 2008. *Russia's European choice*. New York: Palgrave Macmillan.

Kononenko, V., 2008. Boundaries of sovereignty, frontiers of integration: Rethinking 'conflict' between Russia and the EU. In: T. Hopf, ed. *Russia's European choice*. London: Palgrave Macmillan, 187–214.

Krok-Paszkowska, A., Zielonka, J., and Shevtsova, L., 2005. The European Union's policies towards Russia. In: A. J. Motyl and B. A. Ruble, eds. *Russia's engagement with the West: Transformation and integration in the twenty-first century*. London: M.E. Sharp, pp. 151–169.

Kux, S., 2005. European-Union-Russia relations: Transformation through integration. In: Alexander J. Motyl, Blair A. Ruble and Liliia Fedorovna Shevtsova, eds. *Russia's engagement with the West: Transformation and integration in the twenty-first century*. London: M.E. Sharp.

Leonard, M., and Grant, C., 2007. *Georgia and the EU: Can Europe's Neighbourhood Policy deliver?*. London: Centre for European Reform.

Leonard, M., and Popescu, N., 2008. *A power audit of EU-Russia relations*. London: European Council for Foreign Relations.

Light, M., 2008. Keynote article: Russia and the EU: Strategic partners or strategic rivals? *Journal of common market studies*, 46, 7–27.

Lukyanov, F., 2008. Russia-EU: The partnership that went astray. *Europe-Asia studies*, 60 (6), 1107–1119.

Lynch, D., 2005, From 'frontier' politics to 'border' policies between the EU and Russia. In: O. Antonenko and K. Pinnick, eds. *Russia and the European Union: Prospects for a new relationship*. London: Routledge, pp. 1–19.

Manners, I., 2010. As you like it: European Union normative power in the European Neighbourhood Policy. In: R. G. Whitman and S. Wolff, eds. *The European Neighbourhood Policy in perspective: Context, implementation and impact*. London: Palgrave Macmillan, pp. 29–50.

Medvedev, S., 2008. The stalemate in EU-Russia relations: Between 'sovereignty' and 'Europeanisation'. In: T. Hopf, ed. *Russia's European choice*. New York: Palgrave Macmillan, pp. 215–231.

Najšlová, L., 2010. The EU in the wider Black Sea region: Clumsy but attractive? In: K. Henderson and C. Weaver, eds. *The Black Sea region and EU policy: The challenge of divergent agendas*. Surrey: Ashgate, pp. 29–44.

Nichol, J., 2009. *Russia-Georgia conflict in August 2008: Context and implications for US interests* [online]. Available from: http://www.fas.org/sgp/crs/row/RL34618.pdf [Accessed 15 February 2010].

Pavliuk, O., 2005. Russia's integration with the West and the states 'in between'. In: A. J. Motyl and B. A. Ruble, eds. *Russia's engagement with the West: Transformation and integration in the twenty-first century*. London: M.E. Sharp.

Popescu, N., and Wilson, A., 2009. *The limits of enlargement-lite: European and Russian power in the troubled neighbourhood* [online]. London: European Council on Foreign Relations, pp. 185–208. Available from: http://www.ecfr.eu/content/entry/ecfr_eastern_neighbourhood_wilson_popescu [Accessed 29 October 2010].

Rahr, A., 2005. Russia-European Union-Germany after September 11 and Iraq. In: A. J. Motyl and B. A. Ruble, eds. *Russia's engagement with the West: Transformation and integration in the twenty-first century*. London: M.E. Sharp, pp. 223–227.

Rahr, A., 2007. Germany and Russia: A special relationship. *The Washington quarterly*, 30 (2), pp. 137–145.

Rynning, S., and Jensen, C.P., 2010. The ENP and Transatlantic relations. In: R. G. Whitman and S. Wolff, eds. *The European Neighbourhood Policy in perspective: Context, implementation and impact*. London: Palgrave Macmillan, pp. 135–160.

Sammut, D., 2010. The European Union's increased engagement with the South Caucasus. In: K. Henderson and C. Weaver, eds. *The Black Sea region and EU policy: The challenge of divergent agendas*. Surrey: Ashgate, pp. 79–105.

Schimmelfennig, F., and Scholtz, H., 2008. EU democracy promotion in the European neighbourhood. *European Union politics*, 9 (2), 187–215.

Tardieu, J.-P., 2009. Russia and the Eastern Partnership after the war in Georgia. *Russie Nei Visions*, 43.

Timmins, G., 2005. EU-Russian relations – a member state perspective: Germany and Russia – a special partnership in the new Europe. In: D. Johnson and P. Robinson, eds. *Perspectives on EU-Russia relations*. Abingdon: Routledge, pp. 55–79.

Tonra, B., 2010. Identity construction through the ENP: Borders and boundaries, insiders and outsiders. In: R. G. Whitman and S. Wolff, eds. *The European Neighbourhood Policy in perspective: Context, implementation and impact*. London: Palgrave Macmillan, pp. 51–72.

Trenin, D., 2005. Russia's security integration with America and Europe. In: A. J. Motyl and B. A. Ruble, eds. *Russia's engagement with the West: Transformation and integration in the twenty-first century*. London: M.E. Sharp, pp. 281–293.

Vasilyan, S., 2010. A cacophony: The EU's Security Policy towards the South Caucasus. In: K. Henderson and C. Weaver, eds. *The Black Sea region and EU policy: The challenge of divergent agendas*. Surrey: Ashgate, pp. 87–105.

Weaver, C., 2010. Black Sea or Black Lake? How US-Russian tensions are affecting EU policy. In: K. Henderson and C. Weaver, eds. *The Black Sea region and EU policy: The challenge of divergent agendas*. Surrey: Ashgate, pp. 65–78.

Wolczuk, K., 2010. Convergence without finalité: EU strategy towards post-Soviet states in the wider Black Sea region. In: K. Henderson and C. Weaver, eds. *The Black Sea region and EU policy: The challenge of divergent agendas*. Surrey: Ashgate, pp. 45–63.

Unrecognized and Unwelcome? The Role of the EU in Preventing the Proliferation of CBRN Weapons, Materials and Knowledge

KAMIL ZWOLSKI

ABSTRACT *This article assesses the role of the EU as an actor in the area of non-proliferation of chemical, biological, radiological and nuclear (CBRN) weapons, materials and know-how. It focuses primarily on the Russian Federation. Russia's extensive CBRN programmes, combined with bad economy, weak security and high unemployment among CBRN scientists, have become a major source of concern for the international community following the end of the cold war and after the terrorist attacks of 11 September 2001. The EU is the only non-state actor that got involved in addressing this threat right at the beginning of the 1990s, renewing its commitments after 9/11. This article revisits the concept of 'actorness' in order to examine the past, present and possibly future role of the EU in preventing the proliferation of CBRN capabilities. This means that in addition to evaluating past policies, this contribution analyses the impact of the Lisbon Treaty reforms and the changing international security environment on the position of the EU as an aspiring international non-proliferation actor.*

Introduction

> Proliferation by both states and terrorists was identified in the ESS [European Security Strategy] as "potentially the greatest threat to EU security". That risk has increased in the last five years, bringing the multilateral framework under pressure.
>
> Report on the Implementation of the European Security Strategy
> (European Council, 2008)

The European Union (EU) aspires to become a global security actor in the area of non-proliferation of weapons of mass destruction (WMDs). Importantly, this ambition has been pursued not only within the framework of the Common Foreign and Security Policy (CFSP), but also through the European Community's non-proliferation assistance programmes, mainly to Russia and the Commonwealth of Independent States (CIS) (Höhl et al., 2003; Portela, 2003; Anthony, 2004; Müller, 2007).

This financial and technical assistance, although important in preventing the proliferation threat, was technical in nature. Thus, throughout the 1990s, the EU lacked an overall political direction for its non-proliferation policy. In fact, the EU did not have a clearly-defined non-proliferation policy until 2003, when it adopted the European Security Strategy (ESS), in which proliferation was identified as the key threat to Europe (Council, 2003a, 2003).

More importantly, at the same time, the EU also adopted the strategy against the proliferation of weapons of mass destruction (the WMD Strategy), bringing non-proliferation to the centre of its aspirations to become a global security actor (European Council, 2003; Álvarez-Verdugo, 2006). To demonstrate that the EU was serious about implementing its strategies, the High Representative's Personal Representative on non-proliferation of WMDs was appointed with a small office in the Council building.

These reforms have significantly enhanced the profile of non-proliferation on the EU's international security agenda, but they have also divided EU policies in this area into two pillars: community assistance and the CFSP, leading to some tensions and competition over resources (Zwolski, 2011). The Lisbon Treaty, through reshuffling the institutional structure of the EU's external actions, aims to bring about consistency and consequently strengthen the profile of the EU as an international security actor. What impact are these reforms going to have on the role of the EU as an international non-proliferation policy actor?

This article examines the role of the EU as an actor in preventing the proliferation of chemical, biological, radiological and nuclear (CBRN) weapons, materials and knowledge. It focuses mainly on Russia because the EU's efforts in this geographical region have been slightly overlooked in research terms (Denza, 2005). Instead, the majority of scholarly literature focuses on the negotiations with Iran over its nuclear programme (Denza, 2005; Kile, 2005; Leonard, 2005; Harnish, 2007; Overhaus, 2007). While important, these negotiations do not represent the whole image of the EU as a non-proliferation security actor. Moreover, it can be argued that the threat of CBRN proliferation from Russia has represented a much greater security problem than the Iranian nuclear programme because it potentially involves non-state, unaccountable actors (Alibek, 2000; Baker and Cutler, 2000; Ball and Gerber, 2004; Busch and Holmes, 2009; Turpen and Finlay, 2009).

The article commences by revisiting the concept of actorness, drawing on the rich body of scholarship in this field of academic enquiry. Traditionally, states have been considered the only actors in international relations, so the arrival of the EU encouraged scholars to develop analytical tools that would take account of the *sui generis* nature of this new international entity. This exercise will enable us to establish the framework for assessing the EU's role as an actor in non-proliferation policy in two historical stages. First, the article will examine the dual character of the EU's non-proliferation policy, embedded in the first and the second pillars of the

EU. Second, the article will assess the potential impact of the Lisbon Treaty reforms on the position of the EU as a security actor in non-proliferation.

The EU as an International Security Actor

For a few decades now, European Studies scholars have been preoccupied with developing analytical tools to examine the role of the EU in the world (Cosgrove and Twitchett, 1970; Sjötstedt, 1977; Bretherton and Vogler, 2006; Smith, 2008). Further, scholars have also applied these tools to investigate single case studies, analysing the 'actorness' of the EU in policies such as terrorism, police cooperation and climate security (Jupille and Caporaso, 1998; Larsen, 2002; Groenleer and Van Schaik, 2007; Beyer, 2008; Dryburgh, 2008; Kaunert, 2010; Zwolski and Kaunert, 2011).

In order to establish the framework for examining the role of the EU as an actor in non-proliferation policy, this article draws on the large body of the aforementioned scholarship concerned with the EU's international 'actorness'. In this respect, the argument in this article is based on the observation that the EU is 'an evolving entity, composed of numerous issue areas and policy networks, neither a full-blown polity nor a system of sovereign states, which displays varying degrees of "actorhood"' (Jupille and Caporaso, 1988, pp. 214).

When assessing the role of the EU in international security issues, such as non-proliferation, it is important to capture this complex nature of the EU's *sui generis* actorness. To this end, Jupille and Caporaso (1988) propose a set of criteria that are observable, continuously variable and abstract. The framework developed by the two authors is integrated into this article, although in a slightly modified form, to examine the EU's actorness in preventing the proliferation of CBRN weapons, materials and knowledge. As a result, the role of the EU in this security policy field is assessed against the following criteria of actorness:

- Authority: This criterion refers to the EU's legal competence to act, but also (particularly in the context of the Lisbon Treaty reforms) to its formal membership in international organizations. Thus, the question that must be addressed is: Does the EU have legal instruments to develop non-proliferation policies? If so, what are these instruments?
- Autonomy: This criterion refers to 'a distinctive institutional apparatus' (Jupille and Caporaso, 1998, pp. 217). Consequently, the empirical part of this article asks: Does the EU have a distinctive institutional structure capable of developing non-proliferation policies? If so, what is its nature?
- Resources: This criterion has been extensively conceptualized by Bretherton and Vogler (2006), drawing on the work of Sjötstedt (1977). Resources include diplomacy/ negotiations, economic tools and military means. Thus, the following question must be addressed: Does the EU have the necessary resources to conduct non-proliferation policies? If so, what are they?
- Recognition: This criterion refers to the political recognition by other state and non-state actors, such as proliferation experts (de facto recognition). The question of the EU's legal (de jure) recognition, such as formal membership in international organizations, is considered part of the EU's authority.

The following empirical part of this article examines the EU as an actor in preventing the proliferation of WMDs, mainly from Russia, with the Table 1 below summarizing the key points. The second part identifies the key innovations introduced by the Lisbon Treaty, with their potential impact on the EU's non-proliferation profile.

Authority: Beyond the CFSP Framework

The Lisbon Treaty, following a prolonged process of ratification (Hoffmann, 2009; Kratochvil and Braun, 2009; Tonra, 2009; Zwolski, 2009), introduced significant changes to the legal setup of the EU's external action. These reforms, along with their potential impact on the EU's non-proliferation policy, are examined further in this article. However, in order to fully understand these modifications, it is first important to briefly examine the evolution of the authority of the EU in non-proliferation policy.

Under the European Political Cooperation (EPC) framework (1970–93), European cooperation on non-proliferation was informal and non-binding (Smith, 2002; Sauer, 2003). The Treaty on the European Union (TEU) integrated the EPC as the second pillar of the newly-established EU, developing it into the CFSP. Consequently, the two new legal instruments of the EU included common positions and joint actions; soon after they became available, the member states started utilizing these instruments to coordinate their positions on non-proliferation, most notably at the Non-Proliferation Treaty (NPT) Review Conferences.

According to Schmitt (2005, pp. 7–8), at the 1995 and 2000 Review Conferences, 'the Union played an active role, establishing itself as a recognized actor in this field'. For example, already in 1995, the EU had prepared for the Conference by adopting a joint action plan, opting for the indefinite extension of the NPT (Council, 1994). In 2000 and 2005, the EU adopted common positions supporting further strengthening of the NPT regime. In 2005, according to some observers, the EU played a more important role than ever before, but nobody actually noticed it (Müller, 2005).

Table 1. The EU as an actor in non-proliferation

Authority	The EU acquired legal authority to act externally on non-proliferation in 1993, with the establishment of the CFSP. Further, 'regulation' as a Community legal instrument enabled it to establish external assistance programmes that the Commission utilized for developing non-proliferation technical and financial projects.
Autonomy	EU institutional 'distinctiveness' in non-proliferation was achieved in 2003, when the permanent non-proliferation office was established in the Council Secretariat, entrusted with the implementation of the WMD Strategy. Until January 2010, the European Commission was also involved in non-proliferation through its external assistance programmes.
Resources	Two categories of non-proliferation resources can be identified. First, there are long-term, capacity-building financial instruments, previously at the disposal of the Commission and now in the EEAS. Second, there are political and diplomatic instruments introduced mainly by the WMD Strategy, such as the non-proliferation clause.
Recognition	The EU tends not to be recognized as an important actor in non-proliferation. There are numerous reasons for this, some of them internal (heavy bureaucracy) and some of them external (the diversity of competing non-proliferation frameworks, which EU member states utilize for their non-proliferation policies).

The non-proliferation policy, as a matter of external security, naturally falls under the CFSP institutional and legal framework. Yet, as this article demonstrates, the European Community had started developing its profile and expertise in this policy area at the beginning of the 1990s with regard to the external dimension, and as far back as the 1950s with the establishment of the European Atomic Energy Community.

Within the Community framework, Article 249 of the Treaty Establishing the European Community (TEEC) introduced legal instruments 'concerned with translating the general principles of the treaties into specific rules' (Nugent, 2003, pp. 238). One of them, a regulation, has been utilized to enable the European Community to provide external assistance to the countries of the dissolved Soviet bloc. In this respect, the Technical Aid to the Commonwealth of Independent States (TACIS) programme was the Commission's main instrument for providing Russia with assistance and recovery funds, including in the area of nuclear safety and non-proliferation. Consecutive Council regulations enabled the Community to acquire important experience in developing non-proliferation projects. Consequently, first-pillar legal instruments cannot be omitted when examining the authority of the EU in this policy field.

Autonomy: From Informal Meetings to Permanent Institutional Structures

Within the cold war context, the institutional instruments of the European Community member states to conduct common foreign and security policy were confined mainly to the informal EPC. This was problematic from the 'actorness' perspective because 'an international organisation, to be an actor, should have a distinctive institutional apparatus, even if it is grounded in, or intermingles with, domestic political institutions' (Jupille and Caporaso, 1998, pp. 217).

The TEU provided the EU with institutional structure in the area of international security policy, but it was only in 2003 that a permanent bureaucratic apparatus dedicated to the non-proliferation policy was established in the Council Secretariat. Following the adoption of the WMD Strategy (European Council, 2003), the Council Secretariat has become home to the EU's non-proliferation office, headed by the Personal Representative on Non-Proliferation of WMDs, Annalisa Giannella.

When Javier Solana appointed his WMD Personal Representative, the post holder was entrusted with the following tasks:

- Contributing to the further development of the EU WMD Strategy;
- Further enhancing the profile of the non-proliferation policy in the EU's relations with third countries;
- Contributing to the implementation of the EU SALW (Small Arms and Light Weapons) Strategy (since 2005);
- Assisting EU member states in their efforts to coordinate policies in the area of conventional arms exports controls; and
- Assisting the E3 (Germany, France and the UK) and the High Representative in negotiations with Iran over its nuclear programme (since Autumn 2004).

The adoption of the WMD Strategy and the consequent establishment of permanent institutional structures in the Council Secretariat mark the most important steps in developing the EU's external non-proliferation policy. Yet, it also contributed to the fragmentation of the EU's efforts, with non-proliferation also being on the agenda of the European Commission through its external financial assistance programmes (further discussed in the next section). As one high-level Council official put it, 'It is a disaster that the EU does not have a unified representation when conducting its policy on the non-proliferation of WMDs. Countries such as the US and Russia are fed up with this situation, it is annoying to them.' (CON01, 2009).

The institutional merging of the non-proliferation bureaucracies of the Council Secretariat and the Commission, as provided for by the arrangements concerning the European External Action Service (EEAS) (Council, 2010), constitutes the most robust attempt to assure institutional consistency. Earlier attempts in the non-proliferation policy include the WMD Monitoring Centre, created in 2006 and located in the Council Secretariat (Council, 2006). The Centre proved to be a valuable forum for various parties, including the Commission (De Jong et al., 2010).

Resources: A Project-Based Vs. Policy-Based Approach

Before the EEAS merged the EU's non-proliferation bureaucracies in January 2010, there was an inter-institutional controversy about which resources were the most important in developing the EU's non-proliferation policy.

On the one hand, the officials of the European Commission pointed to the instruments of the European Community, the Instrument for Stability (IfS) and the Instrument for Nuclear Safety Cooperation (INSC). These financial tools were created in 2006 as part of the overall reform of the Community's external assistance instruments (Bartelt, 2008). They enabled the Commission to finance non-proliferation and nuclear safety initiatives in the countries and regions of proliferation concern. Following the Lisbon Treaty reforms, both instruments are now 'programmed' in the EEAS and only executed by the Commission (Council, 2010).

On the other hand, Council officials underline the importance of the political dimension of the EU's non-proliferation capacities. As one Council Secretariat official pointed out (CON04, 2011): 'Now, the EU's non-proliferation policy is not merely about having some funds and spending money on projects; instead, now the EU has a policy. Of course, budgetary elements play a role in our policy, but we have the political direction introduced by the WMD Strategy. Since 2003, the EU is a political actor, not just a funder.'

Where did this divergence of resources and approaches to non-proliferation in the EU originate? Since the beginning of the 1990s, the European Community has been the only non-state actor providing non-proliferation assistance to the former Soviet Union (Höhl et al., 2003). The focus of this assistance (TACIS) was on training and developing studies analysing the Soviet nuclear installations (Commission, 1993).

For example, the Community got involved in supporting the redirection of scientists. This was achieved by co-financing the International Science and Technology Centre in Russia and, later, also the Science and Technology Centre in Ukraine. The idea behind these initiatives is to support unemployed Soviet-era scientists with knowledge related to WMDs and missile delivery systems so they can use this knowledge and skills for peaceful purposes.

TACIS expired in 2006. Subsequently, some of its tasks were assigned to the two new instruments of the European Commission, the IfS and the INSC. The IfS, through its long-term component (Article 4), allowed the Commission to provide assistance in the context of stable conditions for cooperation (European Parliament and the Council, 2006). Non-proliferation was identified as one of the priority areas for the years, 2007–13.

Importantly, the IfS continues to fund the redirection of scientists, but it has broadened its geographical scope. Currently, it also contributes to non-proliferation initiatives in regions such as Africa, the Middle East and South Asia (Commission, 2009). While the INSC focuses on financing nuclear safety projects, the IfS used to be (before it was moved to the EEAS) 'the sole Community instrument that can directly address issues relating to the risks presented by the weaponisation of chemical, biological, radiological and nuclear agents' (European Commission, 2007, pp. 20).

Over the period of 1991–2006, the Commission allocated €1.3 billion from the TACIS budget for non-proliferation and nuclear safety projects in the former Soviet Union (Commission, 2007). Under the budgetary framework covering the years 2007–13, the IfS and INSC have average annual budgets of €112 million for non-proliferation and nuclear safety. At same time, the CFSP budget for non-proliferation has been much more modest at just above €22 million in 2010 (Council, 2011).

However, as already mentioned, Council officials underline the fact that funding constitutes only one (minor) component of the EU's non-proliferation policy. Importantly, the WMD Strategy equipped EU non-proliferation efforts with a sense of strategic direction and a strong political dimension, in contrast to the depoliticized character of budgetary programmes. In order to 'mainstream' the non-proliferation policy into the EU's relations with third countries, the EU introduced, also in 2003, the non-proliferation clause (Council, 2003b), which is an important diplomatic resource at its disposal. Since 2003, the non-proliferation clause has been inserted into all the so-called mixed agreements between the EU and third countries.

The first section of the clause commits parties to fully comply with their existing obligations. Although these obligations are not explicitly mentioned, it is understood that they encompass the NPT, including safeguards, the Chemical Weapons Convention, the Biological and Toxic Weapons Convention and the United Nations (UN) Security Council resolutions, most notably Resolution 1540. The second section encourages parties to join any other relevant international non-proliferation frameworks and to establish an effective system of export control (Council, 2003b). This diverging set of non-proliferation resources at the disposal of the EU was moved into the EEAS at the beginning of 2011. The opportunities and challenges that this reform brings to the role of the EU as an international non-proliferation actor are discussed further in this article.

Recognition: EU Member States over the EU?

The extent to which the EU is recognized as an important non-proliferation security actor depends on who is asked. EU officials underline the fact that the adoption of the WMD Strategy significantly enhanced the EU's recognition by external partners and among the EU member states (CON04, 2011). Yet, this view is not widely shared outside of the EU. In fact, external actors, such as non-proliferation experts, tend to disregard the role of the EU as an actor in non-proliferation policy; this section identifies the main reasons for this.

First, the extensive EU bureaucracy is considered one of the key factors undermining EU recognition in non-proliferation policy. As one non-proliferation expert notes, 'If the UK runs a project worth €70 million and the Commission contributes €3 million, the paper-work for spending €70 million and €3 million is similar' (WMDExp1, 2009). Marc Deffrennes of the European Commission underlined these difficulties, pointing to the 'heavy procedures, heavy bureaucracy' and the fact that there is a long time span 'between a decision-making process to run a programme or a project, the start of implementation, and the end of implementation' (House of Lords, 2005, pp. 55).

Second, in addition to internal EU problems, there are also significant external factors that negatively affect the recognition of the EU as a non-proliferation actor. For example, even though Russia has traditionally been the main recipient of the EU's non-proliferation technical and financial assistance, the EU has never been Moscow's favourite partner. In fact, Russia has a hierarchy of preferred partners. These include:

- The US: Working with Washington on non-proliferation validates the Russian position as an important actor on the world scene (WMDExp1, 2009). Furthermore, Washington is perceived to have the largest resources at its disposal;
- EU member states: Working with individual states is a preferred option for Moscow because the work tends to be more flexible and the discussions take place at the working level and are not highly politicized (WMDExp1, 2009); and
- The EU is only the third of Russia's preferred partners because it is considered less flexible than its individual member states and generally more complicated to work with.

Third, there are differences concerning the priorities for the EU's involvement. Deffrennes admits: 'Working with Russians is very hard (...) It is as difficult today as it was at that time [1992] because they have their own priorities' (House of Lords, 2005, pp. 56). Other Commission officials specify that Moscow would like the EU to become more involved in chemical weapons destruction and in nuclear submarine dismantlement (COM10, 2009).

Yet, the Commission is reluctant to become more involved in these priorities. Not only are they very expensive, but the culture of secrecy surrounding all military activities in Russia prevents the Commission from scrutinizing the implementation of such projects. Instead, the Commission would prefer to focus on nuclear safety, where it has developed extensive expertise. It would also like to continue to support projects contributing to the redirection of CBRN scientists, which give the EU firsthand knowledge about Russian programmes (COM10, 2009).

Former Commission officials admit that this exchange of information is particularly important in the area of bio-security and bio-safety because, officially, the EU is not allowed to know anything about these programmes (COM10,

2009). John Mattiussi (2006), a former Commission official working in the area of non-proliferation, admits: 'The Soviet Union maintained a large and sophisticated bio research programme – what happened to the materials/expertise? We do not know. Russia refuses to discuss past programmes' (Mattiussi, 2006, pp. 2).

Fourth, 'the proliferation' of international non-proliferation frameworks undermined the attractiveness of the EU in this area. The G8 Global Partnership constitutes one significant example. It brings together countries, including EU member states, to cooperate on non-proliferation projects, and it initially focused on Russia. One American non-proliferation expert noted in this context that the G8 had emerged as the primary forum for dealing with non-proliferation for EU member states (WMDExp2, 2009).

Importantly, all of these factors affecting the recognition of the EU as an actor in non-proliferation policy concern the provision of non-proliferation assistance. They indicate that the EU has not been considered an important player in this respect by either external observers or by Russia, even if Moscow has benefited hugely from the EU's funding. This, in turn, indicates that the EU has also not acquired a high level of recognition as a non-proliferation actor in a more political or strategic sense, contrary to what some EU officials suggest. Thus, it is important to assess the opportunities to enhance the EU's non-proliferation profile introduced by the Lisbon Treaty.

Lisbon Treaty Reforms: Filling the Frame

The institutional reforms introduced by the Lisbon Treaty provide an opportunity for the EU to enhance its international profile as a non-proliferation actor, but this process is not going to be automatic. It will depend on a few crucial factors, such as the leadership role of the High Representative and intra-institutional consistency within the EEAS. Before examining these factors in more detail, this section first outlines some of the key changes to the EU's external action brought about by the Lisbon Treaty (Whitman and Juncos, 2009; Missiroli, 2010; Vanhoonacker and Reslow, 2010).

Bringing consistency to the EU's external actions lies at the core of the reforms. At the leadership level, the High Representative has become the Vice-President of the European Commission, in addition to presiding over the Foreign Affairs Council. The intention is to ensure that the external activities of the Commission and those of the member states are mutually supportive and reinforce each other.

On the bureaucratic level, the Directorate General, External Relations (DG Relex), of the Commission was moved to the EEAS, as was the 'foreign policy' part of the Council Secretariat. In this newly-established EU diplomatic service, roughly one-third of the officials come from the Commission, one-third from the Council and one-third from the member states (COM16, 2010). This is a truly unprecedented composition, further supporting the argument about the *sui generis* character of the EU's international actorness. However, what impact are these and other novelties likely to have on the EU's role as an actor in the non-proliferation policy? The Table 2 below summarizes the key points.

Table 2. The EU as an actor in non-proliferation after the Lisbon Treaty reforms

Authority	The key innovation introduced by the Lisbon Treaty is located in its Article 47, establishing a legal personality of the EU. This offers the potential to strengthen the EU's legal presence in non-proliferation regimes.
Autonomy	The Lisbon Treaty reforms strengthen the institutional distinctiveness of the EU through establishing the EEAS and transforming Community delegations into Union delegations. Yet, while potentially strengthening the leadership of the EU, the reforms can also lead to new tensions, mainly between the High Representative and the European Council President.
Resources	EU's financial resources in non-proliferation will not be affected by the Lisbon Treaty reforms, apart from the fact that they will now be 'programmed' by the EEAS. Diplomatic and political resources can be strengthened significantly, depending on the High Representative's determination, priorities and leadership role in coordinating all non-proliferation resources at the EU's disposal.
Recognition	Recognition of the EU as a non-proliferation actor will be closely linked to its perception as an actor in foreign and security more broadly. Paradoxically, strengthening of the EU's external action institutional structure can further contribute to the capability-expectation gap.

Authority

The authority of the EU, that is, its legal competence to act, has been potentially reinforced by eliminating the Community-Union dichotomy and, consequently, granting the EU a legal personality. The confusion in this respect has been long-lasting, amply demonstrated by the ambiguous character of the EU's membership in various non-proliferation regimes. For example, even though the EU is not party to the NPT, the Commission has long been recognized by the International Atomic Energy Agency and the EU has been acting, more or less, as a single actor at the NPT Review Conferences. Similarly, even though the EU is not a full member of the G8, it has been recognized within the G8 Global Partnership framework.

Article 47 of the Lisbon Treaty offers an opportunity to overcome these ambiguities by granting the EU a legal personality. Koehler (2010, pp. 63) observes that:

> These amendments clearly strengthen the EU's status as an international actor, since the Treaty explicitly regulates the legal personality of the EU, and, furthermore, it clarifies the question concerning the Union's diplomatic relations and the status of its institutions, which solidifies the EU's position in the international arena under international law grants the EU with legal personality.

These reforms indeed provide the means for the EU to ascertain its position in international non-proliferation regimes and organizations, thus strengthening its authority. Yet, the eventual materializing of this potential will depend on the political will of the member states. They have already undertaken precautionary measures in this respect in the form of the declaration in the Lisbon Treaty, which states that 'the fact that the European Union has a legal personality will not in any way authorise the Union to legislate or to act beyond the competences conferred upon it by the Member States in the Treaties' (Council, 2008, pp. 438).

Autonomy

The establishment of the EEAS and the transformation of the Commission's delegations into the EU's delegations offer an opportunity to strengthen the EU's institutional autonomy. However, this will depend largely on the leadership role of the High Representative and the speed at which the new institutional ethos will replace old loyalties in the EEAS (Whitman, 2011). This is important because the EEAS is composed of officials coming from different institutional backgrounds, with diverging traditions of approaching problems. In the area of non-proliferation, this requires mutual understanding and support between diplomats, who have been traditionally involved in international negotiations, and civil servants, who are experienced in developing long-term capacity-building projects of a technical nature.

If autonomy is understood as 'institutional distinctiveness', the post-Lisbon institutional reforms can prove to be a double-edged sword. On the one hand, the intention was to establish a greater sense of leadership. Thus, instead of a separate High Representative and Commissioner for External Relations, now the High Representative performs a double-hated role. Further, the Lisbon Treaty replaced the rotating Presidency of the European Council with a permanent President, who shall 'ensure the external representation of the Union on issues concerning its common foreign and security policy (...)' (Council, 2008, pp. 30).

On the other hand, this can lead to confusion or even competition over competencies. Controversies in the non-proliferation policy, in particular, may arise between the High Representative and the President of the European Council. For example, it was Herman Van Rompuy who represented the EU at the 2010 Nuclear Security Summit in Washington, not Catherine Ashton, who has at her disposal the EEAS with a separate non-proliferation team (European Council, 2010).

Resources

It has already been established that the non-proliferation resources at the EU's disposal can be grouped broadly into two categories. First, there are long-term capacity-building financial and technical projects developed through geographical and thematic financial instruments, including TACIS, the INSC and the IfS. Traditionally, these resources have been focused on preventing the threat of proliferation of CBRN materials and knowledge from Russia and former Soviet Union countries. The European Commission invested millions of euros in initiatives such as scientific centres in Russia and Ukraine, which provide opportunities for thousands of CBRN scientists to redirect their skills to peaceful purposes.

Second, there are political and diplomatic resources available for the EU within the CFSP framework, based on the guidelines of the WMD Strategy. These include, most importantly, the non-proliferation clause included in agreements between the EU and third parties. They also include the diplomatic efforts of the EU based on the mandate provided by joint actions and common positions, most notably at the NPT Review Conferences. Council officials emphasize the importance of this political dimension introduced by the WMD Strategy. They point to the fact that even though financial assistance plays some role in non-proliferation efforts, the EU used to lack the political direction for its policy prior to adopting the strategy and appointing the Personal Representative on Non-Proliferation of WMDs in 2003.

The EEAS brings these two categories of resources together so that officials who used to work in the Council Secretariat will now have more say in 'programming' long-term financial projects and former DG Relex officials will have more influence over diplomatic policies. However, what do these reforms mean for the resources as such?

On the financial side, not much will change, as the capacity-building instruments (the IfS and the INSC) are still separate from the CFSP budget and other political instruments. Thus, in the long term, competencies and resources have to be converged, in addition to institutions and processes. This will result in enhancing the overall impact of the EU's non-proliferation policy. On the political side, the EU's diplomatic and political impact can increase, provided that (a) the High Representative will reflect in her policy the fact that the non-proliferation policy was identified as a top security priority for the EU in the European Security Strategy; and (b) the High Representative and the European Council President will quickly reach a consensus concerning their competencies in this policy area.

Recognition

The possible causal relationship between the Lisbon Treaty reforms and the political recognition of the EU as an actor in non-proliferation is a rather speculative exercise at this early stage. However, it is certain that this recognition will be closely linked to the broader recognition of the EU as a foreign and security actor. In the broader sense, the capability-expectation gap (Hill, 1993, 1998) became prominent once again recently, when the EU and the High Representative were criticized for failing to speak with one voice and convey a strong message from the EU with regard to the revolutions in Egypt and Libya.

This criticism demonstrates a rather paradoxical situation in which strengthening the institutional capacity of the EU's High Representative can actually lead to more disappointments among those who expect a stronger EU voice in international politics. This will inevitably affect the recognition of the EU as an actor in non-proliferation.

However, a few other factors will also play key roles. First, recognition will depend on whether the EU will be able to take advantage of its newly-acquired legal personality in order to seek full membership in international institutions and regimes concerned with non-proliferation. Second, the leadership role of the High Representative will be important both at the international level and in developing the institutional ethos of the EEAS. Third, the EU will not be recognized as an important non-proliferation actor unless member states decide to channel more of their policies and resources through the EU rather than bilaterally or through other frameworks.

Conclusion

The empirical evidence suggests that the EU now has all the necessary means to become an important actor in preventing the proliferation of WMDs. First, it has authority, including international legal personality. Legal competence to act includes regulations (establishing capacity-building instruments) as well as CFSP instruments of a more political nature. Second, the EU has autonomy; this includes in particular the EEAS, which enables better aligning of the different categories of resources at the EU's disposal. Third, the EU has a variety of resources to prevent the proliferation of CBRN weapons, materials and knowledge. They range from financial assistance programmes for building capacities in regions of proliferation concern, to diplomatic and political measures, including the non-proliferation clause. Most importantly, the EU has the WMD Strategy and a team of experienced civil servants and diplomats, now working in the EEAS.

Yet, recognition of the EU as an actor in non-proliferation remains relatively low. This is partially because even though the EU has all of these means to enhance its profile, its member states must be willing to shift the larger portion of their non-proliferation policies to Brussels. In theory, this should not be as controversial as the coordination of EU actions in other areas of international security because an important framework (and a strong commitment) for cooperation already exists in the form of the WMD Strategy, not to mention the European Security Strategy.

However, disagreements remain, particularly between nuclear (NWS) and non-nuclear (NNWS) states. According to the analysis by Friedrich Ebert Stiftung, '[t]hese differences result in various intra-EU cleavages and ultimately enable or encourage individual member states to engage in various interest coalitions outside the EU' (Katsioulis and Mölling, 2010, pp. 5). Further, none of these groups is homogenous. Diverging approaches exist between France and the UK with regard to disarmament and nuclear deterrence, as well as among the NNWS states (NATO members versus countries such as Ireland and Sweden) (Katsioulis and Mölling, 2010). Until these differences between NWS and NNWS as well as NATO and non-NATO EU member states are resolved, the EU's role as a non-proliferation actor will be hampered.

In addition to analysing these differences and the extent to which they can be overcome, further research will be necessary to assess the impact of the Lisbon Treaty reforms on the EU's stance as an international actor in non-proliferation. It is suggested in this article that this treaty provides the frame, but it needs to be filled with substance. For example, the High Representative must assume a leading role, not just internally, when coordinating EU policies, but also strive to enhance the EU's profile within multilateral frameworks such as the NPT Review Conferences.

References

Alibek, K., 2000. *Biohazard.* London: Arrow Books.
Alvarez-Verdugo, M., 2006. Mixing tools against proliferation: The EU's strategy for dealing with weapons of mass destruction, *European foreign affairs review*, 11 (3), 417–438.
Anthony, I., 2004. Reducing threats at the source: A European perspective on cooperative threat reduction. SIPRI Research Report no. 19. London: Oxford University Press.
Baker, H., and Cutler, L., 2000. A report card on the Department of Energy's nonproliferation programs with Russia. Washington, DC: The Russia Task Force of the Secretary of Energy Advisory Board, January.
Ball, D. Y., and Gerber, T. P., 2004. Will Russian scientists go rogue? A survey on the threat and the impact of Western assistance. PONARS Policy Memo 357. Washington, DC, November.

Bartelt, S., 2008. The institutional interplay regarding the new architecture for the EC's external assistance. *European law journal*, 14 (5), 655–679.

Beyer, C., 2008. The European Union as a security policy actor: The case of counterterrorism. *European foreign affairs review*, 13 (3), 293–315.

Bretherton, C., and Vogler, J., 2006. *The European Union as a global actor*. London: Routledge.

Busch, N. E., and Holmes, J. R., 2009. Russia's nuclear security culture. In: N.E. Busch and D.H. Joyner, eds. *Combating weapons of mass destruction: The future of international nonproliferation policy*. University of Georgia Press, 352–342.

COM10, 2009. Research interview at the European Commission, June 2009.

COM16, 2010. Phone research interview at the European Commission, November 2010.

Commission, 1993. TACIS: Annual report from the Commission, 1991 and 1992. COM (93)362 final. Brussels: Commission of the European Communities.

Commission, 2007. Nuclear safety strategy for community cooperation programmes, 2007–13, and Indicative Programme for 2007–09. Revision 17. Brussels: European Commission.

Commission, 2009. The Instrument for Stability – Multi-annual Indicative Programme, 2009–11. C(2009)2641. Brussels: European Commission.

CON01, 2009. Research interview at the General Secretariat of the Council of the European Union, March 2009.

CON04, 2011. Phone research interview at the General Secretariat of the Council of the European Union, March 2010.

Cosgrove, C., and Twitchett, K., 1970. International organisations as actors. In: C. Cosgrove and K. Twitchett, eds. *The new international actors: The UN and the EEC*. London: Macmillan, 11–54.

Council, 1994. Decision 94/509/CFSP concerning the joint action regarding preparation for the 1995 Conference of the States Parties to the Treaty on the Non-proliferation of Nuclear Weapons. OJ L 205. Brussels: Council of the European Union.

Council, 2003a. A Secure Europe in a Better World: European Security Strategy. 15895/03. Brussels: Council of the European Union.

Council, 2003b. Fight against the proliferation of weapons of mass destruction: Mainstreaming non-proliferation policies into the EU's wider relations with third countries. 14997/03. Brussels: Council of the European Union.

Council, 2006. EU strategy against the proliferation of WMD: Monitoring and enhancing consistent implementation. 16694/06. Brussels: Council of the European Union.

Council, 2008. Consolidated versions of the Treaty on the European Union and the Treaty on the Functioning of the European Union. 6655/08, 15 April 2008. Brussels: Council of the European Union.

Council, 2010. Council decision of 26 July 2010 establishing the organisation and functioning of the European External Action Service. (2010/427/EU), L 201 (OJEU). Brussels: Council of the European Union.

Council, 2011. 2010 CFSP Budget – Final update of the 2010 CFSP Budget. 5230/11. Brussels: Council of the European Union.

De Jong, S., Sterkx, S., and Wouters, J., 2010. The EU as a regional actor: Weapons of mass destruction. *EU-GRASP*, Working Paper No. 10. Bruges: United Nations University.

Denza, E., 2005. Non-proliferation of nuclear weapons: The European Union and Iran. *European foreign affairs review*, 10 (3), 289–311.

Dryburgh, L., 2008. The EU as a global actor? EU policy towards Iran. *European security*, 17 (2), 253–271.

European Commission, 2007. The Instrument for Stability: Strategy Paper 2007–11 [online]. Available from: http://ec.europa.eu/europeaid/how/finance/documents/eidhr/ifs_strategy_2007-2011_en.pdf [Accessed 11 August 2010].

European Council, 2003. Fight against the proliferation of weapons of mass destruction – EU strategy against proliferation of weapons of mass destruction. 15708/03. Brussels: European Council.

European Council, 2008. Report on the implementation of the European Security Strategy – Providing security in a changing world. S407/08. Brussels: European Council.

European Council, 2010. Statement by President Herman Van Rompuy on behalf of the European Union at the Nuclear Security Summit in Washington. PCE 68/10. Brussels: European Council.

European Parliament and the Council, 2006. Regulation (EC) No. 1717/2006 of the European Parliament and the Council of 15 November 2006 establishing an Instrument for Stability. L 327 (OJEU), 24 November.

Groenleer, M., and Van Shaik, L., 2007. United we stand? The European Union's international actorness in the cases of the International Criminal Court and the Kyoto Protocol. *Journal of common market studies*, 45 (5), 969–998.

Harnish, S., 2007. Minilateral cooperation and transatlantic coalition-building: The E3/EU-3 Iran initiative. *European security*, 16 (1), 1–27.

Hill, C., 1993. The capability-expectations gap, or conceptualizing Europe's international role. *Journal of common market studies*, 31 (3), 305–328.

Hill, C., 1998. Closing the capabilities-expectations gap? In: J. Peterson and H. Sjursen, eds. *A common foreign policy for Europe?* Abingdon, UK: Routledge, 18–38.

Hoffmann, L., 2009. Don't let the sun go down on me: The German Constitutional Court and its Lisbon judgement. *Journal of contemporary European research*, 5 (3), 482–490.

House of Lords, 2005. Preventing Proliferation of Weapons of Mass Destruction: The EU Contribution. HL Paper 96, 13th Report of Session 2004–2005. London: Stationery Office Limited.

Höhl, K., et al., 2003. EU cooperative threat reduction activities in Russia. Chaillot Papers No. 61. Paris: *Institute for Security Studies*, June.

Jupille, J., and Caporaso, J., 1998. States, agency, and rules: The European Union in global environmental politics. In: C. Rhodes, ed. *The European Union in the world community*. Boulder, CO: Lynne Rienner, 213–229.

Katsioulis, C., and Mölling, C., 2010. *NPT Review 2010: What role for the EU?* Berlin: Friedrich Ebert Stiftung.

Kaunert, C., 2010. Europol and EU counterterrorism: International security actorness in the external dimension. *Studies in conflict and terrorism*, 33 (7), 652–671.

Kile, S., 2005. *Europe and Iran: Perspectives on non-proliferation*. SIPRI Research Report No. 21. Oxford University Press.

Koehler, K., 2010. European foreign policy after Lisbon: Strengthening the EU as an international actor. *Caucasian review of international affairs*, 4 (1), 57–72.

Kratochvil, P., and Braun, M., 2009. The Lisbon Treaty and the Czech Republic: Past imperfect, future uncertain. *Journal of contemporary European research*, 5 (3), 498–504.

Larsen, H., 2002. The EU: A global military actor? *Cooperation and conflict*, 37 (3), 283–302.

Leonard, M., 2005. *Can EU diplomacy stop Iran's nuclear programme?* London: Centre for European Reform.

Mattiussi, J., 2006. *External relations perspectives: Informal seminar on bio-preparedness of the European Union*, July 2006 Brussels. Available from: http://www.ebsaweb.eu/ebsa_media/Downloads/EU Seminar/Mattiussi.pdf [Accessed 12 August 2010].

Missiroli, A., 2010. The new EU 'foreign policy' system after Lisbon: A work in progress. *European foreign affair review*, 15 (4), 427–452.

Müller, H., 2005. *The 2005 NPT Review Conference: Reasons and consequences of failure and options for repair*. Stockholm: The Secretariat of the Weapons of Mass Destruction Commission.

Müller, H., 2007. Europe and the proliferation of weapons of mass destruction. In: P. Foradori, P. Rosa and R. Scartezzini, eds. *Managing multilevel foreign policy*. Lanhan, MD: Lexington Books, 181–200.

Nugent, N., 2003. *The government and politics of the European Union*. Basingstoke, UK: Palgrave Macmillan.

Overhaus, M., 2007. *Analysis: European diplomacy and the conflict over Iran's nuclear programme*. [online], 19 July. Available from: http://www.deutsche-aussenpolitik.de/resources/dossiers/iran06/Dossier-Iran-Introduction.pdf [Accessed 12 August 2010].

Portela, C., 2003. The role of the EU in the non-proliferation of nuclear weapons: The way to Thessaloniki and beyond. *PRIF Reports* No. 65, Zurich, December.

Sauer, T., 2003. How 'common' is European nuclear non-proliferation policy. Joint session of workshops of the European Consortium for Political Research [online], March 2003. Edinburgh. Available from: http://www.essex.ac.uk/ECPR/events/jointsessions/paperarchive/edinburgh/ws12/Tom%20Sauer.pdf [Accessed 12 August 2010].

Schmitt, B., 2005. Introduction. In: B. Schmitt, ed. *Effective non-proliferation: The European Union and the 2005 NPT Review Conference*. Chaillot Papers No. 77. Paris: Institute for Security Studies, 7–9.

Sjöstedt, G., 1977. *The external role of the European Community*. York, UK: Saxon House.

Smith, H., 2002. *European Union foreign policy: What it is and what it does*. London: Pluto Press.

Smith, K., 2008. *European Union foreign policy in a changing world*. Malden, MA: Polity.
Tonra, B., 2009. The 2009 Irish Referendum on the Lisbon Treaty, *Journal of contemporary European research*, 5 (3), 472–479.
Turpen, E., and Finlay, B. 2009. U.S.-Russia cooperative nonproliferation. In: N. E. Busch and D.H. Joyner, eds. *Combating weapons of mass destruction: The future of international nonproliferation policy*. University of Georgia Press, 302–334.
Vanhoonacker, S., and Reslow, N., 2010. The European External Action Service: Living forwards by understanding backwards. *European foreign affairs review*, 15 (1), 1–18.
Whitman, R., 2011. The rise of the European External Action Service: Putting the strategy into EU diplomacy? [online]. Available from: http://www.euce.org/eusa/2011/papers/8l_whitman.pdf [Accessed 2 April 2011].
Whitman, R., and Juncos, A., 2009. The Lisbon Treaty and the foreign, security and defence policy: Reforms, implementation and the consequences of (non-)ratification. *European foreign affairs review*, 14 (1), 25–46.
WMDExp1, 2009. Phone research interview with a WMD expert, April 2009.
WMDExp2, 2009. Phone research interview with a WMD expert, April 2009.
Zwolski, K., 2009. Euthanasia, gay marriage and sovereignty: The Polish ratification of the Lisbon Treaty. *Journal of contemporary European research*, 5 (3), 489–497.
Zwolski, K., 2011, forthcoming. The external dimension of the EU's non-proliferation policy: Overcoming inter-institutional competition. *European Foreign Affairs Review*, 16 (3), 325–40.
Zwolski, K., and Kaunert, C., 2011 The EU and climate security: A case of successful norm entrepreneurship? *European security*, 20 (1), 21–43.

Russia's Energy Leverage over the EU: Myth or Reality?

TOM CASIER

ABSTRACT *Today, the EU is less dependent on Russian energy than it was two decades ago. Nevertheless, EU-Russia energy relations are more widely understood in terms of power, security and zero-sum geopolitical competition. This article challenges this Neo-Realist argument. Drawing on Keohane's and Nye's concepts of interdependence sensitivity and vulnerability, it both tests the actual degree of EU energy dependence and the extent to which dependence may create Russian leverage. It is found that the actual EU supply dependence is overrated and is mainly due to the EU's internal divisions. Secondly, Russia's potential leverage is undermined by its high dependence on EU energy demand. Thirdly, its potential energy leverage is at least counterbalanced by other dimensions of asymmetrical interdependence outside the energy context. Explaining how geopolitical power-related explanations became dominant in the analysis of EU-Russia relations, this article refers both to structural changes in the energy market and also to new perceptions that resulted from a renewed geopolitical logic in early decisions over pipelines, changing attitudes as Russia grew stronger and the different nature of the energy markets in the EU and Russia. While geopolitical considerations may occasionally sneak in, the core of EU-Russia energy relations is still predominantly economic and commercial.*

Introduction

When the Soviet Union collapsed, the European Union (EU) countries were proportionally importing more Russian gas than today. The term, energy security, however, was largely absent from the political discourse. Today, energy issues, in particular in relations between the EU and Russia, are understood mainly in terms of security, dependence, political influence, threats, and geopolitical gains and losses. Why are policy-makers so concerned about dependence on Russia today when they did not have similar concerns in the last days of the cold war? What explains this shift in the understanding of EU-Russia energy relations if not the increased dependence on energy imports from Russia?

This article first presents the arguably most dominant view in the study of energy relations. It reflects a vague Realist perspective in which control over energy flows is approached as geopolitical competition over power. Energy resources and control over transmission networks are seen as a source of power. The EU and Russia are presented as entangled in a zero-sum game, in which the gains of one party automatically imply the loss of the other.

Against this dominant perception, this article posits an analysis of EU-Russia energy relations that puts the emphasis on the complexity and multidimensionality of energy relations. It distinguishes between different aspects such as gas and oil markets, as well as supply, demand and transit. Drawing on the distinctions posited by Keohane and Nye between interdependence sensitivity and vulnerability, the article gives a more nuanced image of EU-Russia energy relations and the power resulting from asymmetries.

The last part seeks to explain why we have evolved from a virtually absent threat perception related to the EU's dependence on Russia in the 1990s towards an understanding of EU-Russia relations, not only in terms of excessive dependence, but even by some as a potential threat. What explains this radical shift in perception, which is not supported by actual trade flows? Here we introduce a third, thin Constructivist perspective, focusing both on material changes in the global energy market and issues of identity and perception in the relations between the EU and Russia.

Energy: From Economic to Geopolitical Issue

The understanding of EU-Russia energy relations as a competitive process is arguably the most dominant approach in contemporary research (for e.g., Smith, 2010; Paillard, 2010; Baran, 2007). Though seldom expressed in explicit terms, many analyses can be situated within a vague Neo-Realist approach to energy (Waltz, 1979; Mearsheimer, 2007). Energy relations are understood as a crucial element in the struggle of power between states. The possession of energy resources is seen as an essential latent source of power, increasing the relative capabilities of states vis-à-vis others. Hydrocarbons, as increasingly scarce goods, have become a crucial capability in the relative distribution of power in the international system. They are regarded as crucial for a state's power and its capacity to provide for its own security. By trying to get control over energy production and transmission (pipelines), states seek to strengthen their relative position in the international system. The possession of traditional energy resources is largely given, thus a determining material fact. As a result, the struggle for power happens mainly in the realm of transmission: States are seen as actors that make strategic calculations to maximize control over pipelines or minimize their dependence. In this setting, stronger states are capable of exploiting their energy strength, while weaker states are forced to bandwagon and to accept unfavourable deals. The power struggle over energy, as a crucial latent source of power, is mainly about geopolitical choices: Pipelines are constructed predominantly as a function of strategic considerations, such as bypassing a particular country to avoid the leverage that transit through its territory would give it.

Energy is seen as an increasingly important asset, creating competitive advantages. It increases the chances of strong energy powers to project their national interests and increase their influence. Many analysts understand energy relations as a zero-sum game: What one party gains is the loss of the contending party.[1] For Paillard, '[e]nergy, already an important security concern, will continue to shape future military and political relations' (Paillard, 2010, p. 65). Keith Smith (2010) analyses energy relations in terms of 'national security risks'. He considers European dependency on Russian energy not only 'a threat to the sovereignty' of the EU's new member states, but also holds it directly responsible for the 'corrosive effect' on transatlantic relations (Smith, 2010, p. 1). Baran writes: 'Russian power and influence is no longer measured in ballistic missile accuracy or bomber production but in miles of pipeline constructed and barrels of oil per day exported, and for Europe, this energy invasion has already begun' (Baran, 2007, p. 131). And further: 'The unjust manipulation or interruption of energy supplies is as much a security threat as military action is...' (Baran, 2007, p. 132).

Increasingly, these views have been challenged (see, for e.g., Goldthau, 2008; Kaveshnikov, 2010; Götz, 2007; Noël, 2008). Several researchers have cast doubt on the one-sided approach, reducing energy to geopolitics, power and security. Several have also nuanced the assumed strength of Russia as an energy giant and the nature of its ambitions. Some of these aspects will be dealt with below. At this point, we want to challenge the Neo-Realist geopolitical approaches because of their reductionism: Energy relations are reduced to issues of power and security, making abstractions of other non-security related aspects and ignoring the complexity of energy relations.

First of all, energy is not per definition and by exclusion a geopolitical and strategic asset. There are two different narratives on energy relations (Aalto and Westphal, 2008; Clingendael, 2004). One is a political narrative, in which the Neo-Realist approach is to be situated. Energy is tied to national interests: Control is seen as enhancing the national interest, dependence is seen as undermining the national interest. The second narrative is an economic narrative. Energy is in the first place a commodity, which is traded on the international market. Economic rules of supply and demand dominate the interaction and the ultimate interest is commercial profit. What we have witnessed is an evolution from a predominantly economic logic in the 1990s to the perception of a predominantly political logic. This gave rise to a variety of terms that were hard to retrieve in both academic and political discourse in the 1990s: energy security, energy diplomacy, energy dependence, the geopolitics of energy, etc. Brzezinski's classic of geopolitics, *The grand chessboard*, illustrates this shift very well (Brzezinski, 1997). Written in 1997, it deals with the geopolitical issues and challenges of the Eurasian continent after the collapse of the Soviet Union. What is considered by many as the geopolitical issue par excellence today, energy, features rather marginally in his analysis. In today's context, it is an issue that few books on post-cold war geostrategic analysis would skip. The same holds for scholarly work on EU-Russia relations in the 1990s. Energy was usually a rather marginal theme, often treated in chapters on economic or trade issues.

Secondly, international energy relations are a complex and multidimensional matter. Most importantly, energy relations and markets have substantially diverging features for different energy products. When EU-Russia energy relations are analysed, the main focus is on oil and gas,[2] and not all analysts acknowledge the crucial difference between the two fields when it comes to both the structure of the market and the political influence or power they may generate (Goldthau, 2008a). In simple terms, oil is traded on international markets and can be transported by several means, of which one is maritime transport by oil tankers. This allows for flexibility in trading. Gas, on the other hand, is mainly transported through pipelines and subject to long-term contracts. The liquefied version of gas, LNG, may also be transported by tankers, but this requires huge investments. As a result, it still takes a rather marginal place in the gas market. This has important implications for the potential to use these energy resources for political purposes. If the transit of gas through pipelines gets interrupted, as the gas spats of 2006 and 2009 have demonstrated, this has important consequences for the economies and households of the countries that are strongly dependent on that transit. At least in theory, shutting down gas pipelines can always be used as a potential threat. Imagine, on the other hand, if Russia were to stop all oil supplies to Europe – the consequences would be much more limited. Europeans would buy their oil elsewhere on the international market. International prices would probably go up, but Russia would be unable to keep the EU in a stranglehold. In other words, while, theoretically, gas can be used as a political weapon by one state against another, this is not the case with oil. The latter can only be used for political purposes if the most important oil producing countries group themselves in a cartel, such as OPEC (Organization of Petroleum Exporting Countries).[3] The rest of our analysis will, therefore, focus mainly on gas relations.

Some further obvious distinctions need to be made, not only between energy producers (supply) and energy consumers (demand), but equally including the interfaces for transmission (transit). Around 78 per cent of the pipelines that bring Russian gas to the EU, for example, transit Ukrainian territory (Aalto and Westphal, 2008, p. 1). This figure, however, is expected to decrease substantially when alternative corridors become operational. Transit is important both from an economic perspective and from a geopolitical perspective. A transit country has an economic interest in pipelines crossing its territory because of the transit taxes it can levy. Secondly, making abstractions of all other factors at this point, they potentially hold political control over pipelines, giving them a degree of leverage or influence.

It is also useful at this point to put things in a historical perspective. No doubt Russia is an energy giant. It is the world leader in oil and gas production. It has the largest proven reserves of gas. This, however, is not a novelty. As Table 1 shows, the

Table 1. Russia's production of oil and gas, 1990–2010

Russia	Production in 1990	Production in 2000	Production in 2010	Share of world production in 1990	Share of world production in 2000	Share of world production in 2010
Natural gas	640 bcm	583 bcm	647 bcm	31%	23.2%	19.7%
Crude oil	524 mt	322 mt	507 mt	16.5%	8.9%	12.9%

Source: Enerdata global energy statistical yearbook 2011 (data based on a wide variety of reliable sources) and own calculations.
Notes: Figures for 1990 for the Russian Republic specifically (not the USSR).
bcm = billion cubic metres.
mt = million tonnes.

absolute production volume of Russian oil and gas today is comparable to that of 1990, while Russia's share in global production is substantially lower than it used to be, in particular for gas.

In the oil sector Russia reached its post-Soviet peak in 2010, with an oil production of 10.15 million barrels a day. This is still below the production level at the end of the 1980s, when the Russian Republic produced 11 million barrels a day out of a total Soviet production of 12 million (Chow, 2004, p. 27).

Interdependence in Energy Relations: A Different Perspective

Challenging Neo-Realist geopolitical approaches, I add an alternative theoretical perspective to understanding EU-Russia energy relations. Keohane and Nye (1989) approach world politics from a perspective of complex interdependence. They define interdependence as 'mutual dependence': 'situations characterized by reciprocal effects among countries or among actors in different countries' (Keohane and Nye, 1989, p. 8). Interdependence produces 'reciprocal (although not necessarily symmetrical) costly effects of transactions' (Keohane and Nye, 1989, p. 9). It is precisely the asymmetry of the interdependence, i.e. the fact that potential costs are higher for one party than the other, that creates a potential source of influence (Keohane and Nye, 1989, p. 10–11).

One of the advantages of this approach is that it departs from the state-centric perspective, taking into account both governments and transnational actors (Keohane and Nye, 1989, p. 18). This is particularly well suited for energy, where major companies are the central actors. First, I introduce Keohane and Nye's distinction between the two dimensions of interdependence: sensitivity and vulnerability. This will serve as a basis to present EU-Russia energy relations in its complexity, rather than in a reductionist form.

When Does Asymmetrical Interdependence Generate Power?

Interdependence creates costly effects, which, in the case of asymmetry, are higher for one party than for the other. Let us assume there are two countries, A and B, with a strong asymmetrical interdependence in favour of A. In the case of energy relations, we can hypothesize country A to be Russia and country B to be an EU member state importing high quantities of Russian natural gas. Interdependence sensitivity then refers to the immediate costly effects for A, i.e. before it had the chance to change its policies. There is a high degree of interdependence sensitivity for country B if interactions with A create considerable costly effects in the short term. In our example, the EU state undergoes immediate costly effects if Russia decides to cut off gas supplies.

Interdependence vulnerability, on the other hand, refers to the costly effects in the longer term, i.e. after country B had the opportunity to change its policies. If country B has no alternatives at its disposal and cannot alter its policy, then it is highly vulnerable. If, however, it has alternative policy options, it will only be sensitive. In our example, if country B can replace Russian gas imports by imports from elsewhere (e.g., because its pipelines are connected to the gas supplies of other states that are not importing from Russia), then it is only sensitive, but not vulnerable. If it does not have these alternatives at its disposal, it is also highly vulnerable. The distinction is important, because vulnerability interdependence adds a strategic dimension (Keohane and Nye, 1989, p. 16).

This has important implications for power. Keohane and Nye look at power, not just as 'control over resources', but as having 'the potential to affect outcomes' (Keohane and Nye, 1989, p. 11). One, the possession of energy resources, does not automatically imply the other, the capacity to influence certain outcomes. The context will be determining, for example the degree to which this is an institutionalized environment or the commitment of the actors involved (Keohane and Nye, 1989, p. 18). 'There is rarely a one-to-one relationship between power measured by any type of resources and power measured by effects on outcomes. Political bargaining is the usual means of translating potential into effects, and a lot is often lost in the translation' (Keohane and Nye, 1989, p. 11).

To represent the complexity of EU-Russia energy relations and their power implications, we can now combine the distinction between sensitivity and vulnerability with the distinction made earlier between supply and demand. This leads to the matrix presented in table 2.

Table 2. Matrix of supply/demand and sensitivity/vulnerability in the energy sector

	Sensitivity	Vulnerability
Demand	Demand sensitivity	Demand vulnerability
Supply	Supply sensitivity	Supply vulnerability

While Russia can be said to have control over resources because of its large oil and gas fields, its potential to affect outcomes in EU-Russia relations will be subject to a double condition. First, the EU should have a high degree of supply vulnerability. In other words, the asymmetrical interdependence between the EU and Russia should be such that it might not only create costly effects for the EU, but also do so in the longer term. This would be the case if the EU is strongly dependent on Russian gas and has no energy alternatives in the longer term were Russia to decide to shut off energy supplies. This is a necessary, but not a sufficient condition. Demand vulnerability should also be minimal on the Russian side. In other words, the costly effects of shutting down gas supplies to the EU should not create high costs for Russia in the longer term. In other words, energy dependence can work in both directions, as 'the user acquires power and influence over the supplier' (Quester, 2007, p. 445).

To what extent are both conditions fulfilled – supply vulnerability on the EU's side and the absence of demand vulnerability on the Russian side?

To answer the first question, we first have to find out how we can measure dependence. If we measure the EU's dependence on Russian gas, what exactly do we measure? Most studies look at the Russian share in EU imports of natural gas. Figures found often refer to a Russian share in EU gas imports of 40 per cent (while, for oil, this is around 30 per cent). Using imports as a criterion indicates that the EU's dependence vulnerability is distributed highly unevenly over the member states (see Eurostat 2010). While some of them import no Russian gas at all, other countries import all their gas from Russia. These are mainly the new member states, who are historically connected to the Russian gas networks (Bulgaria, Romania, Slovakia and the Baltic states), and Finland. On the other side of the spectrum, some EU states do not import any Russian gas at all (Denmark, Ireland, Portugal, Spain, Sweden and the UK). In between, we find countries with varying import dependence rates (for e.g., Poland, 89.5 per cent, Greece, 52.8 per cent, and Germany, 37.1 per cent) (all figures from BP, 2011; comparable figures in other sources). While it could be argued that the countries importing all their gas from Russia are highly sensitive and also considerably vulnerable (as alternatives in the mid-term are lacking), this point is much harder to make for the EU as a whole: Russian gas qualified in 2008 for 31 per cent of the EU's gas imports (figures for 2008, see table 3). If looking at longer term trends, the Russian share in the EU's import of gas has declined drastically. In the late Soviet years, in 1990, the Russian share in EU imports was 55 per cent (based on Eurostat 2011), a lot higher than it is today[4]. Volumes in absolute figures have remained fairly stable. The large share of Russian imports in the early 1990s is mainly the result of a policy in Western Europe to reduce dependence on OPEC oil after the oil crisis.

Stating that Russia provides 31 per cent of the EU's gas imports does not mean, however, that 31 per cent of the gas consumed in the EU is of Russian origin. EU countries, in particular the UK and the Netherlands, produce their own gas. EU production constitutes 40 per cent of its total gas supply. This means that Russian gas imports provide around 25 per cent of EU gas consumption (Noël, 2008, p. 4), a figure that has remained fairly stable for the last one and a half decades. In other words, roughly a quarter of the gas consumed in the EU is Russian. The same goes for some individual countries. Romania, for example, is often presented as a country that is 100 per cent dependent on Russian gas because all its gas imports are Russian. However, it produces 10.6 bcm (billion cubic metres) of gas itself, five times more than it imports from Russia (2.15 bcm). Therefore, its dependence on Russia is very limited.

This can be taken one step further. Instead of measuring the share of Russian gas in the total EU gas supply, we can measure its share in the total primary energy consumption. This share is only around 6.5 per cent and has remained fairly stable since 1990 (Noël, 2008, p. 5; Kaveshnikov, 2010, p. 597). Considering that only gas creates real dependence issues, for the reasons mentioned above, the EU's effective supply dependence on Russian gas has thus been overrated. The three ways of measuring energy dependence are summarized in Table 3.

Reducing energy dependence is a strategic priority for the EU. It has diversified its gas imports since 1995 (Noël, 2008, p. 3) and reinforced its diversification policy in

Table 3. Comparison of Russian share in EU-27 natural gas imports, natural gas consumption and primary energy consumption[4]

	1990	2000	2008
Russian share in EU gas imports	55.3%	40.4%	31.5%
Russian share in EU total gas consumption	30.6%	24.8%	24.9%
Russian share in EU primary energy consumption	6.0%	6.3%	6.8%

Sources: Eurostat 2011.

the different Strategic Reviews of the last decade (European Commission, 2006, 2008, 2010). The EU seeks to diversify both its energy sources (reducing the dependence on oil and gas), the countries of origin and the transit routes (see, *inter alia*, European Commission, 2010). Pipeline projects, such as Nabucco, play an important role in this, but the EU also aims at establishing energy relations with alternative suppliers and transit countries. The latter was one of the main reasons for the EU to reinstate relations with Libya before the Arab Spring and with Belarus before the December 2010 presidential elections. Many member states have similar diversification strategies. Poland, for example, has concluded a deal with Qatar on LNG deliveries of a million tonnes per year to reduce its one-sided dependence on Russian gas (Baxter, 2009). Furthermore, the EU is also working on interconnecting different networks across the borders of member states so that energy shortages in certain member states can be compensated more easily. It aims at establishing 'market coupling' by 2014 (European Commission, 2010, p. 12).

To what extent is the second condition of minimal Russian demand vulnerability fulfilled? The Russian energy strategy till 2030 (Ministry of Energy, 2010) is quite revealing. Energy security is seen as the most important guideline of the strategy.[5] The 'diversification of export energy markets' and 'guaranteed demand' are mentioned as strategic objectives of Russia's foreign energy policy (Ministry of Energy, 2010, p. 57). The Russian Federation also wants to reduce its economic dependence on the energy sector, stating its goal to reduce the share of energy in the GDP by 1.7 times and the share of energy exports in the GDP by three times by 2030 (Ministry of Energy, 2010, p. 19).

The demand dependence of Russia exists both at the general economic level and in the gas sector specifically: 60 per cent of its exports go to the EU; of its gas exports, that is 70 per cent. On the basis of this strong demand dependence in the energy sector, Kaveshnikov goes so far as to state that 'the EU is a monopolistic client to a greater extent than Russia is a monopolistic supplier' (Kaveshnikov, 2010, p. 598). Immediate alternatives for this export are lacking. Most Russian pipeline projects go West. Russia is delivering oil to the markets in the Far East through its Eastern Siberia-Pacific Ocean pipeline, with a total capacity of 80 million tonnes of oil per year (Ministry of Energy, 2010, p. 56). A parallel gas pipeline is still under construction. Overall, the volumes remain far below those of the dense pipeline network with Europe.

Russia has a lot to lose if it risks its reputation as a credible supplier. The gas spats in 2006 and 2009 between Russia and Ukraine (though complicated in terms of responsibility) and the shock effect they caused in the EU made many Russian decision-makers more aware of the importance of being perceived as a reliable energy supplier. As a result, the EU and Russia signed a memorandum on an Early Warning Mechanism in case of disruptions of energy supplies.[6] The mechanism was activated when Russia reduced its gas deliveries to Belarus in June 2010. According to Energy Commissioner Oettinger, it has functioned fairly well.[7]

When is Asymmetrical Interdependence a Security Threat?

For Keohane and Nye, 'contemporary world politics is not a seamless web, it is a tapestry of diverse relationships' (Keohane and Nye, 1989, p. 4). In other words, there is a complex web of diverse relations of interdependence between the EU and Russia with asymmetries going in different directions. The hierarchy of issues is not given.[8] This implies a possibility to move from one power resource or one set of interdependence to another. If, in our example above, country B (being vulnerable in the energy sector) is militarily and economically superior to country A (being vulnerable in the military and economic sector), it may always have the possibility to shift to one of those power resources, even if it implies higher costs. For Keohane and Nye (1989, p. 17), this shift is most likely to happen 'as the interests at stake become more important' and when the incongruity between different dimensions of interdependence (military, economic, energy, etc.) is substantial. In the most simple terms, what this implies for our analysis is that we cannot reduce EU-Russia power relations to energy asymmetries only. Other contexts and other asymmetrical interdependences should equally be taken into account, even if they do not appear as the field in which 'power' is most visible at a given time.

Forms of asymmetrical interdependence between the EU and Russia exist in different contexts, with the imbalance often in favour of the EU. In economic terms, the EU's economy is 15 times bigger than that of Russia. Only in 2007 did Russia manage to reach the production levels it had at the time the Soviet Union collapsed (Sakwa, 2008, p. 246). Even if the Russian economy has been thriving on rising energy prices after 2000, it has not managed to become an important global economic player beyond the energy sector and it is certainly not the BRIC or emerging economy some have taken it for. As Macfarlane argues: 'Russia is more properly seen as a state that has recently experienced substantial damage and is attempting to stop the bleeding' (Macfarlane, 2006: 43).

Even in the military field, though Russia is still one of the world's leading nuclear powers, its military spending is far behind that of the West. While the US stands for around 46 per cent of global military spending, Russia spends around 3 per cent only (SIPRI, 2008). The EU-27 combined military budgets account for 21 per cent of global military expenditure, still seven times higher than that of Russia. These figures are nothing but selective and isolated indicators. The point is that we simply cannot make abstractions of them when auditing power relations between the EU and Russia. Energy is definitely not the only issue determining Russia's power and capacity to influence the international agenda. There is no such a thing as an automatic spill-over from the asymmetries in the energy relationship to other aspects of the power relationship.

Finally, speaking about Russia using energy for leverage or as a political weapon assumes that there is a clear political objective and that energy asymmetries are used to reach this objective. While political objectives can be discerned in Russia's energy policy towards the post-Soviet space (e.g., as in the case of the deal made with Ukraine in 2010), this point is hard to make in the case of relations with the EU. If the gas spats of 2006 and 2009 are seen as aimed against EU countries, as some analysts have perceived it, the question still needs to be answered: What exactly does Russia want to obtain from the West. As Hadfield states: 'On its own, Russian energy dominance is a *necessary* but insufficient explanation for alleging that energy is a tool of Russian foreign policy. The addition of an external *political* goal however represents a *sufficient* factor' (Hadfield, 2008, p. 327). Moreover, energy is a blunt weapon (Goldthau,

2008b). Like a nuclear weapon, it can at the most act as a deterrent, but it is very impractical to achieve precise political targets. If Russia wants to see a change in the Commission's Third Energy Package, to allow more favourable conditions for Russian energy companies to enter the Single Market, it is unlikely it will reach that objective by cutting off gas supplies altogether. The weapon would be in no proportion to the objective, but there is also no guarantee that it would be effective in reaching this goal. Rather, it would undermine Russia's reputation as a reliable energy supplier, which would have disastrous long-term effects for its energy-dependent economy.

How Energy Came to be Perceived as a Geopolitical Issue

What then can explain the shift in our thinking on EU-Russia energy relations from a dominant economic to a geopolitical story? Why did we start to perceive excessive EU dependence on Russian energy as a determining feature of their relations? How did energy make it to the top of the security agenda, with Russia's energy power being perceived as an increasing threat to the EU?

First of all, if we compare the 1990s and the first decade of the new millennium, we will see that the global energy market has undergone profound change. Energy consumption has increased dramatically. Booming economies, like the Chinese one, have tried to gain access to energy resources in different parts of the world. As a result, fears about scarcity of traditional energy resources have increased. Energy prices have risen dramatically from less than US $20 per barrel throughout the 1990s to around US $100 per barrel in 2008. In 2010, oil prices recovered from the downfall during the financial crisis and were again at around US$ 80 (all figures BP, 2011). Rising energy prices have no doubt strengthened Russia's economic position. It is estimated that between one-third and two-fifths of Russia's economic growth is due to rising energy prices (Sakwa, 2008, p. 247). No doubt this has contributed to more assertive foreign policy rhetoric in Putin's second term as President. In the first place, however, Russia has used this stronger position vis-à-vis Europe to negotiate better conditions for its own energy companies. This was, for example, clearly visible in the Sakhalin II conflict. Under the pretext of environmental concerns, Western energy companies were stripped of their licences, leading to major indignation in the Western press. What got less attention is the fact that, afterwards, new contracts were signed, most of them with the same companies. Royal Dutch Shell, for example, saw its share reduced to the advantage of Gazprom, but still holds a 40 per cent share in the Sakhalin II project. What the Russian government wanted to achieve was primordially a stronger position for its own energy companies and more favourable commercial conditions for Western investments.

A second factor that has altered energy relations between Russia and the EU was the enlargement of the latter. With former communist states and satellites of the Soviet Union joining the EU in 2004 and 2007, two things changed. Firstly, the energy dependence of the EU increased, as demonstrated above. Secondly, relations between the EU and Russia soured over the enlargement. Several of the new member states were among the more vocal supporters of a tougher stance on Russia. Many of their bilateral issues with Russia got uploaded onto the European agenda. It is interesting to note here that there is no positive correlation between energy dependence on Russia and the willingness to engage pragmatically with Russia. As mentioned earlier, several of the new member states are strongly dependent on the import of Russian gas. This, however, has not stopped them from calling for a tougher EU policy.

Furthermore, a long list of events undermined the trust between the EU and Russia and led to a mini escalation of suspicion. These events included the deprivatization of oil company Yukos (demonstrating the politicized and selective use of the judicial apparatus), the growing role of the Russian state in the energy sector, expelling Western companies from the Sakhalin II and Kovykta projects, the use of price differentiation in the post-Soviet space, Russian companies buying themselves into the energy sectors of different states and the gas spats between Russia and Ukraine in 2006 and 2009 – the latter having a tremendous psychological effect on policy-makers in the EU. All these events reinforced the perception that Russia was back and willing to play the energy card to reinforce its power position.

The effects of a changing global energy market and of the EU enlargement are definitely not to be underestimated. Yet, there may be even more fundamental reasons explaining the dramatic shift in the perception of energy relations. We will take a thin Constructivist perspective here (Fierke, 2007), integrating both material factors and social processes. Changing material circumstances – such as the rising energy prices – play a role, but they do not come to us as an objective fact. They always require social mediation and interpretation. In other words, the material facts are not given, but get a particular meaning in a social process, in a context of meanings (Wendt, 1992). When looking at the social contexts determining energy-related policy-making in Russia and the EU, I will single out three factors of importance. These three factors help us to understand the discrepancy between the enormous rise in the 'social' understanding of energy dependence and the actual change in 'material' energy dependence.

First, after the end of the cold war, we saw the return of a geopolitical logic creeping in silently in the 1990s, before becoming dominant in the next decade. The decision of the Clinton administration to build the pipeline linking the energy-rich Caspian Sea basin with the Mediterranean can be seen as a milestone in the return of geopolitics on the energy agenda. This Baku-Tbilisi-Ceyhan (BTC) pipeline served a clear geopolitical purpose. The choice for this all but evident route served one central purpose: It was meant to transport oil from the Caspian Sea basin to the West bypassing the territories of two countries, Iran and Russia (Joseph, 1999, p. 13; Heslin, 1997). As an advisor to Clinton stated, the objective was to prevent either of those countries obtaining dominant control over the energy resources of the Caspian (Heslin, 1997). Of course, this geopolitical logic was not entirely new. Back in the Soviet days, the geopolitical importance of pipelines had already become a major issue. In the early 1980s, the United States imposed sanctions on the export of oil and gas equipment to the Soviet Union, trying to prevent the construction of the Euro-Siberian gas pipeline. While West European countries were seeking ways to reduce their dependence on OPEC oil, the Reagan administration in the US feared that this would make its European NATO allies too dependent on Soviet gas. The sanctions threatened to hit European companies hard and led to a rift between the NATO allies until the US lifted the sanctions at the end of 1982 (Smeenk, 2010, pp.

127–128). Many geopolitically inspired projects on both sides would follow in the slipstream of the BTC pipeline.

The point here is that geopolitical considerations followed not so much from compelling material circumstances (in the mid-1990s, energy scarcity and rising prices were not a prevalent issue), but from a larger context of understanding, from a logic of appropriateness resistant to change. Within this context, Russia was still very much mistrusted and the post-Soviet space was increasingly seen as an area of competing national interests. The Russian Ambassador to the EU, Chizhov, referred to this as a 'phantom pain of the past'[9] of the West vis-à-vis Russia. In his view, the policy of the West continues to be driven by fears and images of the threat of the Soviet Union, even if the country itself disappeared a long time ago.

Secondly, Russia's economic growth and regained assertiveness after 2000 affected its relations with the EU and changed attitudes. In the 1990s, Russia was a strongly weakened player and the EU's policy was to a large extent aimed at exporting EU rules and norms to the post-communist country. The relations between them had a strong EU-centric bias. In the energy field, this is reflected in the Energy Charter Treaty signed in 1994, which seeks to introduce a number of neoliberal principles in the energy market as favoured by the EU. The Treaty thus reflected both Russia's weakness and the EU's preference to align international energy agreements with internal market rules (European Commission, 2010, p. 18). While Russia was willing to make concessions in the 1990s, this was no longer the case in the first decade of the new millennium, when it increasingly sought recognition as an equal partner of the EU. Its reluctance to accept the EU's neoliberal approach to the energy market resulted in Russia's refusal to ratify the Energy Charter Treaty, which it had signed in 1994. The main bone of contention was the so-called Transit Protocol of this Treaty, which introduced market principles for transit. This was at loggerheads with the trend under Putin's Presidency to consider the energy sector, in particular pipelines, as a sector of strategic importance, requiring a certain degree of control by the state. This policy went hand in hand with an attempt to reinstate state control of some sort in the energy sector. In particular in the oil sector, throughout the 1990s, Russia had followed a predominantly liberal model. With the Yukos affair and the deprivatization of part of the oil industry, this definitely came to an end. It allowed the Kremlin to get better control of strategic energy assets, through more 'reliable' companies such as Rosneft. Sakwa, however, warns that this deprivatization should not be understood as a renationalization of the energy sector. The state does not fully own the energy companies, nor does it manage the energy sector in its entirety. Rather, it gains control over the energy sector, which is considered to be so important that it cannot be left to pure market forces. As a result, corporate autonomy is reduced. Rather than speaking of nationalization or a state economy, Sakwa suggests that this is '"bureaucratic capitalism", a variant of ordo-liberalism ..., where property rights were fungible, seeping between the state and private owners, in an informal assertion of regime power over the economy' (Sakwa, 2011, p. 149).

This takes us to a third factor explaining why energy is often a source of conflict between both players. What is often seen as a clash of paradigms – the neoliberal paradigm of the EU and the state-interventionist paradigm of Russia – is maybe not so much a matter of ideological preferences, nor a clash between a norm-based and an interest-based approach. Rather, it is the result of diverging economic interests, following from the substantially different nature of the energy markets on both sides (Kaveshnikov, 2010, p. 598). The EU projects its position as energy consumer onto the international stage. It seeks to change the rules of the international trade regime to create a 'consumer market' with maximal competition between the suppliers, leading to lower energy prices. Russia, however, seeks to maintain the current 'producer market', which keeps the energy suppliers in control, for example, through long-term contracts and separate investment deals. As Kaveshnikov argues convincingly, '[T]hese differences are by no means rooted in diverging political positions. On the contrary, political differences logically evolve out of actual dissimilarities of the Russian and European energy sectors' (Kaveshnikov, 2010, p. 599). He points out that 'energy security cannot be a spontaneous result of market self-regulation' (Kaveshnikov, 2010, p. 590).

Thus, at the heart of the energy 'conflict' are diverging economic interests. All the countries involved, the EU member states, Russia and the transit countries, have primordially commercial interests and most concerns and conflicts can be explained from this perspective. If we look at the EU-Russia agenda, the predominant concerns have to do with access to markets. The EU is concerned about its access to the production market in Russia and fears that legal uncertainty will undermine the investment climate. Russia is equally concerned about access to the EU's internal market. The bone of contention here is the so-called 'reciprocity clause' proposed in the Commission's Third Energy Package. The original version of the clause would prevent energy companies from third countries from controlling distribution networks in the EU unless they grant EU companies equal access to their markets, hence a reciprocity clause. The provision was mainly seen as aimed at Russian companies, fearing that they would get too much of a grip on the EU market. For this reason, it was nicknamed the 'Gazprom clause'. At the EU-Russia summit of October 2007, Putin stated that the Gazprom clause was misconceived, as EU investments in Russia were 10 times those of Russia in the EU (Youngs, 2009, p. 88) The final version of the reciprocity clause was eventually watered down, allowing member states to conclude a bilateral political agreement instead of an EU-endorsed one. This leaves the member states with full discretion to negotiate investment clauses with Russia. The weakening of the clause symbolizes the dividedness of the EU in its energy relations with Russia. Again, if the EU appears as the weaker player in its energy relations with Russia, it has more to do with this internal dividedness than with real dependence.

Conclusion

While European dependence on Russian energy is lower today than it was in the early 1990s, we have moved from a predominantly economic understanding of EU-Russia energy relations to one in terms of a power struggle, geopolitical competition and security. This article sought to explain this paradox. It challenged the dominant Neo-Realist geopolitical argument and its reductionist approach. An alternative theoretical perspective was used to assess to what extent asymmetries in EU-Russia relations may generate power and pose security threats. On the basis of Keohane and Nye's interdependence theory, an analysis was made of interdependence sensitivity and vulnerability for both supply and demand in the natural gas market. Drawing on this theory, we indicated two key conditions that have to be fulfilled if we expect asymmetrical interdependence to generate an uneven power relationship. First, the EU has to be strongly dependent on Russian gas. This was found to be the case to a limited extent only. The supply vulnerability of the EU is fairly high if we measure it in terms of Russia's share in gas imports, but it is much lower when measured as its share in the total gas supply and small when measured in terms of its share in the EU's primary energy consumption. Moreover, EU dependence was found to be unevenly distributed over different member states, with mainly some of the new member states and Finland being strongly dependent. The second condition is limited Russian dependence on demand from the EU. It was found that Russia displays considerable demand vulnerability, exporting most of its gas to the EU. Furthermore, one cannot make abstractions of the other dimensions of the EU-Russia relations, where diverse asymmetrical forms of interdependence exist, more often in favour of the EU-27 than not.

Why we have moved to a geopolitical logic in energy relations while real dependence has not increased, was explained by both material and social changes. First of all, the changes in the global energy market and the EU enlargement had a profound effect. Secondly, perceptions have been affected by the return of a geopolitical logic in energy matters fed by distrust surviving the end of the cold war, by Russia's stronger position and growing assertiveness and by the different nature of the EU and Russian energy markets, fostering conflicting perceptions of their economic interests.

In conclusion, Russia's energy leverage over the EU is highly overrated. One could even state that if the EU was not divided, it would not find itself in a weaker position. Against common sense opinion, EU-Russia energy relations are not about geopolitics, security and the struggle for power. Geopolitical considerations definitely play a role, but the first concerns of the actors involved are of an economic nature: commercial profits, low energy prices, lucrative contracts, etc. Where geopolitical calculations are at risk of becoming dominant, this is often the result of a self-fulfilling prophecy. How this self-fulfilling prophecy works is illustrated very well by the recommendations of an influential report on energy (Clingendael, 2004). The report states that the energy world has changed: It has moved away from a market logic to a geopolitical 'logic of empires'. It recommends that the EU adapts to this logic and makes energy an integral part of its Common Foreign and Security Policy (CFSP), using the tools of 'prevention, deterrence, containment and crisis management' (Clingendael, 2004, p. 26). Self-evidently, this reinforces a logic where energy issues predominantly get a meaning of geopolitical competition: If all actors believe energy relations are about geopolitical gains and see their national interests in this light, the competition will eventually become geopolitical.

Notes

[1] Similar security-related views appear selectively in political discourse. Energy security, for example, made it to the NATO agenda (see Gallis, 2007). In a speech in 2008, Secretary-General de Hoop Scheffer said: 'Energy security is too important to be left only to market mechanisms. ... NATO can and should act as a catalyst in persuading our countries to take a more strategic look at energy security and to develop a more collective approach' (de Hoop Scheffer, 2008).

² Also, this article is limited to the role of gas and (to a lesser extent) oil in EU-Russia relations, as they constitute most of the trade in energy resources.
³ Russia, though one of the world's leading oil producers, is not a member of OPEC.
⁴ Noël 2008 mentions a figure of 75 per cent for 1990, but this figure was not confirmed by other sources (Eurostat 2011, Smeenk 2010). Note on the statistics: There is considerable divergence among the energy statistics, even within the Eurostat data. Longer term comparisons (1990–2010) are difficult because of changes on the supply side (demise of the USSR) and the demand side (EU enlarging from 12 to 15 to 24 to 27 members). Many studies and databases do not specify clearly how they define actors (for example is the EU in 1990 counted as the 12 member states or is this a simulation for the 27 states that now form the EU). This explains some divergences in statistics. Table 3 in this article is based on data for all 27 states, currently members of the EU, and for the Russian Federation as separate entity (not the Soviet Union).
⁵ 'Energy security is the country's security, that of its citizens, society, state and economy from the threats to reliable supply of fuel and energy. These threats are determined by external (geopolitical, macroeconomic, market) factors, as well as by the condition and operation of the country's energy sector' (Ministry of Energy, 2010, p. 28).
⁶ See the full text of the memorandum on: http://ec.europa.eu/energy/international/bilateral_cooperation/russia/doc/reports/2009_11_16_ewm_signed_en.pdf [Accessed 15 June 2011].
⁷ Written answer to a parliamentary question, 16 August 2010: http://www.europarl.europa.eu/sides/getAllAnswers.do?reference=E-2010-4931&language=EN [Accessed 15 June 2011].
⁸ Keohane and Nye indicate that military force may be more dominant than forms of economic interdependence, but that it is very costly and will only be used in extreme circumstances (Keohane and Nye, 1989, p. 16–17).
⁹ V. Chizhov, Permanent Representative of the Russian Federation to the EU, lecture at BSIS, 16 February 2011.

References

Aalto, P., and Westphal, K., 2008. Introduction. In: P. Aalto, ed. *The EU-Russia energy dialogue: Securing Europe's future energy supply*. Aldershot: Ashgate, pp. 23–42.

Baran, Z., 2007. EU energy security: Time to end Russian leverage. *The Washington quarterly*, 30 (4), 131–144.

Baxter, K., 2009. Qatar to supply LNG to Poland [online]. Available from: http://www.arabianoiland gas.com/article-5300-qatar_to_supply_lng_to_poland/ [Accessed 21 June 2011].

BP, 2011. Statistical review of world energy 2011: Workbook of historical data from 1965–2010 [online]. http://www.bp.com/sectionbodycopy.do?categoryId=7500&contentId=7068481 [Accessed 15 June 2011].

Bzrezinski, Z., 1997. *The grand chessboard: American primacy and its geostrategic imperatives*. New York, NY: Basic Books.

Chow, E., 2004. Russian pipelines: Back to the future? *Georgetown journal of international affairs*, 27 (5), 27–33.

Clingendael International Energy Programme 2004. *Study on energy supply security and geopolitics: Final report*. The Hague: Clingendael.

De Hoop Scheffer, J., 2008. Energy security in the 21st century. Keynote speech at the *Economist* Energy Security Dinner [online], 23 October London. Available from: http://www.nato.int/docu/speech/2008/s081023b.html [Accessed 3 March 2010].

DG Energy and Transport, 2011. EU energy in figures 2010 [online]. Available from: http://ec.europa.eu/energy/publications/doc/statistics/part_2_energy_pocket_book_2010.pdf [Accessed 15 June 2011].

Enerdata, 2011. *Global energy statistical yearbook* [online]. Available from: http://yearbook.enerdata.net/ [Accessed 15 June 2011].

European Commission, 2006. *Green Paper: A European strategy for sustainable, competitive and secure energy*, COM (06)105.

European Commission, 2008. *Communication from the Commission to the European Parliament, the Council, the European Economic and Social Committee and the Committee of the Regions – Second Strategic Energy Review: An EU energy security and solidarity action plan*, COM (08)781, final.

European Commission, 2010. *Energy 2020: A strategy for competitive, sustainable and secure energy. Communication from the Commission to the European Parliament, the Council, the European Economic and Social Committee and the Committee of the Regions*, COM (10)639, final.

Eurostat, 2010. Energy yearly statistics, 2008 [online]. Available from: http://epp.eurostat.ec.europa.eu/cache/ITY_OFFPUB/KS-PC-10-001/EN/KS-PC-10-001-EN.PDF [Accessed 15 June 2011].

Eurostat, 2011. New Cronos (Data downloaded: 10 March 2011). ESDS International, University of Manchester. DOI: 10.5257/eurostat/nc/2011-03-10 [Accessed 28 October 2011].

Fierke, K.M., 2007. Constructivism. In: T. Dunne, M. Kurki and S. Smith, eds. *International relations theory: Discipline and diversity*. Oxford University Press, 166–184.

Gallis, P., 2007. NATO and Energy Security, *CRS Report for Congress* (Washington: Congressional Research Service, RS22409, 15 August 2007), see: http://www.usembassy.it/pdf/other/RS22409.pdf (Accessed 3 March 2010).

Goldthau, A., 2008a. Resurgent Russia: Rethinking Russia Inc. *Policy review*, 147 (2008), 53–63.

Goldthau, A., 2008b. Russia's energy weapon is a fiction. *Europe's world* [online], Spring 2008. Available from: http://www.europesworld.org [Accessed 3 March 2010].

Götz, R., 2007. Russian gas and European energy security. SWP Research Paper No. 10.

Hadfield, A., 2008. Energy and foreign policy: EU-Russia energy dynamics. In: S. Smith, A. Hadfield and T. Dunne, eds. *Foreign policy: Theories, actors, cases*. Oxford University Press, 321–338.

Heslin, S., 1997. The new pipelines politics. *The New York Times*, 10 November. Available from: http://chss.montclair.edu/english/furr/pol/wtc/heslinnwpipelinepols.html [Accessed 3 March 2010].

Joseph, J., 1999. Pipeline diplomacy: The Clinton administration's fight for Baku-Ceyhan. WWS Case Study 1/99 [online]. Available from: http://wws.princeton.edu/research/cases/pipeline.pdf [Accessed 21 June 2011].

Kaveshnikov, N., 2010. The issue of energy security in relations between Russia and the European Union. *European security*, 19 (4), 585–605.

Keohane, R., and Nye, J., 1989/1977. *Power and interdependence*. New York, NY: Harper Collins.

Macfarlane, S., 2006. The 'R' in BRICs: Is Russia an emerging power? *International affairs*, 82 (1), 41–57.

Mearsheimer, J., 2007. Structural realism. In: T. Dunne, M. Kurki and S. Smith, eds. *International relations theory: Discipline and diversity*. Oxford University Press, 71–88.

Ministry of Energy of the Russian Federation, 2010., Energy strategy of Russia for the period up to 2030. Approved by Decree No. 1715-r of the Government of the Russian Federation, 13 November 2009. Moscow: Institute of Energy Strategy.

Noël, P., 2008. Beyond dependence: How to deal with Russian gas. Policy Brief ECFR/09.

Paillard, C.A., 2010. Russia and Europe's mutual energy dependence. *Journal of international affairs*, 63 (2), 65–84.

Quester, G., 2007. Energy dependence and power: Some paradoxes. *Demokratizatsiya*, 15 (4), 445–453.

Sakwa, R., 2008. New cold war or twenty years' crisis? Russia and international politics. *International affairs*, 84 (2), 241–267.

Sakwa, R., 2011. *The crisis of Russian democracy: The dual state, factionalism and the Medvedev succession*. Cambridge University Press.

SIPRI, 2008. Summary. *SIPRI Yearbook 2008* [online]. Available from: http://yearbook2008.sipri.org/files/SIPRIYB08summary.pdf [Accessed 3 March 2010].

Smeenk, T., 2010. *Russian gas for Europe: Creating access and choice*. Den Haag: Clingendael International Energy Programme.

Smith, K., 2010. *Russia-Europe energy relations: Implications for US policy* [online]. Centre for Strategic and International Studies. Available from: http://csis.org/publication/russia-europe-energy-relations [Accessed 21 June 2011].

Waltz, K., 1979. *Theory of international politics*. New York, NY: Addison Wesley.

Wendt, A.E., 1992. Anarchy is what states make of it: The social construction of power politics. *International organisation*, 46 (2), 391–425.

Youngs, R., 2009. *Energy security: Europe's new foreign policy challenge*. London: Routledge.

Index

Page numbers in *Italics* represent tables.
Page numbers followed by n represent endnotes.

Aceh 56
Action Plans 66–9, 87–8; EU-Libya 87
actorness concept 117–28, *120*, *126*
actors: non-state 48–52, 89
Afghanistan 105
Africa 5, 60–79, 107, 123; North Africa 74, 96; sub-Saharan 68
African Union (AU) 94
Agadir Agreement 64
Alliance of Liberals and Democrats for Europe (ALDE) 38; rapporteur 40
Alvaro, A. 40
Amsterdam Treaty 83
Anderson, R. 54
Arab League 94
Arab Maghreb Union 87
Arab Spring 7, 60–79, 140
Area of Freedom Security and Justice (AFSJ) 32, 33, 83–4; Strategy for the external dimension 83
Armenia 107
Article 29 Working Party 36
Ashton, C. 64, 74, 104, 127
Asia 56
Assembly of the Western European Union 23
Association Agreement 86–7, 94
Attinà, F. 55
authoritarianism 62–3, 66, 69, 76, 76n, 80–101
autocratic regimes 80–101
Azerbaijan 107

Baku-Tbilisi-Ceyhan (BTC) pipeline 143–4
Baltics 106
Baran, Z. 135
Barcelona Process 63–5, 67–8, 70, 86–7, 94
Barroso, J. 74
Bauer, P. 7, 60–79
Belarus 7, 140; coercive conditionality 88–93, 96; EU foreign policy 80–101; Interim Trade Agreement 85; opposition protests 82; passive leverage failure 89–90; population 88–91, 97; post Cold War 85–6; pragmatic engagement 90–1; presidential elections (2010) 93–4, 97–8, 140, *see also* Union of Soviet Socialist Republics (USSR)
Belarusian government 88–91, 93, 96–7
Belarusian Oblast 90
Belgium 34
Berlin 85, 112
Biden, Vice-President J. 39
Bigo, D. 52
Black Sea fleet 107
Black Sea Synergy 111
Bosse, G. 7, 80–101
Bourdieu, P. 14
Bretherton, C.: and Vogler, J. 119
Britain 106, 124, 139
Brussels 13, 18, 91, 104, 109, 129
Brzezinski, Z. 135
Bures, O. 31
Bush, President George W. 39, 54
Busuttil, S. 41
Buzan, B. 51

Canadian government 4
Caporaso, J.: and Jupille, J. 119
Casier, T. 8, 133–48
Caspian Sea Basin 143
chemical biological radiological and nuclear (CBRN) weapons 7–8
CBRN weapons non-proliferation 117–32, *120*; international security actor 119–25; Lisbon Treaty reforms 125–8
Central and Eastern European (CEE) countries 50, 80–1, 106, 110–12
Cercone, M. 95
Chernobyl catastrophe 89
China 107, 142
Chizhov, Ambassador V. 144
Chouala, Y. 14
Christiansen, T. 22
Christou, G. 107, 110
Committee on Civil Liberties, Justice and Home Affairs (LIBE) 32–3, 39–40

INDEX

civil society 24–6, 47, 51, 64, 74–5, 84; Belarus 89; Egypt 68
Committee for Civilian Aspects of Crisis Management (CIVCOM) 13, 18, 22
Clinton, Hillary 35
Clinton, President William 'Bill' 143
Cold War 8, 51–3, 57, 81, 85–6, 96, 98n, 121, 133, 143, 146
Common Foreign and Security Policy (CFSP) 2, 6, 117–18, 120–1, *120*, 127, 129, 146; budget 123, 128; and EC 11–29
Common Security and Defence Policy (CSDP) 12–29, 102–3, 108; epistemic communities 13
Commonwealth of Independent States (CIS) 118
community instruments 14–16, 22, 25
comprehensive security 51–2
conflict 4, 51, 56, 64; prevention and methods 14, 16–20, 64
Conflict Prevention Partnership (CPP) 19
Congo: Democratic Republic of Congo (DRC) 19
Cooperation for Security and Defence Research framework 16, 23
Copenhagen School 51
corruption: elections (Egypt) 76; public service 50–1
Council of Ministers 86–7
Council Secretariat *120*, 121–2, 125, 128
Country Reports 88
Country Strategy Paper 66
crisis response 17–20, 23
cross-border cooperation (CBC) programmes 90

Darfur 19
data protection 30–46; data retention 33–4; institutional conflicts 32–4; Passenger Name Record (PNR) Agreements 30–3, 39, 41
Data Protection Directive (DPD) 32
Data Retention Directive (DRD) 33–4, 41
decision-making procedures 13, 18, 40, 124; non-state actors 49
deep democracy concept 74
defence market 20–1
Defence Package 12, 15–16, 20–1, 26
Defence and Procurement Directive 21
Deffrennes, M. 124
democracy 49, 56; maximalist / minimalist definition 83–4; reforms 88, 91
democracy clause 83
democracy promotion 86–8, 96–8, 108
Democratic Republic of Congo (DRC) 19
democratization 7; autocratic regimes 80–101; conditionality 84–5, 88–93, 96–7;
contagion 84, 88; convergence 84, 90; Egypt 60–79
Directorate Generals (DGs) 16, 22; of Development 14; External Relations (DG Relex) 13, 15, 17–18, 22, 90, 125, 128
drug strategy 53
drug trafficking 53–4
Drugs Action Plans 53
drugs (illegal): Bureau of International Narcotics and Law Enforcement Affairs (INL) 54; European Monitoring Centre for Drugs and Drug Addiction 53
Druzbha pipeline 91
Dura, G. 88

Eastern enlargement 15, 63–5, 80, 83, 142–3, 146
Eastern Europe 80–1, 106, *see also* Belarus
Eastern Neighbourhood: EU Membership 108–9; EU's impact 109–12; regional conflicts 112
Eastern Partnership (EaP) 81–2, 93–4, 105, 108–9, 111–12; Belarus 93–4
Eastern Siberia-Pacific Ocean pipeline 140
Egypt 7, 67–76, 128; democracy movement 76; economy 67–71; energy strategy 68; ENP Action Plan 66–9; Ministry of Foreign Affairs 68; political elite 65–6, 76; politics 62–3, 75–6; Spring 2011 revolution 7
Egypt Country Strategy Paper (2007–13) 70–4
Egyptian Foreign Ministry 65, 68–9
Egyptian government 68–9, 75
Egyptian transition and ENP 60–79; analytical framework 61–4; ENP's background 64–6; policy components and instruments 67–74; recent developments 74–6, *see also* European Neighbourhood Policy (ENP)
energy 8, 77n, 89, 91–2, 96, 102–4, 107, 133–48, *139*; Early Warning Mechanism 140; European Atomic Energy Agency 121; Libya 94–5; market 133–48; Neo-Realist approach 133, 135, 137, 145; OPEC 136, 139, 143; power 133–48; prices 142–3; Russia 103–4, 106, 108–9, 133–48; Third Energy Package 142, 145, *see also* gas; oil; Russian energy leverage
Energy Charter Treaty (1994) 144
Energy Policy for Europe 91
Euro-Siberian gas pipeline 143
Europe Aid Cooperation Office 14
EuropeAid 18, 22
European Aeronautic Defence and Space (EADS) 24
European Arrest Warrant (EAW) 32

INDEX

European Atomic Energy Agency 121
European Bank for Reconstruction 104
European Commission (EC) 2–3, 5–8, 11–29, 32, 36, 42, 63–70, 74–5, 82, 86–97, 104–7, 110–13, 121–7; Article 29 Working Party 36; Belarus *Non-Paper* 88, 90, 93; *European defence industrial and market issues* 20; *A European security research and innovation agenda* 15; Third Energy Package 142, 145
European Commission (security position) 11–29; actors interface 21–5; conflict prevention 17–20; defence procurement 20–1; internal and external security connections 25; multidimensional role 14–21; relations configuration 12–14; security research 15–16
European Community 85, 118, 121–2, 126
European Council 12–13, 21–5, 30–4, 37–42, 81–91, 112, 121–7; President 128; *A secure Europe in a better world* 53
European Data Protection Supervisor (EDPS) 36, 38
European Defence Agency (EDA) 16, 23
European Defence Equipment 20
European Defence Technological and Industrial Base (EDTIB) 23
European External Action Service (EEAS) 26, 122–3, 125, *126*, 127–9
European Instrument for Democracy and Human Rights (EIDHR) 89
European integration 3, 11, 52, 65, 112
European Investment Bank 104
European Mediterranean Partnership (EMP) 60–79, 81–2, 86
European Monitoring Centre for Drugs and Drug Addiction 53
European Neighbourhood Policy (ENP) 5, 7, 14, 81–101, 105, 107–12; background 64–6; Egyptian revolution (2011) 60–79; Progress Reports 69–70, 75; Strategy Paper (2004) 86, 90, *see also* Egyptian transition and ENP
European Neighbourhood Policy Instrument (ENPI) 66, 70, 87, 89–90, 94, 97; Memorandum of Understanding 70
European Parliament (EP) 3, 12, 17, 21, 23, 25, 87, 105, 112; institutional tools 40–1; international agreements power 32; Napolitano Report (2003) 87, *see also* data protection
European People's Party (EPP) 38–9
European Political Cooperation (EPC) 120–1
European Security and Defence Policy (ESDP) *see* Common Security and Defence Policy (CSDP)
European Security Research Advisory Board (ESRAB) 15
European Security Research and Innovation Forum (ESRIF) 16
European Security Research Programme (ESRP) 12, 15–16, 26
European Security Strategy (ESS) 3, 5, 17, 20, 25–6, 53, 55–6, 117–18, 128–9
European Security and Supranational Governance Conference 1–2
European Transparency Initiative 24
European Union Simulation (EUSIM) 1–2
Europol 37; Joint Supervisory Board (JSB) 38, 41
External Relations Council 93

Ferrero-Waldner, B. 109
financial aid 63, 66, 70–1
financial crisis 21, 107, 142
Finland 139, 146
Foreign Affairs Council 94, 125
Foreign Ministers 87
foreign policy 60–116, 125; Belarus and Libya post Cold War 85–6; competing policies 83–5; institutionalizing partnership 93–6; paradigm shifts 80–101; practicing neighbourhood relations 89–93; rhetoric differences 86–9
France 96, 102–6, 109, 111, 113, 129
Free Trade Area 94
FRONTEX 68, 92
Füle, S. 74, 94–5, 113

G8 Global Partnership 125–6
Gaddafi, Colonel Muammar 7, 81–2, 85, 91, 93–8
gas 92, 106, 112, 133–48, *136*; Euro-Siberian gas pipeline 143; imports (member states) 138–40, 143; LNG 136, 140; market 136, 138–40, *139*; North Stream project 105; Russia 133–48; Russia-Ukraine gas row (2006) 91, *see also* energy; oil
Gazprom 105, 142, 145
Geithner, T. 35
geopolitics 134–7, 142–6
Georgia 104, 106–7, 109
Germany 68, 77n, 102–6, 109, 111, 113
Giannella, A. 121
Global Mediterranean Policy 85
global security 47–59
globalization 49, 54–5, 57
governments 4, 6, 11–12, 21, 26, 37, 48, 52, 84, 112, 137
The Grand Chessboard (Brzezinski) 135
Greens and European United Left/Nordic Green Left (GUE/NGL) 38

INDEX

Hadfield, A. 141
High Representative 26, 53–4, 87, 118, 121, 125, *126*, 127–9
Hills, General J. 54
Howorth, J. 13
Human Development Report (1994, UNDP) 4–5
human rights 7, 30–1, 33, 76n, 83, 94, 96, 110; autocratic regimes 80–101; Egypt 62, 64, 67, 69–71, 74; Libya 81, 92; policies 84; Russia 104, 113
Human Rights Watch 95
human security 1, 3–6, 52, 55–6
Hustinx, P. 36–7
Hyde-Price, A. 84

identity 107–8, 111
immigration 7, 68, 96; Annual Action Programme 92; illegal 54, 84, 89, 91; Libya 87, 91–2, 94–5; management 91, 93; Migration Cooperation Agenda 95; policies 84, 87
Instrument for Nuclear Safety Cooperation (INSC) 122–3
Instrument for Stability (IfS) 12, 15–20, 22–6, 75, 122–3
interdependence 137–42, 145–6; asymmetrical 137–42, 146; sensitivity 137–8, *138*, 145–6; vulnerability 137–8, *138*, 146
International Atomic Energy Agency 126
international cooperation 53, 55–6
International Monetary Fund (IMF) 56
international political system 48, 57
International Relations theories 48
International Science and Technology Centre 122
Iran 105, 121, 143
Iraq War 109
Irrera, D. 8, 47–59
Israel 24
Italy 104, 106, 113

Japanese government 4
Jean Monnet Centre of Excellence (JMCE) 2
Joffé, G.: and Paoletti, E. 92
Jupille, J.: and Caporaso, J. 119

Karski, K. 111
Kashmir 56
Kaunert, C. 32; and Léonard, S. 1–10
Kaveshnikov, N. 140, 145
Kefauver Committee 54
Keohane, R.: and Nye, J. 8, 133–4, 137–8, 140–1, 145
Kirchner, E. 14
Knight, W. 52
Koehler, K. 126

Kosovo 50
Kremlin 144
Kubicek, P. 84
Kyoto Treaty 108

La Belle disco bombing (Berlin 1986) 85
Lappin, R. 83
Latin America 50
Lavallée, C. 6, 11–29
left-wing groups 38
Léonard, S.: and Kaunert, C. 1–10
liberals 38–9
Libya 7, 80–101, 128, 140; arms embargo 91–2, 97; EU foreign policy 80–101; Framework Agreement 94–5; light conditionality 89–93; Memorandum of Understanding 95; post Cold War 85–6; uprising 82, 95–8
Libyan government 91–3, 95–6, 97
Lifelong Learning Programme 2
Lisbon Treaty: Article (47) 126; co-decision procedure 21, 33–4, 40–1; consent procedure 33, 40–1; organized crime 47–59; policy impacts 6–8; reforms *126*; security environment change 1–10; weapons non-proliferation 117–32
Lockerbie bombings (1988) 85
Lukashenka, President A. 81–2, 85–6, 88, 91, 97
Lukyanov, F. 104

Maastricht Treaty 83
Macfarlane, S. 141
MacKenzie, A.: and Ripoll Servent, A. 6–7, 30–46
Madrid terrorist attacks 15
Mafia 50, 54, *see also* transnational organized crime (TOC)
Malmström, Commissioner C. 40, 95
Mattiussi, J. 125
Mediterranean Policy 66
Medvedev, President Dmitry 104
member states 22–3, 25–6, 39, 48, 53, 62, 82, 84, 96, 124–9; CEE 110–11; crisis management 23; defence 20–1; gas imports 138–40, 143; Russian relations 102–16, 133–48
Members of the European Parliament (MEPs) 33, 35, 39–42
Merkel, Chancellor Angela 105
Mexico 54
Middle East 97, 105, 123
migration *see* immigration
Migration Cooperation Agenda 95
military 2–3, 17–18, 23, 51, 95–6, 106, 109, 141, 147n; Russia 108, 124, *see also* weapons

INDEX

Ministry of Foreign Affairs (Egypt) 68
Minsk 90
Moldova 50, 81, 87, 104, 112
Moscow 7, 102–16, 124–5
Moscow State Institute of International Relations 113
Mubarak, President Hosni 61–2, 74–6
multilateralism 8, 47–59, 64, 66, 107, 113

Nabucco pipeline 140
narcotics *see* drugs (illegal)
National Indicative Programme (NIP) 66, 70–5, *71*, *72–3*, 94–5
National Security Strategy (USA) 54–5
Neighbourhood Programmes (2005–6) 89
Netherlands 139
New York Times 34
Nitoiu, C. 7, 102–16
non-governmental organizations (NGOs) 19, 68, 89
Non-Proliferation Treaty (NPT) 123, 126; Review Conferences 120, 126–7, 129
normative approach 97–8, 102–16
North Atlantic Treaty Organization (NATO) 23, 129, 143, 146n
North Stream gas project 105
Norway 92
nuclear power: European Atomic Energy Agency 121; International Atomic Energy Agency 126
nuclear safety 124
Nuclear Security Summit (2010) 127
Nye, J.: and Keohane, R. 8, 133–4, 137–8, 140–1, 145

Odessa 93
Oettinger, Commissioner G. 140
oil 91–2, 133–48, *136*; Baku-Tbilisi-Ceyhan (BTC) pipeline 143–4; Druzbha pipeline 91; Eastern Siberia-Pacific Ocean pipeline 140; Nabucco pipeline 140; OPEC 136, 139, 143, *see also* energy; gas
Ojanen, H. 13
Organization of Petroleum Exporting Countries (OPEC) 136, 139, 143
organized crime 47–59; Mafia 50, 54, *see also* transnational organized crime (TOC)

Paillard, C. 135
Palestine conflict 64
Paoletti, E.: and Joffé, G. 92
paramilitaries 51
Partnership and Cooperation Agreement (PCA) 85, 87, 96–7, 111
Partnership for Democracy and Shared Prosperity 74

Passenger Name Record (PNR) Agreements 30–3, 39, 41
Peacebuilding Partnership 19
Poland 89, 111, 140
policy-making 11–14, 22, 24, 62–3
Polish government 93
Political and Security Committee (PSC) 13, 18, 22
Popescu, N.: and Wilson, A. 108
power: hard 108, 110; soft 108–9
Prague 93
Putin, President Vladimir 104, 106, 142, 144–5

Qatar 140

Rapid Reaction Mechanism (RRM) 17–18, 20
Reagan, President Reagan 143
Reding, Commissioner V. 95
Regional Core Group 56
Regional Strategy Paper (2007–13) 87
Register of Interest Representatives 24
religion: Orthodox Church 107
Ripoll Servent, A.: and MacKenzie, A. 6–7, 30–46
Romania 112, 139
Rosneft 144
Royal Dutch Shell 142
Russia 7–8, 8, 50, 85, 90–2, 102–16, 117–48, 133–48, *136*; bilateral relations 103–9; CBRN/WMD proliferation 117–32; Eastern Neighbourhood 109–12; energy 8, 91, 102–16, 133–48; foreign policy 104, 140–2; language 107; reconceptualizing cooperation 102–16
Russia-first policy 105, 108, 113
Russia-Ukraine gas row (2006) 91
Russian energy leverage 133–48; economic to geopolitical issue 134–7; energy relations interdependence 137–42
Russian government 142
Russian-Georgian War (2008) 106, 109

Sakhalin II conflict 142–3
Sakwa, R. 144
Sarkozy, President N. 96, 111
Schengen Agreement 32
Schmitt, B. 120
Schroeder, Chancellor G. 105
Schulz, M. 37
Schumpeter, J. 83
Science and Technology Centre 122
A secure Europe in a better world (European Council) 53
security: internal 83–5, 87, 89, 96–7
security agenda 1–10, 52–4, 57, 83, 118, 142

INDEX

security environment 1–10, 52; CBRN weapons 117–32, *see also* CBRN weapons non-proliferation
security threats 3, 18; energy 133–48; non-traditional 1–3; organized crime 47–59; soft issues 68
Šefcovic, M. 113
September 11th terrorist attacks 8, 33–4, 52, 54–5, 57, 117–32
Serbia 50
Single European Market 32, 142
Single European Payments Area (SEPA) 35–6
Sjötstedt, G. 119
Smirnov, I. 107
Smith, K. 135
socialists 38–9
Society for Worldwide Interbank Financial Telecommunications (SWIFT) Agreement 6–7, 30–46; background 34–5; EU scrutiniser 36–8; outcome 35–7; permanent agreement results 36–7; pull system 36–7; twin-track approach 38–9
Söderköping Process 91
soft power 108–9
Solana, J. 53, 121
Southern Caucasus 19, 88
Southern Mediterranean 60–79
sovereignty 49, 107, 135
post-Soviet space 106–9, 111–12, 141, 144
Spain 104
Spanish Presidency 35, 40
stability goals 61
states: captured 50; de-structured 50; failed 50, 55; fragile 50; kleptocratic 50; Mafia 50; weak 50–1
Stiftung, F. 129
supranational institutions 6, 11–13, 26, 49
Supreme Council of the Armed Forces 61
Sweden 105, 111
Swedish government 93
Swedish Presidency 34, 37
Switzerland 34

Tampere European Council 83
Technical Aid to the Commonwealth of Independent States (TACIS) 89, 121, 123
technology 15–16
terrorism 8, 15, 33–7, 52, 55, 57, 82, 96; counter-terrorism 7, 31–4; counter-terrorism EP's and EU's role 31–4; international 47–8, 85–6; La Belle disco (Berlin 1986) 85; Lockerbie (1988) 85; Madrid terrorist attacks 15; Passenger Name Record (PNR) Agreements 30–3, 39, 41; September 11th terrorist attacks 8, 33–4, 52, 54–5, 57, 117–32

Terrorist Financing and Tracking Programme (TFTP) 31, 34; EU system 36–8, 40–1
Timmins, G. 104
Tonra, B. 111
Trade and Cooperation Agreement (TCA): Belarus 85
transnational organized crime (TOC) 8, 47–59; EU security agenda 52–3; non-state actors 48–52; transatlantic cooperation 55–6; US security agenda 54
Transneft 91
transparency 24, 113
Treaty Establishing the European Community (TEEC) 121
Treaty of European Community (TEC): Article (296) 20
Treaty on the European Union (TEU) 120–1
Treaty on the Functioning of the European Union (TFEU) 20, 84
Tripoli 91, 95
tsunami (2004) 56
Tunisia 60, 62, 76

Ukraine 81, 87, 91, 104, 107, 122, 127
Union for the Mediterranean (UfM) 82, 94–6
Union of Soviet Socialist Republics (USSR) 122–3, 125, 127, 133, 135, 139, 141, 143–4; post-Soviet space 106–9, 111–12, 141, 144, *see also* Belarus
United Kingdom (UK) *see* Britain
United Nations (UN) 8, 18, 24, 48, 56; Libyan Resolution 95–6
United Nations Development Programme (UNDP) 4–5; Human Development Report (1994) 4
United Nations High Commissioner for Refugees (UNHCR) 95
United States of America (USA) 7–8, 55–7, 122, 124–5, 143; bulk data transfer 30–46; EP relations 39–40; foreign policy 109; government 39, 143; security agenda 54; security authorities 34
US Department of State 54
US Department of the Treasury 34–5
USAID 71

Van Rompuy, H. 74, 127
Vogler, J.: and Bretherton, C. 119

Waltz, K. 51
Warsaw 111
weapons: arms embargo (Libya) 91–2, 97; Code of Conduct on Arms Exports 92; Instrument for Nuclear Safety Cooperation (INSC) 122–3; non-proliferation 117–32; Non-Proliferation Treaty (NPT) 120, 123, 126–7, 129, *see also* military

INDEX

weapons of mass destruction (WMDs) 53, 96; Personal Representative on Non-Proliferation of WMDs 121, 128; WMD Monitoring Centre 122; WMD Strategy 121–4, 127, 129
Weaver, C. 105
Webber, M.: *et al* 14
White Paper on European Governance (2001) 24
Wider Europe-New Neighbourhood Strategy 86, 88
Wilson, A.: and Popescu, N. 108
Wolczuk, K. 111

World Bank 56
World Trade Organisation (WTO) 108

Yeltsin, president Boris 104
Yukos 143–4

Zimmermann, D. 31
Zwolski, K. 7–8, 117–32

www.routledge.com/9780415688826

Related titles from Routledge

Developing European Internal Security Policy
After the Stockholm Summit and the Lisbon Treaty
Edited by Christian Kaunert and Sarah Leonard

The European Union (EU) is making strong inroads into areas of security traditionally reserved to states, especially into internal security, or Justice and Home Affairs. The Area of Freedom, Security and Justice (AFSJ), as it has been renamed in the Amsterdam Treaty, has seen significant policy developments since the late 1990s. After major treaty revisions in Maastricht, Amsterdam, Nice, and, finally the Lisbon Treaty, which entered into force on 1 December 2009, as well as an increased political impetus through the European Council Summits in Tampere (1999), the Hague (2004), and Stockholm (2009), the area appears as one of the most promising policy fields for integration in the EU in the foreseeable future. This book is the first to analyse these hugely topical developments in European internal security at both the treaty and policy levels, as well as its implementation at the national level, from various disciplinary perspectives (political science, law, criminology, etc).

This book was published as a special edition of *European Security*.

Christian Kaunert is Lecturer in EU Politics and International Relations at the University of Salford, UK.

Sarah Leonard is Lecturer in International Security at the University of Salford, UK.

December 2011: 246 x 174: 208pp
Hb: 978-0-415-68882-6
£85 / $145

For more information and to order a copy visit
www.routledge.com/9780415688826

Available from all good bookshops

www.routledge.com/9780415695671

Related titles from Routledge

European 'Security' Governance

Edited by George Christou and Stuart Croft

This book argues that we can understand and explain the EU as a security and peace actor through a framework of an updated and deepened concept of security governance. It elaborates and develops on the current literature on security governance in order to provide a more theoretically driven analysis of the EU in security. A theoretical framework is constructed with the objective of creating a conversation between these two literatures and the utility of such a framework is demonstrated through its application to the geospatial dimensions of EU security as well as specific cases studies in varied fields of EU security.

This book was originally published as a special issue of *European Security*.

George Christou is Associate Professor in European Politics, Department of Politics and International Studies, University of Warwick, Coventry, UK.

Stuart Croft is Professor of International Security, Department of Politics and International Studies, University of Warwick, Coventry, UK.

December 2011: 246 x 174: 208pp
Hb: 978-0-415-69567-1
£80 / $125

For more information and to order a copy visit
www.routledge.com/9780415695671

Available from all good bookshops